from Landi Kotal *to* Wagah

SALMAN RASHID

Page
i
Foreword

Pages
ii-iii
Introduction

Pages
iv-v
Acknowledgements

Chapter 1
Passing into History

Pages
1-17

Chapter 2
Peshawar: the First City

Pages
18-59

Chapter 3
East of the Indus
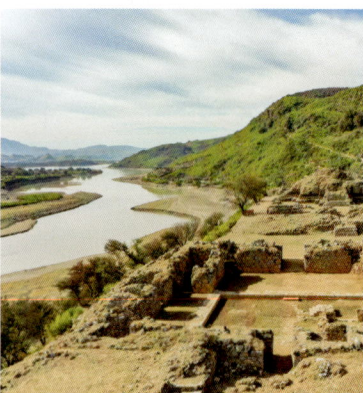
Pages
60-99

Chapter 4
Over the Cut Throat Pass

Pages
100-149

Chapter 5
In the Land of Raja Paurava

Pages
150-165

Chapter 6
Maharaja Ranjit Singh Ruled Here

Pages
166-207

Chapter 7
The City that Loh Built

Pages
208-249

Foreword

On a bright summer morning in April 2018, officials from UNESCO Islamabad and the Department of Archaeology and Museums, Government of Pakistan, visited Rawat Fort to assess the conservation work underway at the site, which is located just outside Islamabad. For centuries, the Rawat Fort served as a caravanserai, an inn with a central courtyard, for traders, adventurers, pilgrims and travelers, traversing across the mountains of Afghanistan into present-day Pakistan, and onwards to the Bay of Bengal. Located in proximity to a prominent Buddhist stupa at Mankiala, the Hindu temples of Gujar Khan and the Sikh havelis of the Potohar, the area consists of countless historical sites that narrate stories of the rich and diverse heritage of this region. Hence, the idea of a book on the heritage along the Grand Trunk Road was born.

From Landi Kotal to Wagah: Cultural Heritage Along the Grand Trunk Road portrays the history and diversity of cultural and religious heritage along the Grand Trunk Road in Pakistan with an acute eye. Salman Rashid, the pre-eminent Pakistani travel writer and a Fellow of the Royal Geographical Society, takes us on a fascinating journey along the Grand Trunk Road, describing the architectural marvels built over millennia and their history, highlighting the diverse cultural, religious and architectural expressions that have helped shape the identity of the people of Pakistan.

The book, unique in its kind, serves to encourage the people and the government of Pakistan to protect and preserve the heritage which marks the ancient landscape of Pakistan. We are confident that *From Landi Kotal to Wagah* will encourage the tourists to explore the country in depth.

In the spirit of the global Sustainable Development Agenda 2030, the production of this book has been a true partnership. The Federal and Provincial Governments of Pakistan, the Delegation of the European Union to Pakistan, the Embassy of Switzerland in Pakistan, The World Bank and UNESCO have collaborated to support the project. We are especially grateful to Salman Rashid, and Dr. Abdul Azeem, Director of Archaeology and Museums, who often traveled together on the journey described in the book. We are delighted to present it to you.

Patricia McPhillips	Bénédict de Cerjat	Najy Benhassine	Androulla Kaminara
Director/Representative UNESCO Islamabad	Ambassador of Switzerland, Islamabad	Country Director, Pakistan World Bank	Ambassador of the European Union to Pakistan

Introduction

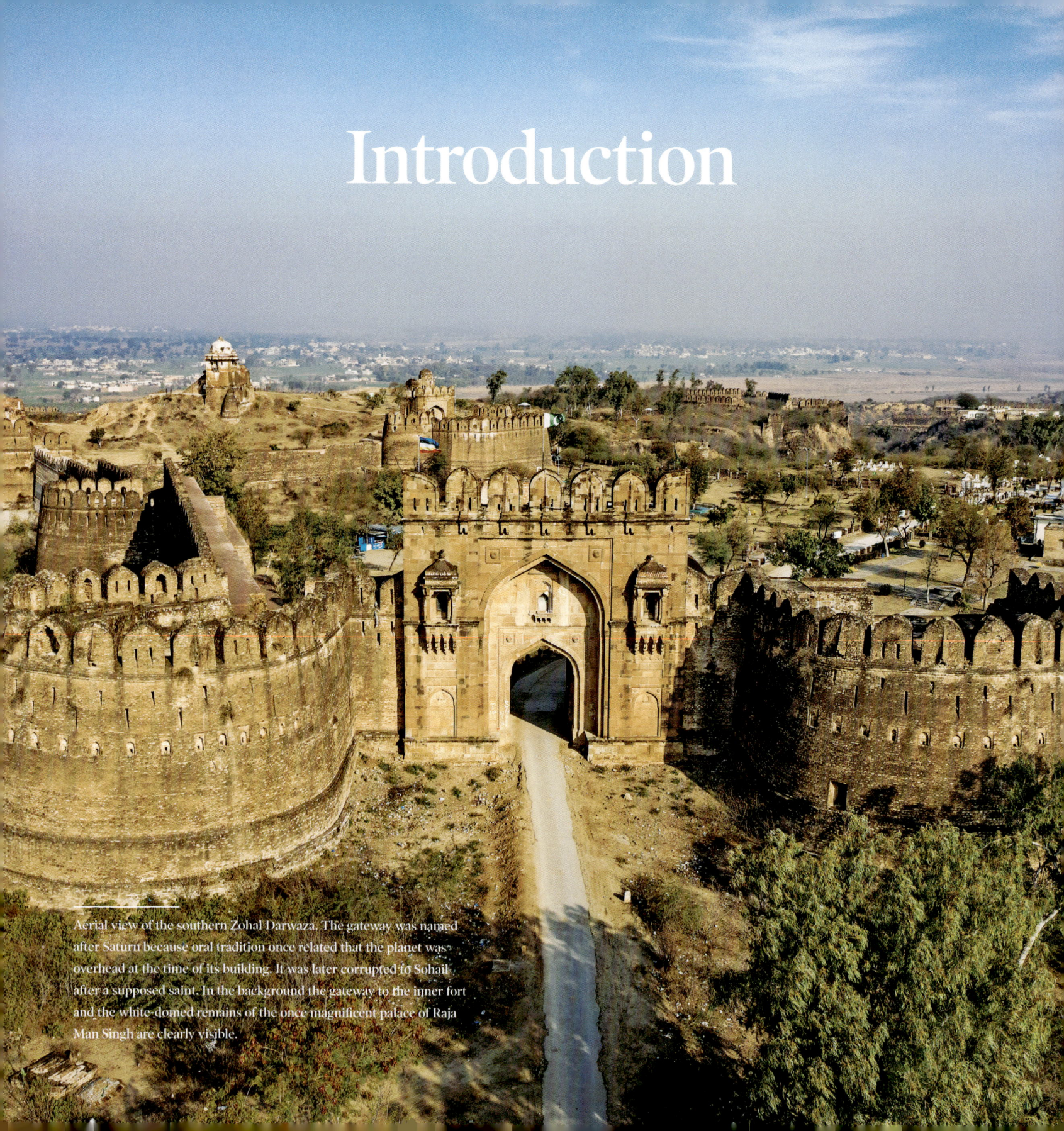

Aerial view of the southern Zohal Darwaza. The gateway was named after Saturn because oral tradition once related that the planet was overhead at the time of its building. It was later corrupted to Sohail after a supposed saint. In the background the gateway to the inner fort and the white-domed remains of the once magnificent palace of Raja Man Singh are clearly visible.

Pakistan is a country of limitless tourism potential ranging from the lakes of Sindh, ideal for windsurfing, through the plains rich with cultural and historical sites, to the high mountains of the northern areas. Yet, over the past seven decades, little attention has been paid to this component of national importance. Boosting tourism for the economic growth of the country is among the top priorities of our government. I am glad to see the manuscript of the book, which highlights the lesser known but amazing sites of Pakistan, identifying potential opportunities for promoting tourism in the country.

It is a matter of great satisfaction to note that both individuals and organizations have extended full support to accomplish this significant project. I wholeheartedly acknowledge the support of UNESCO, World Bank, European Union and Embassy of Switzerland in Islamabad, who put a joint effort to bring out a monograph titled *From Landi Kotal to Wagah: Cultural Heritage Along the Grand Trunk Road*. I am delighted to know that this is the first book of its kind on heritage sites along the ancient Grand Trunk Road and provides a complete compendium of important historical and cultural sites spread along four hundred odd kilometres of the ancient highway.

The most pleasing aspect of the book is the narrative that connects each monument with historical fact and modern belief(s) - providing a wonderful bridge between the present and distant past. Equally interesting is the research undertaken by Salman Rashid, going back to the origin of this grand highway to the 4th century BCE, in the time of the Mauryans. He takes us on a fascinating journey of Buddhist, Mughal, Sikh and British eras, bringing to fore vibrant & diverse history of Pakistan.

The book focuses mainly on highlighting the importance of Pakistan's cultural heritage. I believe, through this book, a significant effort has been made to raise awareness regarding need to preserve these milestones pointing to our collective past. The book clearly reflects dedication and commitment of those, who put their efforts in compiling this informative monograph. For this, I acknowledge the concerted efforts of the Department of Archaeology and Museums under National Heritage & Culture Division, who had completed the initial task of survey along this ancient highway and had identified all important sites and monuments. I am sure this effort will prove a milestone in preserving our built heritage and with it our history and this is what we owe to our future generations.

Shafqat Mahmood
Federal Minister for National Heritage & Culture Division

Acknowledgements

Fresco painting at Bedi Palace in Kallar Syedan.

The force driving this book from concept to fruition was Vibeke Jensen of UNESCO who conjured up the idea. And there was Junaid Akhlaq, then of the Department of Archaeology and Museums, who had that misplaced trust in me being able to do it in record time. I did not, and I griped about the rain whenever he asked how things were getting along. At UNESCO thanks is also due to Samar Majid and Jawad Aziz, to the latter especially for putting up with my colourful outbursts and his unfailing propriety.

Nothing would have taken off without Nicole Malpas of European Union who held the purse strings to the travel expenses that I expended so liberally. And to Maha Ahmed of World Bank for not letting funds lapse and paying me in full well before the book was completed which so tempted me to run away with the money. To her colleague and my old friend Kamran Akbar also my gratitude.

The several archaeologists in Peshawar, Taxila, Islamabad, Rohtas and Lahore were invaluable with their advice and guidance which added so much value to the writing. In Peshawar I owe much to my civil service friends Ikram Khan and Shakil Qadir Khan for their efforts to keep me out of trouble. I am grateful to my friend Irshadullah Khan (major, retired) for his hospitality in Nowshera. In Lahore Raheal Siddiqui was equally helpful with stories.

In the end, my gratitude to the designer Halima Sadia, the photographer Asad Zaidi and to Afzaal Ahmad of Sang-e-Meel Publications for bringing out this book.

———

Salman Rashid

The word 'pass' rings of romance and adventure; and not just in English. No matter what language the word comes from, it raises goose bumps and a burst of adrenaline in the hearer and the reader. Of them all, Khyber is ever more so. It has long been the passage way into and from the subcontinent of peaceful migration and sanguinary invasion and everything else in between. It has truly been the busiest route to shape the history of the subcontinent.

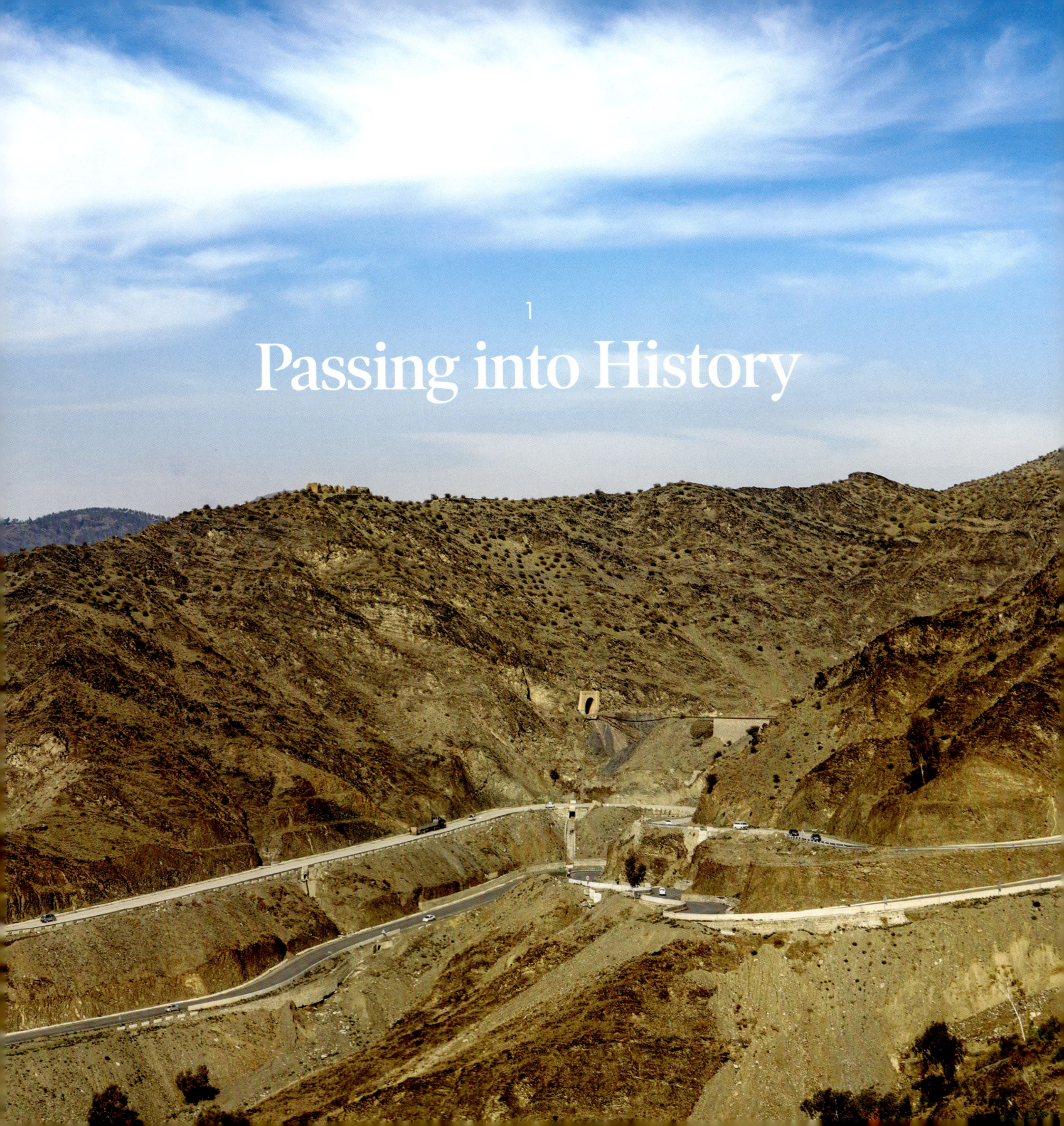

1
Passing into History

'Roads make all the difference to women. They have little meaning for men who can ride horses that we women can't,' said octogenarian Maranjan of the recently renamed village Ali Mohammad Killi. Situated almost midway between Peshawar at the bottom of the Khyber Pass and Landi Kotal at its head, the village now bears the name of a local journalist who had died in an accident.

I had asked Nusrat Naeem of Mardan to travel with me up the Khyber Pass from Peshawar so that we could get a women's perspective on roads and transportation. Nusrat Apa to all of us who know her from her decades of social work, is a Punjabi who has lived all her life in Mardan and speaks perfect Yusufzai Pushto.

'Even when they are unwell, men can ride horses as they used to when I was child, Maranjan explained, 'but a pregnant woman cannot, especially one with a complication. For women, the practice was to tie them on a charpoy to be carried down from the village to the road. There she was put on a camel and taken down to the nearest medical facility.'

This happened mostly when a pregnant woman developed complications near delivery time. In normal conditions the matron of the family, much experienced in motherhood and who had helped deliver all the babies in the extended family, would be in charge of operations in attendance with the village midwife. The sound of the smack and the thin yowl would then signal a happy end to the pregnancy. The woman expecting the baby had to face the charpoy treatment only when things got out of hand and the mother's life was thought to be in peril.

Maranjan had heard these stories from her mother. Her memory went back to the mid-1940s when the British had much improved the winding road through Khyber Pass and a once-a-day bus service plied up and down the gorge. A railway line, which provided a daily up and down service, had opened only a decade and a half before Maranjan was born.

Maranjan herself had been tied to a charpoy and brought to the road to ride the bus to Jamrud for treatment in the early 1950s. Then her family lived some ways off the road, her home inaccessible to wheeled traffic. But now, she said, roads go everywhere.

'It was such a hassle. Four men carried the bed and four marched along as replacement detail for when the carriers tired. Also, another woman had to accompany the procession to deal with the patient's problems. The jolting ride over rough ground sometimes brought on the labour and the baby would be delivered right there by the side of the path.'

Maranjan went silent perhaps thinking of her own long ago predicament. 'Many times women died because of improper care. But that was the will of God,' she added. 'Now you say roads go everywhere. Does that mean women don't have to be brought down tied to a bed?' asked Nusrat Apa.

'No. They are still tied to the charpoy. Only now they ride a pick-up truck to the medical facility.'

'That means a lot of lives must have been saved because of the road?'

'Recent improvement of the road means speeding drivers and accidents. And there are many. Women still die, sometimes in road accidents and sometimes even as they are borne away to the maternity home by pick-up truck. This too is the will of God,' Maranjan, no fatalist, finished with hearty cackling laughter.

But Maranjan did not know if the road that went through the Khyber Pass was the Grand Trunk Road. She only vaguely knew that it was said all roads in the subcontinent were built by the Afghan king Sher Shah Suri.

Sadly for the Suri king, he came a bit too late to lay claim to the artery British officials termed the Grand Trunk Road. Arriving in the sixteenth century, he was late by more than 1500 years after the road was first written of as receiving royal patronage. This road would, however, have existed long, long before that too. Perambulation is a basic primordial action of humans and even before they became traders and pilgrims humans were walking, walking, and walking the earth in search of sustenance, survival and better living. Millions of years of as many pounding feet beat paths across grassland and rocky mountains. These were the alignments that descendants of those early walkers followed on their horses and later in their motor vehicles turning them into highways.

At the western end of Khyber Pass looking towards the border post of Torkham. The distant mountains lie in Afghanistan.

In January 326 BCE, Alexander of Macedonia descended upon India. He claimed this invasion was to satisfy his desire of standing on the shore of the Eastern Ocean to see the sun emerge out of the sea. In reality, he was drawn to the subcontinent by word of its immense material wealth and intellectual development. At modern day Jalalabad in Afghanistan, he divided his force into two: he himself led the bulk of his multi-national army by way of Nawa Pass to enter modern day Bajaur, while two of his generals, Perdiccas and Hephaestion, brought their divisions across the Suleman Hills through the contours of the Khyber. They passed through Peshawar without pausing as they hurried on to lay low the fortified town of Pushkalavati (Peucelaotis to the ancient Greeks, whose ruins sit outside Charsadda town, thirty kilometres northeast of Peshawar).

That two divisions of infantry and cavalry were able to pass down the Khyber gorge can only indicate that the road was in fairly good condition. The next we hear anything of the great east-west artery is from Megasthenes.

After the death of Alexander in Babylon in 322 BCE, his empire was divided up between his generals. One of them, Seleucus Nikator, succeeded to most of what Alexander had wrested from Darius of Persia. In about 303 BCE, Seleucus resolved to pull another Alexander on India: he marched through Afghanistan to confront the Indian king Chandragupta Maurya in the Khyber Pass. The site of this battle where the Greek invader was roundly defeated is believed to be at the eastern foot of the pass under the Mullagory Hill near Ali Masjid.

Peace was negotiated between the warring sides and in consequence, ambassadors were exchanged. In 300 BCE, Megasthenes arrived in the court of Pataliputra (modern Patna, now the capital of Bihar in India) and remained here serving the interests of Seleucus Nikator until 285 BCE. During his tenure, the ambassador travelled extensively across the Mauryan kingdom and became quite well acquainted with its culture, history and geography. Upon his return home, he wrote his *Indica* that still exists today, albeit in fragments. The book is an interesting mix of fact and fable but for the discerning reader there is an ample stock of historical significance.

Megasthenes who became the source for later writers like Strabo and Arrian tells us, among so much more, of excellent administration in the Mauryan Empire that stretched along northern India clear from the Bay of Bengal across the Indus to Pushpapura – City of Flowers – today's Peshawar. The empire also had sway across the Khyber all the way to Ortospana and south to Alexandria Arachosia.

Now, Ortospana was the Greek rendition of the Sanskrit Urdasthana – Lofty Citadel. Today fortifications like the one in Peshawar and the war-ravaged one in Kabul are called Bala Hissar of the same meaning. In the case of the classical Ortospana, scholarly consensus rests on Kabul. Arachosia was the Greek title for the Helmand River valley in southern Afghanistan and Alexandria became Kandahar. Indeed, some believe the name is a corrupted form of Sikandar, the Persian version of Alexander.

The administrative measures of the Mauryan Empire included, among others, a dedicated department looking after roads, taxes, land management and water. Megasthenes wrote, 'They construct roads and at every ten stadia set up a pillar to show the by-roads and distances [to the next station and to outlying towns].' In that far off time, the road was *Rajapatha* – Royal Highway. In fact, since all major highroads received royal patronage, they were known by the same cognomen.

Now, ten stadia of the Greek measure equal an English mile and a half. This in turn is somewhat less than the Indian *kos* in plain country. However, the length of the *kos* varies: in mountainous terrain it can be as little as an English mile, while in plain country it is reckoned between two and three miles. Of the pillars that the Greek ambassador noticed, only two remain in Pakistan, both in Lahore.

Only today, having attributed the road to Sher Shah Suri, we call it *Jarnaili Sarak* – General's Highway. Great as he undoubtedly was, the Suri king, having ousted the inept Mughal king Humayun, ruled India for a mere five years from 1540 to 1545. Much of this time was spent fighting the desert Rajputs and the Rawalpindi Gakkhars who had aided Humayun as he fled before Sher Shah's army. Having supplanted the Mughal kingdom, Sher Shah proved an unbiased, able and ironhanded administrator and in his brief tenure lawlessness was unheard of. However, even he, despite his team comprising the finest of the country, could not have constructed a 3500-kilometre road in five years.

In *Daily Life in Ancient India*, French historian Jeannine Auboyer gives us greater detail. Ports in the gulf of Bengal attracted a great deal of Chinese sea-borne trade through the Straits of Malacca. This trade passed up the country all the way to the marts of Pushpapura and across the pass to Urdasthana. The passage of trade which could only have been possible by good roads meant custom duties, and road toll which went to government coffers. It was therefore the express interest of kings and emperors to maintain the road in the best fettle.

Auboyer tells us that even in ancient times all highroads in the country had, besides toll posts, travellers' rest houses at regular intervals, each with its well to provide water for human consumption and a large tree-shaded pond for animals. The road itself was always raised on a bed above the surrounding surface to ease travel during rain. Trees lined all roads and water-filled ditches ran alongside. This paraphernalia could only be maintained in top class condition by a well-staffed department such as the one Megasthenes tells us of.

The superintendent of roads was not just in charge of the facilities along the roads; it was also within his purview to arrest and punish robbers on the way. Two thousand years ago, writes Auboyer, 'there were unscrupulous merchants who attempted to defraud the revenue officials by taking to side-roads when approaching toll-points.' Understandably enough, old habits die hard.

Modern day smugglers, coming down from the duty-free haven of Landi Kotal at the top of Khyber Pass, give up the

The covered stairway leading up to the loop-holed blockhouse of the British fortress overlooking Torkham. Common misconception makes it a slaughterhouse where Temur the Lame executed his foes.

With the railway line covered by tarmac, there is no hope that Digai Tunnel built in 1922 will ever again be used for a train.

Plaque on the Digai Tunnel names Malik Baz Mir Shinwari as the contractor for this structure. In order to keep trouble-makers at bay, British engineers hired local chiefs to work on the project who would keep their clan in check. Mr Shinwari would have been one such person.

road as they approach the customs checkpoint near the town of Jamrud. Laden with their contraband whether in pick-up truck or on foot, they sneak past by a path about five hundred metres to one side, sometimes within sight of customs officials.

While modern customs officials tend to overlook this trickery, those of the past were more vigilant and a cheat discovered was immediately thrown into prison and his goods confiscated. Such goods were sold in auction and the proceeds were shared between the treasury and the community, writes Auboyer.

Most people have only some vague notion of the Grand Trunk Road and have never heard of the great web of officially sanctioned highways intersecting the country in ancient times. As already mentioned, all roads were constructed and maintained under royal orders, and were all known as *Rajapatha*, the more important ones being classified by their geographical location. The Grand Trunk Road that we know in Pakistan was thus the *Utra Rajapatha* – Northern Royal Highway.

Eminent archaeologist Dr Saifur Rahman Dar's *Historical Routes through Gandhara* confirms what Megasthenes tells us about byways when Dar writes that every main artery was joined by side roads at frequent intervals. Similarly, the Grand Trunk Road in our part of the subcontinent was a set of different alignments. Leaving Peshawar, it branched off to the northeast via Pushkalavati whose ravaged remains continue to be pillaged near Charsadda. In the Yusufzai Plain of Mardan, the road rested at modern Shahbazgarhi, so named after a supposed visit by the saint Usman Marwandi better known as Shahbaz Qalandar.

Had it not been for the Chinese pilgrim Xuanzang we would never have known how this ancient prosperous mart and Buddhist centre was known in antiquity. Our pilgrim calls is Po-lu-sha that scholars translate into the original as Varusha. Here the great Asoka ordered stupas and monasteries that no longer exist but whose secrets sleep beneath the foundations of modern housing and today we know Shahbazgarhi only for the inscribed rock that still carries the edicts of that ancient king. From Varusha, the road swung southeast for Hund, the ancient Udabhandapura – Water Pot City – the main ferry across the Indus. This was the very place that Alexander and his legions went over en route to Taxila.

Its other branch passed through Nowshera into the hinterland past Nizampur[1] to reach the less frequented ford of Bagh Nilab into modern Attock city. Babur, the founder of the Mughal dynasty in India, mentions in the early sixteenth century, frequent coming and going by this route indicating that downstream of Hund, this was the major road. In the 1580s, Babur's grandson, Akbar the Great ordered construction of the impressive Attock Fort and, right under its walls, the caravanserai of the Begum. With it, he also had infrastructure built in the riverbed to moor a boat bridge when flow was at low flood. At high

---

1) Nizampur bears the name of one of the sons of the great warrior poet Khushal Khan Khattak. He and his elder brother Ashraf remained steadfast by their father in his revolt against Aurangzeb.

flood, travellers braved the mewing eddies of the mighty Indus in flat-bottomed boats. In Akbar's time, this became the preferred crossing place, while Nilab was relegated to a secondary place. With this route gaining importance, Peshawar and Attock were connected by the shortest route via Nowshera, the very road we use today. In the latter Middle Ages, there were thus three alignments of the old Rajapatha in what we now call Khyber Pakhtunkhwa.

East of the Indus, the alignment from Hund passed through the Chach Plain directly to Taxila in whose waning glory Rawalpindi rose as the halting place to which all southbound traffic came from the three roads. Southward of Rawalpindi one alignment went south through Adiala and Chakwal, through the village of Basharat into Jhangar Valley in the Salt Range. Thence it made for village Ara from where it headed down through a wild and desolate gorge into the short and narrow pass of Nandna. About the ninth century CE, Nandna became home to a school and fortified temple complex whose ruins can be seen to this day. Past the fertile farms at the foot of the Nandna hill, the road reached several ferries on the Jhelum River.

The Haranpur ferry made for Bhera, a thriving salt market until two hundred years ago and believed to be the ancient Jobnathnagar. The other crossing at Rasul (now famous for the barrage and irrigation canal network) went through Phalia to the celebrated ford of Rasulnagar before attaining the vicinity of Eminabad and the main axis of the Rajapatha.

The third branch having passed by Gujar Khan town, swung east into wild and broken country to skirt Dhamiak before coming out just southeast of Sohawa. In 1520, Babur used this way and called it the 'sub-montane road'. Thence through Dina, it reached Jhelum town for the ferry across. From Jhelum to Eminabad, the modern road sits smack on the ancient alignment. At Eminabad, ten kilometres south of Gujranwala, the road meandered eastward into forested hinterland before fetching up at the main ferry on the Ravi at Shahdara outside Lahore.

Regimental crests of battalions that served in the Khyber Pass, by the roadside outside Landi Kotal.

Though there were subsidiary routes, Khyber passed into history because it was this way that nearly every influx into the subcontinent, whether peaceful migration or sanguinary invasion, came. In the second half of the sixth century BCE, the Achaemenian king Cyrus the Great of Persia sent his armies by way of this pass to lay claim to a slice of modern Khyber Pakhtunkhwa and Balochistan as one of his satrapies. For two hundred years, his empire lasted as he and his successors filled their treasuries with tribute received from this possession. Then the powerful kingdom was undone by Alexander the Macedonian.

Inside Tamerlane's gallows.

Alexander was the first European to invade the subcontinent. Thereafter, the pageant of outsiders was endless. Alexander's empire died with him and the brilliant Chandragupta, founder of the Mauryan Empire in northern Indian, laid claim to this land in 322 BCE. Within a century and a half, his empire gave way to an influx of the Greek descendants of one of Alexander's generals. They in turn submitted to the Scythians in the middle of the first century BCE. There followed the Parthians, Kushans, and eventually the Persian Sassanians, each holding Khyber Pakhtunkhwa for varying periods of time. Though the savage White Huns too came by way of the Khyber Pass, they did not hold the country for long. After the rout of their king Mehr Gul (Mihirakula of western literature) in early 528, there followed five hundred years of relative peace as the powerful Hindu Shahya kings of Kashmir gained ascendency.[2] These last were replaced by neo-Muslim Turks, foremost among whom is Mahmud who ruled from the Afghan city of Ghazni from CE 997 until his death in 1030.

But if violent influx by way of the Khyber Pass is recorded, we also hear the jangle of caravan bells as traders went up and down this way between the marts of India and Central Asia. And we know of Buddhist monks spinning their prayer wheels and chanting their mantras as they trudged their determined way up the snaking road in the pass en route to the highlands of Afghanistan and beyond into Central Asia. With them, the tenets of the Great Buddha spread across this land.

The new creed appealed greatly to the highland Fire Worshippers: within a thousand years after they first converted to the new faith, they had painstakingly crafted the great marvel of the gigantic carvings of Buddha at Bamian, sadly destroyed by the Taliban in 2001. One wonders how many believers would have fallen to their deaths from the rickety scaffolding erected to sculpt the face of their Lord fifty-four metres above the valley floor.

---

2) The dynasty rose in the third century CE and remained in power, first in Kashmir and then all the way through Punjab and Khyber Pakhtunkhwa to Kabul, until the beginning of the tenth century.

Our journey began at Landi Kotal at the top of the Khyber Pass. My captain was Dr Abdul Azeem, the archaeologist, for he had travelled here before. From this beginning, we stayed together until the end of our explorations near Wagah outside Lahore. In his fifties, he kept a boyish grin and coupled his deep knowledge of the glorious Gandhara period with a sharp sense of humour and the ability to segue from a very learned discourse on the life and times of Kanishka to a risqué story or a Persian couplet from modern times.

At Michni as we stood at the viewpoint looking west to the distant bustle of the border crossing at Torkham – Black Bend, Azeem pointed to the irregular triangle of a small fortification sitting atop a rocky crag in the middle distance. It was commonly believed that this was the slaughterhouse of Temur the Lame (Tamerlane). If one were to go by the stories, this could only be called a slaughterhouse: here the fourteenth century Barlas Turk king, a descendent of Chengez Khan, would have his prisoners flung from a parapet into a pit equipped with sharp vertical blades.[3] As they were impaled, their cries of agony were heard afar striking fear of the Turk in the hearts of the Khyber tribes. The story is commonly believed by locals and is said to have been passed down through the generations.

It was late on a January afternoon as we stood there with the screams of the unfortunate victims of that long ago ruthlessly savage king ringing in my ears and I knew I would have to return to see those now rusty blades.

Three months later, on a hot and very dry afternoon as believers kept the fast, I was again at the Michni viewpoint with permission from the provincial Home Department to take a guide from the local police force for the short walk down into the gorge and then up to Tamerlane's slaughter house. Young Shavrez Khan, lounging on a charpoy under the shelter of the Michni viewpoint, was assigned as my pilot by an older colleague of his. We descended into the gorge, crossed a dry streambed and climbed a modern looking cemented stairway leading up to the slaughterhouse.

The reputed jailhouse and gallows built by the Mongol Tamerlane. One wonders how the story became so prevalent when the brick building is clearly a British structure. The fortress is tactically situated to provide all round visibility and loop holed positions to engage fire from any side. It reminds us of those uncertain times when the Shinwaris who inhabit this part of the Khyber Pass periodically rose up against the British.

As he led me up the steps, Shavrez Khan spoke in a mixture of Pashto and Urdu telling me Temur's *phansi-ghat*

---

3) The Latinised Genghis is far from the true pronunciation of the Mongol name. I therefore prefer Chengez Khan.

(gallows) was haunted. In the dead of night, one could sometimes hear the screams of those being done to death. As we drew nearer, I said the brick structure clearly dated to the beginning of the twentieth century. It was a British fortress.

'No! You are wrong,' Shavrez said sharply, 'everyone knows this is Temur's phansi-ghat.'

The man resolutely believed in the haunting story, for while I was photographing the exterior, he did not venture in alone. The entrance was from the east into a triangular courtyard which combined the natural defensive nature of the crags on the north side with the fortification. Again, Shavrez who was hanging back called out sharply for me to get out of there. For my lack of Pashto, I could not ask if it was because of the ghosts of Temur's victims or some more natural cause such as snakes.

To the south, a roofed staircase led up to a semi-circular turret connected with an oblong room on the north side. This room with large firing ports on three sides was once roofed, but the rafters and other timber fixtures had long since been cannibalised. There was no pit with the blades and heaps of skeletons from Temur's time. Yet my basic Pashto-Punjabi amalgam could not convince Shavrez that the fourteenth century king had long before turned to dust when the British raised this structure barely a century and a quarter ago.

Back at the Michni viewpoint, a man with lavishly oiled hair and a thick moustache so dark that they could only have been dyed that insane colour, came for me screaming like a banshee. Why, he demanded to know, had I taken his man on the walk in the afternoon when he was fasting. He himself gave them only light work that too only after the fast, he raved. I told him I had permission from the home secretary and asked for his name which he would not reveal. Even so his rant did not end.

What was my business snooping around a sensitive border area, he demanded to know. If it was treasure, he thundered without waiting for my reply, then I was in trouble. As long as he held his post, no treasure-seeker would be able to dig anywhere in Khyber. I wondered how many treasure hunters like me haunted this outpost of Pakistan.

Upon hearing that I was a writer he cooled down a bit. Then he told me I ought to climb the ridge south of the *phansi-ghat* for on the crest I would find the remains of a 'third century BCE' fortification. He offered to send Shavrez with me. Just five minutes earlier he had roundly berated me for taking the man and now he wanted us to climb a rather more difficult hill. He claimed to have seen the interior of the *phansi-ghat* and knew all about the pit with the blades, but he could not tell me where exactly it was. He scoffed me when I offered that the building was only about a century old. He also told me Sphola stupa lower down in the pass was also third century BCE!

Later I related the episode to Azeem and he said it was usual for laypersons to make up stories like that from what they perceived as having gleaned from the conversation of visiting archaeologists whom they accompanied for administration and security. Only some months earlier a team of archaeologists had carried out a survey in the area and it seems the man had listened in to their conversation to create his story of the two millennium old fortification on the ridge.

When the mountaineers of Bamian in Afghanistan were carving their giant Buddha on the cliff face, the believers of Khyber were raising a stupa and a monastery in the tortuous bends of their pass. The Sphola stupa, dating from the second century CE is the sole extant Buddhist relic in the Khyber Pass and a reminder of Kushan rule in the area.

In 2012, I had photographed the stupa and below it the abandoned railway line festooned across a gap in the hill. Then the stupa stood alone on the crest of its low hill. In January 2019, an ugly modern blockhouse was in the final stages of completion. The soldier on site only permitted photography when Azeem had introduced himself as being from the government. The barracks, said the soldier, was being built to house a contingent of the Khyber Rifles and I found myself wondering why some brilliant minds could only think of planting the ugliness right next to an ancient monument instead of a couple of hundred metres to one side.

This was not a stand-alone stupa, said Azeem. A hundred metres to the northeast one could once see the remains of a monastery. That has long since been cannibalised and taken over by modern construction.

No historical building is complete without its tale of buried treasure. Young Waliullah, a colleague of Azeem's who accompanied us, was the teller of this yarn. Sometime in the early 1990s, a local man having either dreamt or heard from a mullah of a great treasure in the stupa began a secret tunnel to reach its core. He was discovered in good time and arrested, so the story goes. Since such stories do not go without their quota of bizarre twists suggesting some evil supernatural influence, this one has the digger going into a fit of crazed frenzy to murder his entire family. Nevertheless, the man seems to have been possessed of singular determination and diligence for to reach the stupa he would have had to dig through a couple of hundred metres of solid rock. But we know of so many historical monuments in Pakistan laid low by ignorant treasure hunters that the Khyber robber does not seem unlikely.

Sphola stupa is the most notable and complete Buddhist monument in the Khyber Pass. Built by the Kushans in the 2nd-3rd century CE, its view is now marred by the structure in front.

At the eastern foot of the Khyber Pass, Ali Masjid is overseen by a British fortress. According to history, it was in this field that Chandragupta Maurya defeated the Greek Seleucus Nicator in the closing years of the fourth century BCE.

Sphola was not the only centre of Buddhism in Khyber. A few kilometres lower down, where the broad Peshawar plain gives way to the first narrowing of the pass, the chunky, green domed Ali Masjid – Mosque of Ali –named after the fourth caliph of Islam was once the site of a Buddhist monastery and stupa. Back in the mid-1980s, when Azeem first joined the Department of Archaeology, he recalls seeing the last vestiges of that ancient monument. Today no sign of it remains.

Though there is no historical evidence of the fourth caliph ever having been in our part of the world, there are dozens of sites across the four provinces connected with him. We see forty-five centimetre long 'footprints' in rock too large for a man reportedly short-statured, we have his pats of butter turned to stone, we have depressions in rocks supposedly made by the hoofs of his mare. The list of evidence of Hazrat Ali's adventures in the subcontinent is long. And so, not to be left wanting, the Khyber Afridis commemorated the visit (that never occurred) of the caliph to their area by raising this mosque at the exact spot where the caliphal forehead purportedly touched the ground in prostration.

In 1519, Babur paused at Ali Masjid and noted that the nearby spring provided excellent water. Rather unlike himself, Babur does not delve into the mosque's history. Nearly a century later (1607) at the same spot his great-grandson Jahangir was mystified by a spider 'the size of a crab' that had grabbed a snake 'one and a half *gaz* (yard)' long by the throat. Within a minute, so Jahangir tells us in his memoir, the snake was dead.

Now, much like Babur, Jahangir was also rather curious and observant who kept a personal diary that comes down to us as the *Tuzk e Jahangiri*. But at Ali Masjid even he was not moved to make any inquiries. Two centuries later, the remarkable Charles Masson, deserter from the army of the East India Company, a much-learned man and a writer of a very interesting log of an extended journey in this region, also failed to comment on the mosque. He only tells us of the clear spring and the 'numerous wasps' that 'good-naturedly allowed [his party] to drink without annoyance.'[4]

We spent more than an hour at the mosque. We found the stream tainted, nary a spider or a snake and in mid-winter no wasps. Every sign of the Buddhist monastery that Azeem knew of had disappeared.

Beyond, hidden from sight, lay the city of Peshawar. The First City for all those who came down the highlands to the rich and fertile plains of the subcontinent.

---

4) Very little is known of this enigmatic explorer. Under the assumed name of Masson, he claimed to be an American, but in reality he was James Lewis, an Englishman, born around 1798, who had for a few years served the Bengal European Artillery as a soldier. He deserted the service in 1826. Thereafter, in fourteen years of travelling around in the area that now makes the four provinces of Pakistan and in Afghanistan disguised either as a mendicant or a Mughal from Delhi, Masson proved himself an unrivalled and exceptionally observant explorer. His journeys are detailed in a set of four very readable volumes; three titled *Narrative of Various Journeys* and the last *Kalat*.

If any edifice is the hallmark of Peshawar, it is Islamia College. It dominates the view as one comes into the Peshawar suburbs down the Khyber Pass. So too for more than a century has it dominated the culture of edification of the city. Founded by the dual endeavours of Sir George Roos-Keppel, chief commissioner Peshawar, and Sir Sahibzada Abdul Qayyum Khan, political agent Khyber, the college opened its first classes in 1913. The name of the institution adheres to the strict religious views of the Pakhtuns, while its architecture is richly redolent of the eastern building tradition.

2

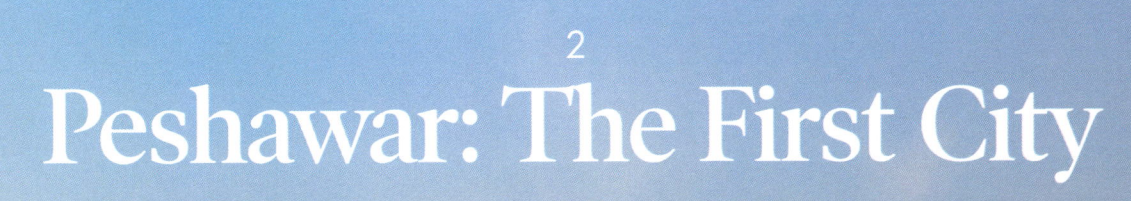

Peshawar: The First City

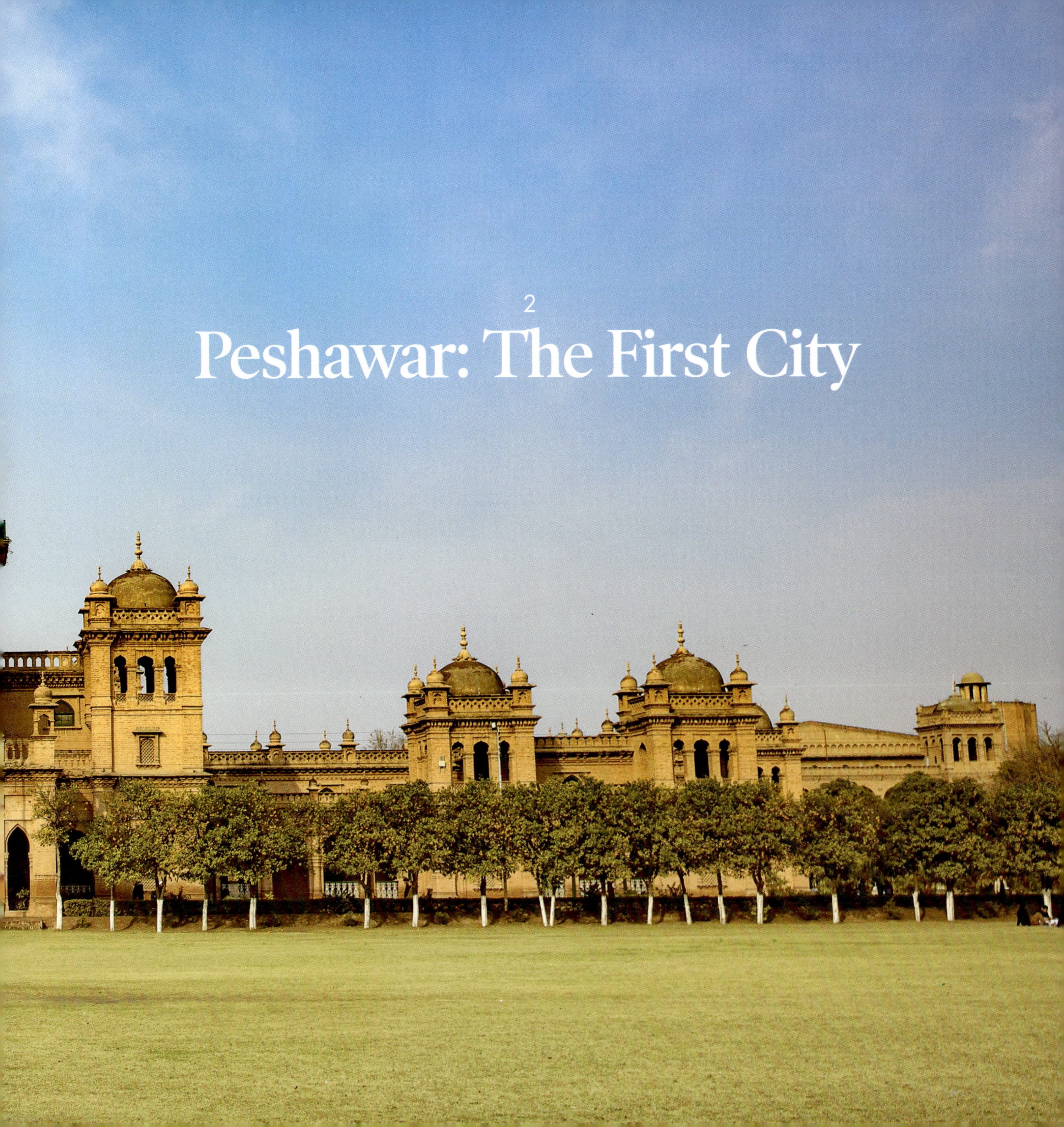

Peshawar is not about the clatter of armoury, the tramp of soldiers' feet and the raging din of battle; it is not of a city on fire and the cries of the dying. Peshawar is about murmured prayer, of the ringing of the temple bell and the call from the minaret, the clang of the *jaras* – the bell around the camel's neck in the caravan – and the soft plop of the animals' feet on unpaved streets, it is of the vendor crying his wares in streets where rows of shops run on either side crowded with buyers and sellers. Above the shops are residential apartments, their ornate balconies festooned with laundry drying in the sun. Peshawar is about long distance travellers, of caravanserais and of storytellers.

Early morning street scene in Peshawar

It was April 1977, and I was wandering about Namak Mandi in Under Sheher (Inner City) Peshawar. In a narrow street lined with stores and *qehvakhanas*, it leapt straight out of a storyteller's repertoire: the caravanserai with its open-to-the-sky courtyard accessible by a gateway twice the height of a man and spacious rooms on all four sides. A timber staircase led to the floor above where smaller rooms were equipped with fireplaces. But in 1977, the fireplaces were cold, the rooms empty and dusty, unused for perhaps a couple of decades with cobwebs dancing in the slanting light of the early morning sun. The downstairs rooms served as warehouse for packaged goods.

The men working in the warehouse did not mind my pottering around and in those few minutes I was taken back through the centuries. I saw the caravans work their way along the street, the camels – all double-humped Bactrians – coming through the high gateway of the serai and crouched in the courtyard to be unloaded. The travellers, dusty and tired, wishing only the bath and then the tryst with those famous tellers of ancient romances and adventures in nearby Bazaar Qissa Khwañ. There, after the meal, the tales would flow over endless cups of qehva. In 1977, the streets of inner Peshawar were still the stuff of stories written centuries before our time.

By all accounts, the city's ancient name was Pushpapura – City of Flowers. Two thousand years after being bestowed this beautiful title, Pushpapura enthralled the Mughal emperor Babur: waxing eloquent, he counts the colours of the flowers grown in plots that 'form a sextuple'. Here 'as far as the eye reached, flowers were in bloom'. He concluded that in spring the fields near the city were truly beautiful with blossoms of every colour.

About the year 510 BCE, Skylax, the sea captain from Karyanda, mispronounced the name of the city. Commissioned by Darius the Great of Persia (reigned BCE 521–485) to map the Indus River, Skylax set down the Kabul River near the city he calls Kaspatyrus. His work, cited by Herodotus and other Greek authors was extant until Alexander's time, but was subsequently lost and we know of no other detail the explorer noted about the city.

One thousand years after our Greek mapmaker, the Chinese Buddhist pilgrim, Fa Hian passed through the city he called Purushapura. And a hundred years later, in 518 CE, came Sung Yun. He was to be followed in the year 631 by the most celebrated Buddhist teacher Xuanzang. The three pilgrims concurred on Purushapura and Xuanzang confirmed that it was the capital of Gandhara.

That all these luminaries setting out of China on their quest for the true word of the great Buddha in India came through Purushapura tells us that the city lay on a major travel route. As the great trans-Asian highway, now called the Silk Road, dipped down from Samarkand to cross the Hindu Kush Mountains into Kabul, it extended eastward across the barren rocks of the Khyber Pass to make Peshawar. The flowers of the city may have been celebrated for centuries, but as traffic to the wealth, culture and learning of our part of the world spread, the City of Flowers became Pesh-Awar – the First Comer – the first city of the subcontinent.

The three Buddhist pilgrims from China noted that Pushpapura had one huge stupa said to be no less than a hundred and twenty metres tall (an obvious exaggeration) and built on the orders of Kanishka, the greatest among the Kushan kings of this land. Beside this towering edifice, there was a smaller one. This, they tell us, appeared miraculously after the main dome was raised. They record that on his visit to Peshawar, Buddha had foretold not only the name of Kanishka but also that he would build a stupa and a monastery. When Fa Hian arrived in Peshawar in 400 CE, Kanishka had been dead for a century and a half. His magnificent stupa, however, was as good as new and it was the centre to which every Buddhist gravitated.[1]

And so a century after Fa Hian, Sung Yun too stood before it in silent prayer with folded hands. He told us that a *pipal* (*Ficus religiosa*) tree shading the stupa with 'thick foliage' was the very one the great Kanishka had himself planted. In 631, Xuanzang described the gilded dome of the main stupa and mentioned a hundred other stupas surrounding it. He also noticed the *pipal* tree which would now have been over four hundred years old. Buddhism, the master lamented, was on the decline and the monastery in decay, however.

---

1) Kanishka's period is somewhat moot. While he is generally placed about the middle of the second century CE, some historians assign him to a hundred years later. As for Buddha's visit to Peshawar or indeed any other city of what is now Pakistan, that is pure fiction.

Of the three Buddhist pilgrims, it was Xuanzang whose account, richly adorned with an adorable piety, is the most detailed. Regarding the stupa, he tells us a very interesting tale of Kanishka out riding by a swamp when he spotted a white hare. Following the animal until it disappeared in its burrow, the king came upon a young shepherd building a small stupa. The shepherd told the king that the Buddha himself had prophesised of the victorious ruler who would raise a stupa to contain a large portion of the Buddha's bodily remains.

As is the wont of royalty, Kanishka flattered himself with the notion that Buddha could only have referred to him and so, surrounding the shepherd's little stupa he ordered his own larger one. As the king's stupa began to rise in height, the smaller one miraculously always rose a metre above it. Persisting in his tussle with divinity, Kanishka kept the building going until it reached a height of a hundred and twenty metres through five storeys. The circumference at the base was then one hundred and forty metres. Only then did the miracle of the smaller stupa cease.

Overjoyed, the king ordered a topping of twenty-five circlets of gilded copper above his stupa. Inside, he ordered the placing of the Buddha's remains. Even as he was making his offering, the smaller stupa once again miraculously appeared on the side of Kanishka's structure. Dismayed at the thought that he may have upset his Lord, the king ordered his building to be demolished. When work reached the bottom of the second storey, the smaller miraculous stupa moved of its own volition to its original place. In the words of Xuanzang, the king concluded,

'When a matter is directed by spiritual power what can human resentment effect?'

In 631 CE, Xuanzang found both stupas still extant. We are told that the stone used in the construction possessed the remarkable quality of appearing 'a brilliant gold colour' in full sunshine and as the light decreased, it turned 'reddish-blue'.

The exterior of the great stupa had carvings of Buddha in different sizes together with a replication of the stupa itself in exact proportions. Such depiction of the elevation of a religious building we see on the façades of Hindu temples from the ninth century onward.

The work of Kanishka, however, was not the only miracle in seventh century Peshawar. Our Chinese pilgrim goes on to tell us another local yarn. Some centuries earlier, as narrated to Xuanzang by the elders, a fissure in the stone foundation of the stupa brought forth a large number of 'gold-coloured ants, the greatest about the size of the finger, the longest about a barleycorn in size'. These ants gnawed on the stones to leave behind a deposit of gold sand and the figures of Buddha on the stupa.

There is something to be said on these peculiar ants. Nearly two centuries after the Maha Pari Nirvana (demise) of Buddha, about the middle of the fifth century BCE, the Greek traveller and historian Herodotus wrote his nine-volume *Histories*. In Book 3 he tells us of the sandy desert that lies near Kaspatyrus – the very same city from which Skylax the sea captain began his voyage on the

Kabul River to map the Indus. Local tribes sent men out to collect gold that was plentiful in this desert. But this precious metal was guarded by ants 'in size somewhat less than dogs, but bigger than foxes.' Never having been to the land of the Indus, our historian gleaned this fanciful tale from Skylax's report.

Burrowing into the ground where they lived, these ants threw up heaps of sand which was laden with gold. The gold-gatherers of Kaspatyrus came to the desert on camels during the hottest part of the day when the ants were resting in the coolness of their burrows. Quickly filling up their sacks, the men made off with the greatest speed possible for if the ants mustered out of their homes, so vicious were they that not a single gold-gatherer or his camel could escape. Herodotus also tells us that several of these ants were kept as a novelty by the Persian king. That is hearsay for the writer does not appear to have visited the Achaemenian court.

Though the story of the ants, whether the size of foxes or gold-coloured, is clearly a fable, there seems to have been a legend current in and around Peshawar about a peculiar breed of the insect for a very long time. If Skylax preserved it in his report to Darius the Great, it must have been popular in the sixth century BCE. Thence it came down to the seventh century of the Common Era to Xuanzang. The kernel of truth, if there was any, that lay in the core of this legend is tantalising in the extreme.

Fast forward to 1504 and we have Babur, then ruling over Kabul, in a thrall of the gardens of Parshawar. He divulges something very interesting: he had been told tales of Gorkhatri and that it was a 'holy place of jogis and Hindus who came from far places to shave their heads and beards there'. Gorkhatri (properly Kor Khatri, signifying House of the Hindu), was located in the precinct of Begram in the city. To this house he rode from his camp at Jamrud. He toured the place and even remarked on the 'great tree', surely the very one Kanishka had planted nearly thirteen centuries earlier and on which the Chinese pilgrims had marvelled. Babur made no mention of the great stupa, however. That the place was now called House of the Hindu shows that by this time the stupa had crumbled to dust and Buddhism was all but forgotten in these parts.

But Babur found nothing of interest here. His guide, Malik Abu Said Kamari, thinking his esteemed guest would find the dark and cramped space unsavoury did not show Babur the underground vaults. When, back in Jamrud, Babur complained about uninteresting Gorkhatri, the guide confessed he had on purpose not led him into the vaults because of the difficult and narrow access. Babur roundly upbraided the man, but as the way back to Begram was long and the day almost over, Babur deferred the dungeons for a subsequent visit.

The locality of Begram recalls at least two other similarly named places in Afghanistan. One tradition makes it a corruption of Vikram, while Charles Masson postulates that it is a Turko-Indic compound of bey (chief in Turkish) and gram (town/village in Sanskrit). Archaeologist Ahmad Hasan Dani, however, believes it is a pure Sanskrit title from vara (best) and gram. That would make sense because Peshawar, the first city of the subcontinent that outsiders came to, seems to have captivated one and all. Today the place name Begram is not part of the local idiom; it is preserved only in the minds of readers of history.

In March 1519, on his way to establish the Mughal Empire in India, Babur paused at Gorkhatri for the express purpose of exploring it. He found it 'a smallish abode' much like a hermitage. All around was a large number of smaller cells as in a Buddhist monastery recalling the time when it was indeed that. Holding a lamp, Babur crawled on all fours into the dark oubliette through a mess of human hair. The man was disgusted. He recalled his earlier visit and how he rued being denied a peek. Now he wryly noted, 'but it does not seem a place to regret not seeing.'

The aura of mystery and mysticism surrounding Gorkhatri was not to be questioned, however. In 1581, Babur's grandson Akbar visited the place and Abu'l Fazal, one of the Nine Jewels of Akbar's court and writer of his biographical diary, wrote of it being the abode of saints. He also noted that 'babblers' spoke of the underground chambers as being endlessly long and dark. On a second sojourn, again in 1581, Akbar ordered Abu'l Fazal to go to Gorkhatri and dole out gifts to the hermits. The needful was done and employing journalistic licence the writer tells us that 'thousands of needy persons' benefitted. One can imagine that royal largesse was responded to by the fakirs with vociferous prayers for the long and successful life of his majesty for Abu'l Fazal concludes that 'the treasure-house of prayer was filled'.

In 1607, Akbar's son Jahangir too paused here awhile hoping to confabulate with some fakirs so that he might 'obtain grace'. But like Babur, he was sufficiently disappointed to pass a rather harsh verdict: 'But that was like looking for the phoenix or the philosopher's stone. A herd without any religious knowledge came to my view, from seeing who I derived nothing but obscurity of mind'.

∞

Shortly after Skylax's reconnaissance, Darius enlarged his grandfather's kingdom to include in his empire all of what is now Pakistan. And so, together with Peshawar, the rest of the country became a tribute payer to the King of Kings. Two centuries of peace ensued and here in Peshawar followers of the new religion of Buddha lived besides singers of Vedic hymns and followers of Zoroaster.

In 326 BCE, Alexander's generals Perdiccas and Hephaestion brought down two divisions of the army through Khyber Pass and rested a few days in Peshawar. The Greeks were as tolerant of different beliefs as their predecessors and even if the governor was changed, life went on undisturbed.

But Alexander's kingdom was short-lived. No sooner had his body lost the colour of life in distant Babylon, there began the great struggle among his generals to be 'the strongest'. That is what the comatose king had said when his generals asked him whom the kingdom would go to. The Greek governor left Peshawar to find his fortune in that struggle and Chandragupta Maurya took control of the country. The year was 322 BCE.

Even if Chandragupta and his grandson Asoka are celebrated for the brilliance of their rule, it is only the nature of empires to rise to a zenith and then decay. And the Mauryan Empire fell to the Greeks whose forebears had first entered India with Alexander. Having annexed Afghanistan, the Indo-Greeks, as historians today refer to them, established themselves by 180 BCE over much of modern day Khyber Pakhtunkhwa and Punjab. This was only the beginning of the great pageant of dynasties that ruled over the City of Flowers.

The Greeks gave way to the Persian speaking Parthians who were supplanted by Scythians enriched by Siberian gold who, in turn, succumbed to the Kushans under the brilliant builder Kanishka. By the end of the third century of the Common Era, the wheel had turned full circle to the Persians. Now it was the turn of the Sassanian dynasty.

In the last quarter of the fifth century, the savage Huns poured down the western passes to ravage Peshawar. Uprooted from the wind-scoured grasslands of Central Asia, these squat horse riders, masters of the awesome power of the composite (wood and antler) re-curved bow that could be used from horseback, were the first 'scourge of god' in our history. Xuanzang says that the great Buddha had prophesised that the stupa to be built by the pious Kanishka would be destroyed and rebuilt seven times. Now the first devastation was upon it. Without remorse and without regard for woman, man or child, the Huns, first under Tor Aman and then his son Mehr Gul, raped, killed and sacked. In centuries of political upheaval, Peshawar had seen a few battles, but never such wanton brutality and destruction. The city was left a smouldering ruin and the Chinese pilgrim Sung Yun lamented the 'most barbarous atrocities' of the 'cruel and vindictive' Mehr Gul occurring only a hundred years before his time.
No sooner had the barbarians passed on to the east to be finally defeated by a confederacy of Rajputs in Cholistan in 528, Peshawar rebounded. Once again trading caravans came down the Khyber; the bazaars thronged, the storytellers regaled their audiences and the flowers grew. Once again peace returned to Peshawar, this time for five hundred years. Now amid the ruins of Kanishka's monastery, the sound of Buddhist hymns gave way to the Vedic. In these years of peace in the Khyber Pass, the powerful Hindu Shahya rulers of Kashmir extended their sway through Peshawar to Kabul and all remained well.

In the closing years of the tenth century came the plundering Turks. After the initial excursions of Subuktagin, a Turk from Barskoon in what is now Kyrgyzstan and the founder of the Ghaznavid dynasty, his son Mahmud was unstoppable. Beginning in 997, Mahmud led no fewer than seventeen raids into India, in quest of spoil more than dominion, and Peshawar suffered greatly. In time, however, the city came to be spared vengefulness because of the growing number of Muslims among its populace.

There followed centuries of repeated upheavals with brief peaceful interludes. The Ghaznavids gave way to the Ghorids who were supplanted by the Slave Dynasty. If the tax collectors of these dynasties were harsh, the thirteenth century saw Mongol influx accompanied by horrible rapine. Relative peace came only with the arrival of the Mughals in the early sixteenth century. The worst trouble in these centuries was when the Mughal Empire decayed and the Turk Nadir Shah of Persia set his eyes on its wealth and, starting in 1738, mounted repeated incursions on this sorry land. Peace returned with Ranjit Singh's reign (r. 1801–1839). But that too was relative, for Sikh rule rankled with the Pakhtuns.[2]

Peshawar was never a city of Pakhtuns who spoke a language rising out of ancient Avestan. It was a city of traders, professionals and scholars who spoke a language derived from Punjabi and Kashmiri with a sprinkling of Gujarati from a long way off to the south. Even in the Middle Ages, natives of Pushpapura would have been surnamed Chawla or Arora or Piracha rather than Afridi or Yusufzai. Sometime after the Pakhtuns converted to Islam in the ninth century, the language of Peshawar and indeed of other cities of the province came to be known as Hindko after the largely Hindu population.

As a city whose businessmen dealt with traders from distant lands, Peshawar was multi-lingual. The Hindko speaker was equally comfortable in the Pashto of the man come down from the Khyber defiles or from Waziristan as he was in Uzbek or a couple of other Turkish dialects. Two thousand years ago, even Greek would have echoed off the ancient walls of the city within the walls.

That is how British administrators of the East India Company found the city in the mid-nineteenth century. It was an island of peaceful businesspeople surrounded by a host, staunchly religious, sometimes peaceful, hospitable and friendly, otherwise turbulent and troublesome. They could be seen swaggering about in their large turbans, baggy *shalwars* and flowing collar-less *kurtas* with a tassel, rather than buttons, on the side to tie the dress at the shoulder as they did business with the vest and dhoti-clad storekeeper.

In 1849, the British took Peshawar and strengthened the outer walls of the old fort before they set about constructing a cantonment. Among the earliest buildings was the deputy commissioner's residence built in 1849. On a natural mound that very likely conceals the remains of an ancient past, they raised an edifice that was a clean break from the traditional fortified houses of tribal chiefs just outside the cantonment.

Visiting Pakhtun dignitaries would surely have found madness in the exposed veranda and absence of crenulations or loopholes along the parapet of the building. Why, the very lack of the traditional high compound wall with its turrets could only mean the rulers were possessed of suicidal tendencies. It was either that or some hidden strength the tribal folks failed to see. Whatever was thought of it, the administrators did not alter the building. It was only added to and it eventually became the Governor's House.

---

2) Pakhtun is singular for the race Pakhtana. The kh sound of northern Pakhto (or Pashto) turns to sh as the language progresses southward. The word Pathan is never used by Pakhtuns for themselves. This was a mispronunciation on Turkish and Mongol tongues that became prevalent in the subcontinent after the twelfth century.

Even as the British built their churches, mission schools and the Saddar Bazaar, life in the old city remained unchanged. And so it continued to 1977 when I first became acquainted with Peshawar as a grown up. It was a city to fall in love with. The flowers that Babur had exulted over were everywhere: in parks, in every private garden, in the sprawling grounds of Islamia College and even along the roads and amid the tombstones of the Christian cemetery until then safe from the hands of desecrators. In spring when the millions of roses were in full bloom in Peshawar, the city was awash with fragrance.

Though there were no double-humped camels plodding in with their loads from the marts of Samarkand and Fergana, the bazaars somehow retained the ageless colour. In open-fronted stores, the gentleman shopkeeper with his dark vest and karakul cap leaned forward to speak softly to the Khan from some village in Tirah or deeper still from the land of the Orakzais. You could tell the visitor was a Khan for his chin was clean-shaven, his moustaches neatly trimmed, his *shalwar-kameez* crisp and he too wore the dark vest and karakul hat. But he also carried his pistol and a belt full of ammo slung across his shoulders.

They could well be talking of the next crop of maize to be brought in from the uplands or the set of copperware needed for a wedding in the Khan's family, but the very air of frontier town Peshawar made me feel they were conspiring. At the nearby fabric dealer's outlet women, three or four at a time, shrouded from head to toe in the folds of the shuttlecock burka, whispered to each other and in barely audible voices gave out their demand to the storekeeper. As he laid out bolts of material, not even a finger showed from under the burka as the women swiftly pulled the stuff in for inspection. Once the selection was made, the haggling was done in an undertone whose drift could easily be known by the responses of the shopkeeper. The bazaars of Under Sheher were replete with scenes from an imagination honed by Kipling.

The air was so clean, that in the winter of 1977 when it rained in Peshawar, we could espy new snow on the hills of Landi Kotal. Peshawar was just like that when I left it in August 1978, telling my friends I would come to live here after retirement.

I returned in 1985. It was as if centuries had elapsed to effect the huge change. Local registration plates were outnumbered by TRP (Temporary Route Permit) ones meant since years before the Soviet invasion for visiting Afghan transport. Countless boxy vans emitting dark clouds of smoke drove roughshod around the city. Boy conductors shouted in the Kabul dialect of Pashto (sometimes in Dari) to draw commuters and there were Afghans everywhere. They were termed either mujahedeen or refugees. Though the flowers were still there and Peshawar girls as pretty as ever, there were more burka-shrouded Afghan women in the bazaars. The diesel-smoky, noisy city was no longer the Peshawar I wanted to retire to.

In 2013, my friend Dr Syed Amjad Hussain who had migrated decades ago from his Meena Bazaar home in the city to Boston, took me walkabout in the old streets. We ended up at the excavation at Gorkhatri. There we

Peshawar city's houses dating back to the nineteenth century were celebrated for their fine woodwork (left) and cut brick ornamentation (right). The bridge connecting two structures meant close family connections between owners of the two houses and for the ladies of the families to cross from one side to the other without being seen by outsiders.

The wrought iron filigree in the spandrels of the arches and the balustrades below the railing of the balcony were not local products. The rich, who could afford such pieces of architecture, ordered the wrought iron from foundries in Kolkata and Mumbai. These beautiful structures line the newly restored Bazaar Kalan, restored by the Directorate of Archaeology and Museums, KP, leading up to Gorkhatri.

Top Left: A qehva-maker in Peshawar. The lip-sticking sweet brew of green tea is a delicacy that has made Peshawar famous for centuries. Word has it that it is this brew that keeps Pakhtun bodies lean and fat free.

Bottom Left: The towering dome of the tomb of Sheikh Imamuddin. Revered as a saint in his lifetime, this man of God passed away in 1650. The mausoleum was completed eight years later and surrounded by a garden laid out in the traditional quadrangle style which has now been taken over by cultivation.

Top Right: The restored Bazaar Kalan with the gateway topped by the blockhouse that Paolo di Avitabile used as his private apartment seen on the left.

Bottom Right: The west wall of the Palosi Piran mosque showing the bulge of the mehrab. The dome of Sheikh Imamuddin stands to the left.

Top Left: The tomb of the dynamic and heroic Nawab Saeed Khan, the governor of Peshawar and Kabul under Shah Jahan, was once sited in a garden but is now in the grounds of Mission High School. Saeed Khan died in Kabul in 1651. Between 1849 and 1851, Harry Lumsden, the founder of the Corps of Guides, used this building as residence and headquarters. In 1926, a lintel was added to create an upper floor which has since served as the Mission Hospital Chapel. There is no sarcophagus because the burial was subterranean and the passage to that chamber is blocked off.

Bottom Left: Once a decrepit and dusty heap of timber and metal, this fire truck dating to the first decade of the twentieth century has been faithfully restored by the Government of KP with the support of Vintage & Classic Car Club of Pakistan. Notice the solid rubber tyres and the cranking handle to fire the engine. The Merryweather London radiator top was a recognised symbol of the first name in manufacture of fire appliances during the early decades of the twentieth century.

Top Right: The tomb of Bijo. Tradition has it that the second Saddozai (Durrani) ruler of Afghanistan Temur Shah secretly romanced Bibi Jan. Unfortunately for the lovers, Temur's wife caught on and had the poor woman poisoned. The grieving king buried his lady love in Peshawar. Since the king himself passed away in 1793, the tomb would have been built some years before that. It is said the name Bijo (monkey) was shortened from Bibi Jan to deride the hapless woman.

Bottom Right: The Chamkani baoli. The beautiful pavilion, a usual adjunct to all stepped wells, is among the rarer ones because of the upper floor cubicle. The brink of the stairs leading to the well is just seen but the well itself on the left is now partially filled up. It dates to the early Mughal period.

Mughal period coins recovered from
the archaeological dig at Gorkhatri.

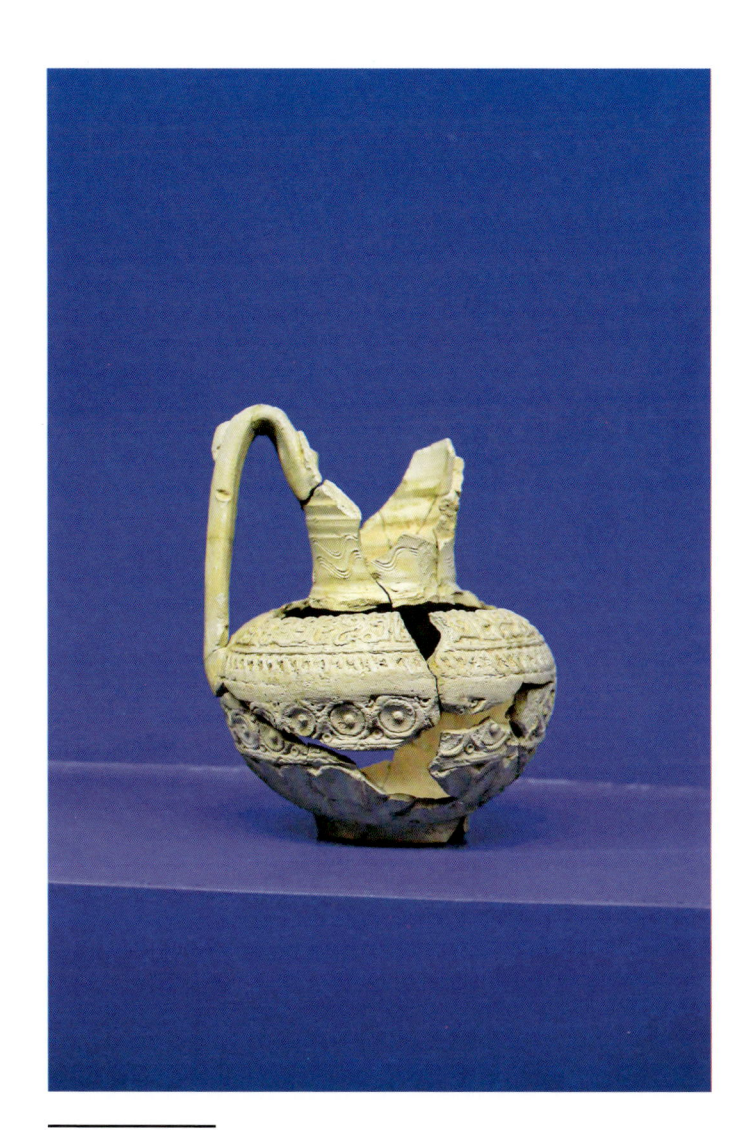

A Ghaznavid period (eleventh century) handled ewer recovered from the archaeological dig at Gorkhatri.

A Mughal period pot with a bird design recovered from the archaeological dig at Gorkhatri.

stood looking down the pit into the layers of habitation spread across two and a half millenniums. They were all there: the Persian Achaemenian, Punjabi Mauryan, Greek, Parthian, Scythian, Kushan, Sassanian, Hun, Hindu Shahya, Ghaznavid, Ghorid, Mughal and Sikh. Gorkhatri was the hub of ancient Pushpapura, said Dr Hussain.

Azeem, my archaeologist captain, brought me back to the present as he drove through the maddening traffic around what was once the south-western side of the walled city. The inhabitants of Peshawar were a peaceful lot, he said. Outside the city, in Serasiya, there lived ruthless brigands who periodically erupted into the city to loot. In the middle years of the nineteenth century, this was such a regular feature, that in order to restrain the bandits British authorities built a wall around Serasiya village. A short stretch of that wall can still be seen near Serasiya Gate in the old protective wall of the city.

We talked of the *pipal* that Kanishka had planted near his stupa and under which fifteen hundred years later Babur had stood. I told Azeem of the beautiful spreading *pipal* trees I had seen in the old city back in 1977-78. He too recalled having played under some of those as a child. On our 2013 walkabout in the city, Dr Amjad Hussain told me that on one of his visits home from the States, he had found his favourite tree gone. The city's lungs were slowly being removed.

'What of the stupa of Kanishka? Where would it have stood in the old city?' I asked Azeem.
'Not inside the city. Recall that Xuanzang says it was built near a swamp, a little beyond crowded habitation. As a child, I remember cycling past Shah ji ki Dheri. Much later I learned that was where the stupa had once stood,' he said.

To many Shah ji ki Dheri, 'Mound of the Shah', would mean it was connected to a personage claiming holy descent. To me it always means the King's Mound. The last time history mentions the great stupa is in *Kitab al Hind* (Book of India) of Abu Rehan al Beruni. This brilliant polymath of Central Asiatic origin was forcibly brought to Ghazni by Sultan Mahmud during one of his depredatory raids to the north. In 1017, Al Beruni succeeded in getting permission to visit India. En route, he paused at Peshawar and was enthralled by accounts of a lofty stupa that no longer existed. He referred to it as Kanik Chaitya – Kanik's stupa – in roughly the same locality as Shah ji ki Dheri. Collective memory has strange ways of reaching back into antiquity and though the stupa and its monastery were very likely laid low in the early sixth century during the barbarous Hunnic invasion, the cognomen connected that old mound with the Kushan king Kanishka.

Azeem said that over the past four decades the mound was built over and was today nothing more than a disorderly jumble of streets and housing. That was before the ancient cultural site could be investigated in any detail to reveal what else had happened there after Kanishka's expression of piety. Yet I wanted to see and photograph it, so he drove me around to the southeast side of town. If I had expected a lofty mound rendered higher still by construction, it was nothing of the sort. It was as Azeem had described it: disorderly and over-crowded. The jumble did not even make for a decent photograph.

A thousand years from today, archaeologists coming upon a mound outside a city that was once called Peshawar would excavate the disintegrating rubble of cement masonry to discover the reality of twenty-first century life. Below this jumble, they will find the remains of life and religion two thousand years older still. For the present at least, the earth holds close to its heart the deeper secrets of life in that far off time.

In 1909, Shah ji ki Dheri was another place, however. Then the mound stood alone with nary a house upon it. That year the archaeologist David Spooner set spade and trowel to the dust of two millenniums. From its depth, he retrieved a relic casket, 'a round metal vessel, five inches in diameter and four inches in height. The centre of the lid supports three metal figures arranged in a semi circle; a seated figure of the Buddha in the centre, Indra the god of heaven to his right, and Brahma the creator to his left, both of whom are standing in a state of adoration.'

Inside this casket was a 'six-sided crystal bottle' sealed with a clay seal of Kanishka. Inside the sealed container was yet another casket, gold this time, containing three tiny fragments of burnt bone. Spooner concluded that the bones could only be the mortal remains of Buddha. For the archaeologist this would surely have been a triumphal Eureka moment for until then the location of Kanishka's stupa was only conjecture. The crystal bottle and the gold casket was gifted to the Buddhist community of Burma (now Myanmar) who reburied the relics in Mandalay and raised a beautiful pagoda above them. The metal casket was preserved in Peshawar Museum, while its replica was displayed in the main hall where it can still be seen.

The figures on the casket were in high relief and even though Spooner found them to be 'particularly pleasing', he observed that the carving showed 'manifest proof of artistic decadence'. He concluded that by Kanishka's time the once superlative art of Gandhara was in decline. The inscription on the casket, in Aramaic script in use here since *circa* 500 BCE, sought blessings for 'all creatures' and gave the name of Agisalaos 'the superintendent of works at the vihara of Kanishka in the monastery of Mahasena'.

Here the name of the superintendent, being clearly Hellenic, is of great interest. Agisilaos, and not Agisalaos as spelled on the casket, is a Greek male given name meaning Gift of God. We know that in the second century BCE, the Euthydemid or Indo-Greek rulers controlled what is now Khyber Pakhtunkhwa and Punjab and there was a large European population in this area. For two hundred years after that most educated natives of cosmopolitan towns like Pushkalavati (outside Charsadda) and Taxila were polyglots. Here they fluently spoke, besides their mother tongues, Greek, Avestan and even some Central Asiatic dialects.

That a Greek architect named Agisilaos was living here in the second century CE, tells us that Peshawar was still very much a multicultural city. The misspelling of the name, however, shows that the purer Greek of four centuries earlier had somewhat corrupted. Had the stupa lasted until his time, Spooner would surely have found it adorned with fluted pillars and the much favoured Corinthian capitals besides other features recalling Indo-Greek rule.

∽

Azeem's family, Barakzai Pakhtuns, moved into Peshawar city from an outlying village more than a hundred years ago. He himself was born in the city where he spent his childhood and received his early education. Now in his mid-fifties, his memory goes back to the early 1970s. On the subject of women shoppers, Azeem said the most numbers they would see in the bazaar would be during the months of weddings which in the old days were usually immediately after either the wheat harvest in May or the rice harvest in October. Then teams of men and women from outlying villages would descend upon the city riding oxen and spread out across the bazaar in smaller single-gender groups to make their purchases.

All these buyers from the village were relatives or neighbours of the bride's and groom's families. Since the families alone could not handle purchases and other arrangements, the entire village mustered out to help. Divided into groups, each with a specific order to fill, they shared the burden of the family from both sides. This was an admirable example of collectivism. Azeem added that all such burden-sharers would be guests at the wedding. The lanes these buyers thronged were the Abreshamgran (silk weavers), Bazaar Misgran (Coppersmith's Bazaar), Bajaj Batra (Fabric Dealers' Alley) and Mochi Batra (Cobblers' Alley). Though businesses have shifted, the names have stuck fast. Azeem remembers the nearby Bazaar Pakhisazan – Hand Fan Makers – that now deals in electrical goods. Today the only hand fans to be had are ornate items for those nostalgically inclined to the past.

In Azeem's childhood, the bazaar that we today known as Pipal Mandi after the several spreading *pipal* trees was known as Ganj e Kohna – Ancient Treasure – perhaps recalling a greater glory in years gone by when caravans unloaded in the now demolished caravanserais wares like hand-knotted carpets from Bokhara and Samarkand or silks from distant factories in China. Not far was Shelay Kobañ where sifters removed grit from lentils and grain before passing on the foodstuff to retailers.

As Azeem spoke, I imagined men, and perhaps women too, sitting on the threshold of the stores lining the narrow street repeatedly tossing the grain on tray-like wickerwork items, the *chhaj* in Punjabi, to work the impurities to the edge. In my mind's eye, I saw the award-winning image: early morning or late afternoon sun slanting in from the long side of the alley highlighting the dust rising above the *chhaj* manipulators. Here too things have changed and for some peculiar reason the lane is now Chiri Kuttañ, literally Sparrow-Beaters.

'On the subject of sparrows, Peshawaris love sparrow fried in a spiced batter of ground chickpeas,' said Azeem. Right under the clock tower, Azeem remembered the man with a long, sharp thumb nail that he used as a knife to slaughter the little birds. One swipe, a spurt of blood and the bird was plucked, cleaned and dunked in the batter before going into the pan. Incidentally, however, the bird in question was not a sparrow, but a jungle babbler (*Turdoides striatus*) that visits the northern parts of the country in winter.

Having come through Bazaar Misgran, we had meandered around Chowk Yadgar – Memorial Crossing – commemorating a certain Colonel Charles Hastings who died in Peshawar in 1892. We paused to read the plaque on Cunningham's Clock Tower. Built in 1900, its clock was not working in the late 1970s when I first saw it. But now, thankfully, it has been put in order again. Cunningham was at one time commissioner of Peshawar division and the tower's builder was one R. B. Balmokand. The full inscription on the plaque above the locked door of the tower was quaintly fawning.

At the top of the street, heading east from the tower sits the entrance leading into Gorkhatri that had so disappointed Babur. The lofty gateway was built in the 1830s and topping it is a now ruinous apartment house that folks even today recall as the residence of the tyrant Abutabela. Many years ago, an elderly shopkeeper in the street had recounted how the man would summarily try and hang Afridi or Mohmand men reported for raiding Peshawar.

From a farming family of Naples in Italy, Paolo di Avitabile joined the ascendant army of Napoleon and rose through the ranks as an artilleryman. After the rout of Waterloo, like so many others of his calling, he drifted through Europe to eventually fetch up in the Persian army.

A house in Bazaar Kalan (Great Bazaar) that runs up eastward from Cunningham Clock Tower to Gorkhatri (popularly known as Tehsil). The superlative stone work of the mock domelets and pilasters gives the impression of being carved in wood.

Top Left: Amin Tajik, who runs the antique shop was born and raised in Peshawar. His family are natives of Ghazni from where they migrated in the late 1970s. Tajik believes that the famous Gardner crockery was manufactured in Tajikistan and exported to Russia. This may indicate that there was a copycat Gardner in Central Asia.

Bottom Left: Gardner Crockery. One wonders if this is the genuine item actually manufactured in the Francis Gardner factory just outside Moscow, or a copy. Gardner established his factory in 1766 and it continues in production to this day. After the Bolshevik revolution, the name Gardner was suitably replaced, however, it was restored with the fall of the Soviets.

Top/Bottom Right: Brassware in the antique shop of Amin Tajik in Bazaar Kalan not far from Cunningham Clock Tower.

Top Left: The famous Sethi House in Mohalla Sethian. An affluent business family of the nineteenth century, these Sethis handled trade through Afghanistan to Central Asia and as far away as Russia. Their *hundis* (letters of credit) were honoured across all these countries earning them substantial profits. To match their wealth, this family cultivated fine artistic taste that is evident in the homes they still own.

Bottom Left: The courtyard of Sethi House is an exquisite display of the finest woodwork to be found anywhere in Peshawar.

Top Right: Stained glass in Sethi House.

Bottom Right: Inside the mosque of Mohalla Sethian

If Peshawar can boast of one jewel in its crown, it is surely the mosque of Mahabat Khan with its exquisitely painted interior. There were two men by this name in the seventeenth century Mughal court. Zamana Beg titled Mahabat Khan or Khan Khana I by Shah Jahan died in 1634. Going by the architecture of this beautiful house of worship, it appears to have been built later. This would be his son Lahrasp Khan also titled Mahabat Khan. This latter served both Shah Jahan and his son Aurangzeb in various appointments. For several years the mosque has been in fits and starts of restoration. In 2019, it was impossible to take a reasonable image of the mosque exterior because of the web of scaffolding on the façade.

Fading frescos in the prayer chamber of Mahabat Khan's mosque.

All Saints Church, Kohati Gate. Consecrated in 1883, this beautiful and iconic worship house was built in true oriental style recalling mosque architecture.

Interior showing the altar of All Saints Church. The stained glass window was gifted to the church by Lady Emma Edwardes in memory of the service to Peshawar by her late husband Sir Herbert Edwardes.

یسوع مسیح
دیروز و امروز
و تا به ابد
همان است
تحصیل نجات
بوساطت
خداوند ما
عیسی مسیح

After four years of service there, he arrived in Punjab in 1827 where the brilliant Maharaja Ranjit Singh gave him command of an artillery regiment. By the time he retired and left Punjab in 1843 to return to his native land, he had risen to the rank of general. In between, he served as Ranjit Singh's governor at Wazirabad and later at Peshawar. It was here, in the lanes and bazaars of Peshawar that his name came to be corrupted to Abutabela, a title that has outlived the man by nearly two centuries.

The west gate of Gor Khatri. The towering blockhouse was Avitabile's private residence. After years of remaining abandoned in dilapidated condition, in 2019 it was in the process of restoration.

Europeans visiting him in his governorships were appalled by his harsh and arbitrary methods of awarding punishment, including execution. Henry Lawrence, the brilliant soldier-statesman who died in the War of Independence of 1857, having seen Avitabile at work, referred to him as 'a savage among savages'. Be that as it may, history tells us that during his rule Peshawar was a peaceful city. From the vantage of the rooms above the lofty gateway, Avitabile is said to have kept watch over the crowded bazaars spread out below him.

The east gate of Gor Khatri.

In the years leading up to and during the First Anglo-Afghan War – in which Britain suffered its most humiliating defeat – Avitabile provided liberal logistical and administrative support to the army of the East India Company. Unsurprisingly, in the few years between his departure and the consolidation of British rule over Khyber Pakhtunkhwa, Peshawar remained troubled and anarchic. Surely it would have been at this time that predatory tribes from Serasiya raided the city whose legends were preserved until Azeem's childhood.

Meanwhile, newly posted to Peshawar in 1834, the Neapolitan governor needed accommodation. And so while his blockhouse above the western gateway of Gorkhatri was being built, Avitabile took over a lovely palace that may have been abandoned at that time. Only twenty years before him, the Scottish statesman Mountstuart Elphinstone had noticed this building. Among the abundance of minarets and cupolas of 'Mohammadan tombs', he wrote of one that rose to 'several high towers' and from afar radiated an 'appearance of grandeur'. But on closer inspection he was disappointed. The 'garden-house' built by 'Ali Merdaun Khaun' had once indeed been 'splendid' but in Elphinstone's time, it was ruinous. Relying purely on conjecture and hearsay, he goes on to tell us, incorrectly, that this man had filled the country from Mashhad to Delhi with very fine tombs and religious buildings that were appreciable all the more because of the gardens surrounding them.

In 1832, Mohan Lal, a highly educated Kashmiri, and secretary to the adventurer and part diplomat Alexander Burnes, arrived in Peshawar with his employer. They were on their way to Kabul where Burnes was to earn the hatred of the Afghans for, besides being a tireless womaniser, an active player of the Great Game. In the unrest of 1841, the Scotsman was ruthlessly murdered in the beginning of November. Mohan Lal survived and returned to India. His memoir *Travels in the Panjab, Afghanistan and Turkistan*, written in English, gives us a rare glimpse from Indian eyes into the carryings on of that fateful time in Kabul.

Mohan Lal wrote of visiting the garden of Ali Mardan Khan while in Peshawar and used Elphinstone's line on Ali Mardan filling the country with fine monuments. In the centre of the garden chocabloc with fruit trees and rose bushes, Mohan Lal saw a lovely three storeyed building surrounded by fountains. He said the garden, criss-crossed by tree-shaded walking tracks, was named Shalimar. One would have wished for someone to have described Ali Mardan's villa a little better, but both Elphinstone and Mohan Lal stop short.

But more of Ali Mardan Khan when we reach Lahore where he is buried. For the time being, as we stood in the shadow of Cunningham's clock tower, Azeem suggested a change of direction. We headed away from the old quarter to see the first accommodation for Avitabile: the garden-house that had failed to impress Elphinstone.

Now imprisoned within the protective walls of the Peshawar corps headquarters, the mid-seventeenth century edifice had once stood well outside the bustle of the city. Here on slightly high ground amid open fields, it looked out on a magnificent vista of the hills surrounding Peshawar. Today it is right within the clench of military housing and offices. The good thing is that it has recently been restored to a bit of its old glory. In fact, when we went there in January 2019 and again two months later, the atrium was still criss-crossed by steel scaffolding.

Shortly before conservation work began, there was talk in the corps headquarters of demolishing the three hundred and fifty year-old building. Because of its location inside the military headquarters, it was inaccessible to the public and in its dilapidated condition the building was of no use to the authorities. One sane mind intervened and invited the Department of Archaeology to see what could be done about it. The man was Lieutenant General Nazeer Ahmed Butt.

Having been used at different times as soldiers' quarters and stores, the building was in poor state. It was run-down and literally 'hanging on by a thread,' said the general. Since it was within the premises of his office, he felt it was his obligation to do something to protect it. While the Department of Archaeology raised most of the money, General Butt chipped in with the rest from his headquarters' budget. At his level, most military officers have other priorities making this man a unique example to be emulated.

Today, with the general long since having left the post and retired from the service, the villa of Ali Mardan Khan has been brought back from the brink. While some little bit still remains to be done, it is nevertheless a fine example of how a derelict and ramshackle historical monument can be resurrected. The restoration project has uncovered subterranean conduits that once fed now defunct fountains and flowing water channels and reveal a bit of the genius of Mughal hydraulic engineering.

∞

We meandered through the old city to Dabgari and the Afghan Mission Hospital and school. Inside the compound reared the lofty dome of a Mughal building, surprisingly with a cross on the parapet. Azeem said this was the only Muslim tomb he knew of in Pakistan that had been converted into a church. Acquiring permission to see the church entailed a rather protracted meeting with the principal who thought we were writing a book on her school and provided a lot of detail about achievements of the school. This was followed by a tour of the deserted classrooms (it was summer vacations) before the prelate arrived to escort us to the church.

The Shah Jahan period building was taken over as a residence by the British when they first took over Peshawar in the 1840s. Subsequently, the ground floor fell into disuse. Using the upper floor galleries to anchor girders and beams, a chamber was created under the dome to house a small

The villa of Ali Mardan Khan. Notice the dry water channel in the foreground that was once punctuated by playing fountains. The stubby pillars and arches on either flank of the main building were added during the Sikh period.

chapel. The tomb has since been a worship house. The priest led us up the stairs and told us about his parish. We listened politely, until he said the stairs leading underground (to the burial chamber) actually went into the opening of the tunnel to fort Bala Hissar.

'Rubbish! There is no tunnel here or anywhere else,' Azeem waggled his hand in the priest's face in the subcontinental style of dismissal.

I loved this vehement and outright rebuttal of a foolishness that is rampant across Pakistan. Every medieval monument is supposed to be connected with every other place by a tunnel. Yet we never hear of royalty travelling from, say, Lahore to Delhi by the subterranean route. The poor padre who had proudly peddled his hokum to anyone who cared to listen was swiftly crestfallen.

'But that is what everyone tells us,' he almost pleaded with Azeem to let the tunnel exist. But the archaeologist did not oblige.

Sitting on a high plinth, the octagonal building is said to be the tomb of Nawab Saeed Khan.[3] He was the dynamic, swashbuckling governor of Kabul and Peshawar under Shah Jahan. His military prowess kept the Pakhtuns under his sway in order. Any infringement anywhere and Saeed Khan was in the field swinging his sword or directing artillery fire. If truth be told, he is one character who actually flashes across the pages of the *Shah Jahan Nama* like a lightning bolt.

In 1638, Ali Mardan Khan, whose garden mansion Avitabile later used, bolted from allegiance to the Safvid king of Persia and wrote to Saeed Khan in Peshawar expressing loyalty to Shah Jahan. That he landed right in the Mughal lap was entirely because of the acumen and diplomacy of this brilliant man. For his loyalty to the crown and his unstinting services, Saeed Khan was granted the honorific Bahadur Zafar Jang – Valorous Victor of Battles. After

Detail of partially restored fresco on the first floor of the villa.

years of a vigorous and victorious life on the battlefield and an equally rewarding one as an administrator, Saeed Khan died peacefully of old age in January 1652. The subterranean vault under the dome of the church behind Mission Hospital contains the mortal remains of this truly admirable man.

---

3) There is some confusion about the name. Pakhtuns pronounce it as Sad (with a soft d), while the archaeologist Ahmad Hasan Dani lists him as Sayid. The *Shah Jahan Nama* spells the name as Sa'id Khan making clear distinction between Sad and Sayyid. I therefore prefer Saeed.

From the villa in the garden created by Ali Mardan, Avitabile moved into his new Gorkhatri accommodation as soon as it was ready and from here his proverbial iron thumb came down on the citizens of Peshawar and all those who sought to make trouble in the city. We entered by the east gate of the large compound because the west gate with Avitabile's apartment was closed for restoration. The apartment itself was a jumble of caved in roofs and sagging floors. Clearly it will take a while before it will be open to attract visitors.

In Gorkhatri, Mohan Lal had found Hindu men, women and children bathing in a pond fed by a fountain. He said this was a usual Sunday ritual. He noted that the pond and fountain was fed by the clear water of a river – which could be none other than the now heavily polluted Bara. From his reading Azeem knew that the river did indeed flow through the city in Mughal times. And barely three decades ago when it followed the present bed, it still provided potable water that was considered a curative for arthritis and gastric trouble.

Murder under the misnomer of 'honour' killing was alive in Mohan Lal's Peshawar. We are told of a mullah who had a not-so-secret affair with the wife of a tailor. One afternoon when the tailor was absent, the mullah thought it 'a good opportunity' for a bit of frolic under the covers. It seems, however, that the cuckolded man was not as clueless as the lovebirds would have thought. Finding the door locked, the tailor, quiet as a prowling cat, climbed over a wall, and with his sword killed the pair in bed.

He then hauled the two corpses to the governor Sultan Mohammad Khan who was at that moment entertaining Mohan Lal's employer Alexander Burnes. It seems that Mohan Lal was present in this meeting for he noted that the party 'praised the tailor for his intrepidity and resolution'.

The houses of Peshawar, we are told, were made of unbaked bricks on wooden frames and were three or four storeys high. The streets were narrow but they were paved and were 'larger and cleaner than those of Lahore'. Mohan Lal also noted the branches of the Bara River running through the town.

Four decades after Mohan Lal a most remarkable woman passed through Peshawar. She fell in love with the city and its people, much as most folks did until the late 1970s. Lady Charlotte Canning, wife of the viceroy Lord Charles Canning, was in Peshawar with her husband in March 1860. Charlotte was not just a writer of a very readable diary; she was also an outstanding water colourist. Had it not been for our very own raconteur par excellence Fakir Syed Aijazuddin, her work would very likely have remained hidden from Pakistani eyes ensconced as it is in the home of the Earl of Harewood, a descendent of Her Ladyship's. Aijazuddin accessed the work and turned it into a delightful collection of paintings and prose, a most readable treasure house of history and a collector's item.

When she arrived in Peshawar, Charlotte was taken by Pakhtun looks: she found them better looking than the Sikhs. She thought them vain but 'the finest face' she had ever seen. One of her paintings shows a walled city and another, quite evidently made from the walls of Gorkhatri, looks out to a 'magnificent' view of the fort, trees, valley and distant mountains. As for the city:

> It was crowded & lighted like Lahore only the houses had been dressed up with hundreds of little flags & shawls. The streets are wide & have trees & streams running along many of them. The small painted houses with so much wood about them gives the look of a Turkish town to Peshawur. There is little about it to remind one of India.

Back in the present and in the spacious compound of Gorkhatri, I commented on the rooms running around the walls as if this was a caravanserai.

'It was indeed that,' said Azeem, 'and one that the remarkable Jahan Ara Begum ordered. She named it Jahanabad Serai after her father Shah Jahan, the fifth Mughal king of India.'

And what a woman this Jahan Ara Begum was!

The second of fourteen children of Shah Jahan and Arjumand Bano Begum better known as Mumtaz Mahal of Taj Mahal fame, Jahan Ara (World Adorner) was born in April 1614.[4] The king noted her acumen and gumption early on and upon the death of the queen in June 1631, Jahan Ara, referred to as Begum Sahiba or Badshah Begum, took the role of the First Lady of the empire. Highly educated and cultured, she fulfilled this 'important position with grace and dignity', wrote Annmarie Schimmel in *The Empire of the Great Mughals*.

Shortly after assuming this role, when she was but seventeen years of age, Jahan Ara was granted the very important office of Keeper of the Royal Seal. A year later, she was in charge of preparations for the wedding celebration of her younger, and favourite, brother Dara Shukoh with whom she shared a profound interest in mysticism. The following year, she repeated her success for the wedding of the next brother Shah Shuja. But in 1637, she excused herself when it came time for Aurangzeb to wed, who, it is easy to gather, she was not very fond of.

Like her father, Jahan Ara was a noted builder. Delhi owes its famous Chandni Chowk to her. Here she also built a caravanserai known, appropriately enough, as Begum ki Serai; a garden (now named after Mahatma Gandhi) and a public bath. She also bequeathed mosques, one each to Agra and to Kashmir. As a patron of learning, Jahan Ara commissioned a multi-volume work on Sufism and commentaries on the work of Maulana Rumi. All this she paid for from her own purse that she had inherited over the years from her father.

In 1658, having imprisoned his father, the cruel and malicious Aurangzeb set out to usurp the right of his older brother Dara Shukoh, clearly the heir apparent. Jahan Ara came forward to write an impassioned plea to him to forbear opposition to their father's choice of heir to

---

4) The first born, also a daughter, died in infancy.

the throne. Her appeal fell on deaf ears. Later, after Dara Shukoh was defeated and on the run, she bore priceless gifts to Aurangzeb hoping he would agree to come to his father's terms of dividing the empire four ways between the brothers. But all efforts failed and the heartless Aurangzeb executed his elder brother and his son. In those final eight years of Shah Jahan's confinement until his death in 1666, Jahan Ara was forever by the broken emperor's side.

Though Jahan Ara never travelled to Peshawar, she evidently had an eye even on distant outposts of the empire. She appears to have based her assessment on reports of the need for an inn spacious enough to house a large number of travellers and their draught animals when she ordered her serai on the site of the famous House of the Hindu where jogis resorted. In her lifetime and for almost two centuries after, it was the most spacious inn of the city providing over a hundred rooms for travellers and enough space for over two hundred draught animals. Then it fell into decay.

Long after Paolo di Avitabile had left this home and office and retired back to Italy, Gorkhatri became the administrative office of the sub-division (*tehsil*). Today, a visitor asking for Gorkhatri is met with blank stares and shrugs. But ask for *tehsil* and everyone within earshot opens up with directions.

Waliullah, the young archaeologist assigned at the office in Gorkhatri, spoke of the mosque and the public bath built at the time the serai was raised. Early in the nineteenth century, when the Sikhs took Peshawar they razed the mosque and with the passage of decades, the bath went the way of dereliction and eventual demolition. To my mind, it seems that the pond that Mohan Lal and others refer to as the bathing place of pilgrims could be the last reminder of Jahan Ara's bath. But the temple dedicated to Goraknath, founder of the jogi sect, remains.

∞

In days of old, caravaners having rested in any of the several *serais* of city, would strike out in an easterly direction for the ferries on the Indus. In a line as straight as an arrow southeast of Gorkhatri, our point of reference in Peshawar, and 4.36 kilometres away, the old Grand Trunk Road crosses the Bara River, the very one whose clear branches Mohan Lal noticed running through the city. The river is now tainted with sewage and industrial waste. Yet today dozens of boys frolic in its filth leaving one to wonder if they ever suffer from skin problems or gastric trouble from the water they are sure to swallow. Nearby men wash their pick-up trucks and rickshaws in the river.

The river here is spanned by a beautiful early Mughal bridge. On the far side, a little east of the river, a huge banyan tree shades the road and on either side, amid a growing number of houses, green fields spread into the distance. The notable feature of the bridge are the eight towers, four on either side of the carriageway. The towers are topped by fluted domelets to pleasing effect. The ten openings for the passage of water are flanked by mini towers reaching up only to the parapet. These are topped by half domes of the same design as on the main towers. For symmetry of design, two mini towers are flanked by two main towers.

As I was pottering about with my camera and tripod, a white-bearded man came around to chat. I asked him whom the bridge could possibly be attributed to.
'Sher Shah Suri?' he said a bit uncertainly quickly adding, 'That is what everyone says.'

At least, the man was doubtful of the prevalent belief. I told him that brilliant as Sher Shah was, the Afghan king ruled India only five years. In these brief few years, he had no influence in this part of the country. We talked of the possibility of Akbar or his son Jahangir having ordered this bridge because both made at least two trips each between their capital cities and the outlying possession of Peshawar and Kabul. However, the histories of both kings make no mention of the ordering of this bridge.

On a later trip with my friend Momina Sanam, we got talking to the elderly Mehr Taj Bibi who lives in the house by the right bank right on the side of the river. She said she was born here, wedded here and lived all her life by the Bara River, the bridge and the beautiful banyan tree.
'The tree and the bridge are for each other. They were made for each other and they have always been together. You think of the one and the other comes straight into your mind; they are a unity,' she said. Nearly four decades ago, I had heard a Kalasha shaman speak of rivers and trees with similar feeling.
'The river was once so beautiful and clear,' she sighed.

'During summer rains it was red, but in winters it was clean to drink and you could see the fish in it. People came here to picnic. In summer afternoons my father used to take all of us under the bridge. In the bay that had no water, we would spread out our sheets and nap. The bridge was so beautiful but now no one looks after it.'

The old woman felt someone needs to tend the bridge and keep it in good fettle. As for the river, she rued that they had killed it. Now there were no fish in it and the water could not even be touched, leave alone drinking it. It was nothing but trash, she said vehemently. The folks who came to the bridge are gone. No one comes, she said. The only visitors are filmmakers now. Mehr Taj Bibi had no idea how old the bridge was and if the old Grand Trunk Road passed by her home, but she was remarkable for the way she felt about the world around her. Her feeling for the river, the bridge and the old banyan tree was admirable.

A few degrees north of east from the bridge and exactly 3.88 kilometres away in a very straight line was another marker of the old road. The *baoli* or stepped well of Chamkani. In company with Azeem and his photographer Kashif, we came through the village and past the squat green dome of the tomb of Mian Omar Baba. Locally much revered, the mausoleum draws large crowds every Thursday.

We did not pause at the tomb to meet with the descendants of this holy man as another traveller had done nearly two hundred years before us. In 1827, the tireless itinerant

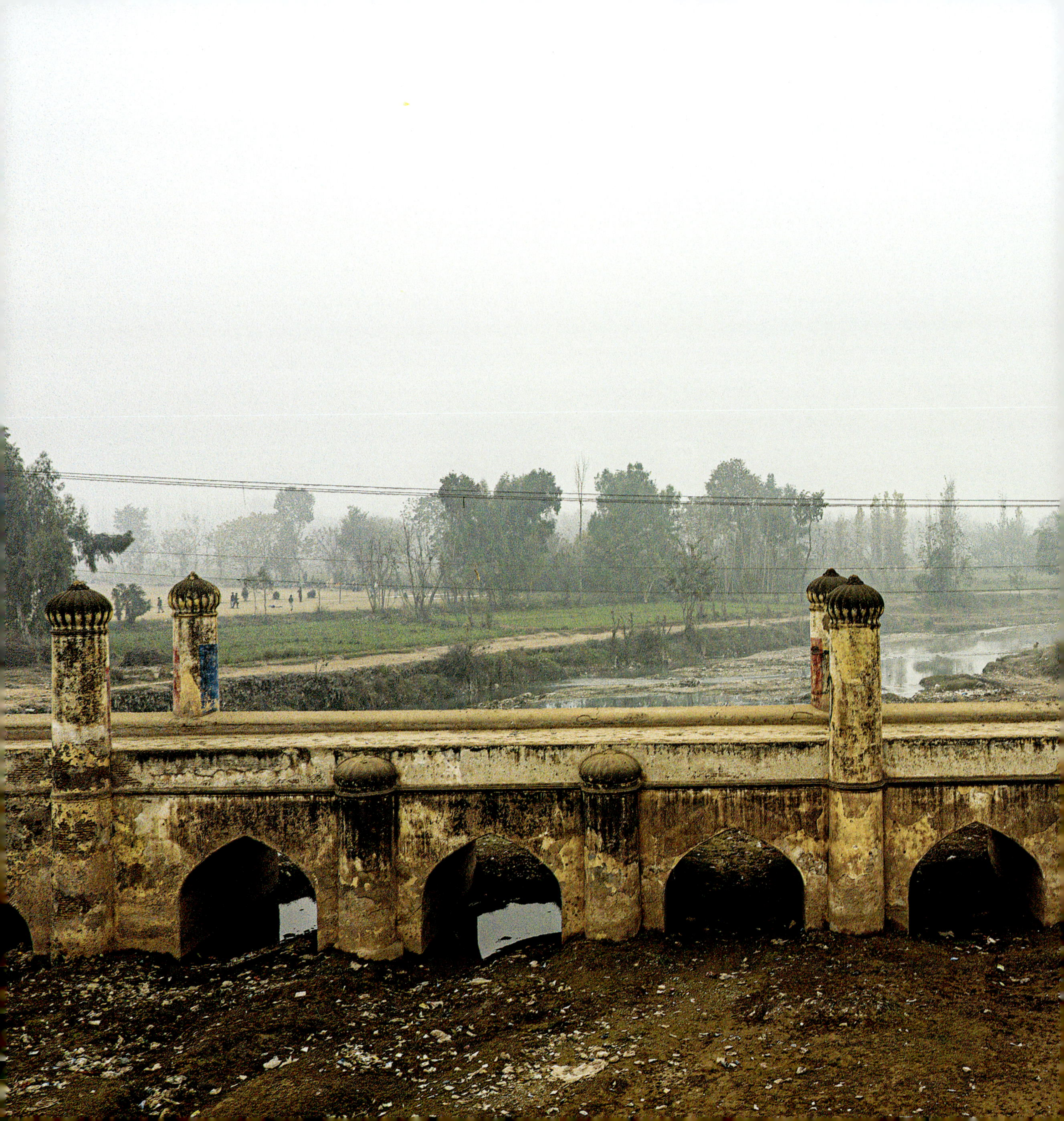

Charles Masson took an outing from Peshawar to Chamkani to visit the widow of 'a celebrated saint, herself eminent for her virtues and liberality'. He gives us no name for this woman who excused herself from seeing him for, since the death of her husband, she had seen no male outside her nearest family. Her messenger also informed Masson that twenty odd years earlier, Mountstuart Elphinstone had come bearing her gifts that she still preserved and cherished greatly.

The traveller recounts that although it was past mealtime, the widow insisted on feeding him and his party. The meal comprising a number of dishes was immediately brought in. Masson admits that he was utterly taken by the high standard of the preparation. He writes that in times gone by this family was very wealthy and famous for 'costly hospitality' and that though times were not the same for them, they kept up appearances.

The nameless widow was remarkable for her time in a Pakhtun setting. That claiming holiness, she was yet able to freely entertain men, shows how much has changed for women in the past two centuries in our part of the world.

Past the jumble of shops and houses, we headed out on a tree-shaded country road southeast of Chamkani. Just a kilometre from the tomb of Mian Omar, by the side of the

---

As the medieval traveller set out of a Peshawar caravanserai they would first of all cross the Bara River by this early Mughal bridge now known after the nearby village of Choa Gujjar. Of all Mughal bridges in Pakistan this is surely the most picturesque with its minarets and onion domes. Today, more than four hundred years after it was built, the bridge can take the weight of laden lorries.

road, stood the stepped well where travellers would once have paused to water their animals and rest a while. The smallish square pavilion and the well were aligned in an east-west direction with the pavilion on the east and the stairs leading down to water level. The interesting feature of the pavilion was the little domed cubicle on the roof accessible by a staircase on the north side of the pavilion.

A man came around to talk and said until a few years ago the steps leading into the well were covered up with earth and brambles. He had no idea who had cleared it out and why they had left the well filled in. His father told him tales of the time when his father was a child who would watch passing caravans halt at the well. He said he was the only old resident of the area, all others were beneficiaries of the burgeoning real estate business around Peshawar and had moved here after selling their properties in the cramped confines of the old city.

The day was still young and we made a beeline for our next marker. In a straight line 37.1 kilometres east of the Chamkani *baoli* was the well-known Rang Mahal – Painted Palace – by the little village of Valai. We took the modern road, past Nowshera turning south at the level crossing of Vatra to reach the monument six kilometres from today's Grand Trunk Road.

Lost Glory were the two words that came to mind as I climbed up the steps into the single ground level chamber. The frescos in the alcoves above the doorways, once bright and lively, were faded and smeared with graffiti of ignorant people, having no regard for their built heritage.

The mortar, three centuries old, was peeling from the foundation upward and a couple of holes in the masonry seemed to indicate the malice of vandals.

It was a classic and true to form *baradari* – twelve-doored apartment. Facing north, it had five doors front and rear and one each on the east and west. The building dates very likely to the mid-seventeenth century, that is, Shah Jahan's period.

Behind the building, on its south side, was a depression that Azeem said was supposed to have been a water tank. But there was no sign of any masonry. A picture of what may have been was given by Anwar Shah who I met on a later visit. In his childhood, he had seen the depression filled with water considered a cure for scabies. Afflicted folks came around and wallowed in the mud as buffaloes do and plastered themselves with it, he said. For him it was not just hearsay because many years ago his daughter, then four years old, suffered from a skin rash which was cured by the mud.

He said his mother was the person to talk to about the baradari. But she spoke only Pashto and so Momina Sanam came in helpful again.

Chaman Bibi estimated she was in her mid-eighties. Going by her heavily wrinkled face, it seemed she had gained one line for every year of her life. But as a youthful woman, she surely would have been very beautiful. She spoke softly in a voice husky with years.

'Rang Mahal has been there long before I was born. Or

even my grandmother. As a child I saw a very pretty building where they held poetry recitals by the side of the pool. The whole was thickly shaded by trees,' she whispered. Literature of the past, she said, had given way to commercial work. She knew that now only ad-makers came there with their cameras and made up models.

We were joined by her daughter-in-law Farzana. In her mid-thirties, she said she too remembered the trees. 'Where are the trees now?' I asked.
'Cut! Gone to the timber markets, all of them. Now everyone wants only money.'

Chaman Bibi spoke again, the same whisper, 'My elders spoke of the Moghul king Shah Jahan who ordered this pleasure garden right by a very ancient road. I remember it as such a joyful and lovely place where visitors came from far off just to spend time among the flowers.' Wistfully she added, 'The area had a profusion of flowers that no one planted. They just sprouted when the season was right. Now there is only perdition.'

Chaman Bibi brought me to the verge of tears. Where, I wondered, are people of my generation and those after me with such intense emotion for history and for nature as this wonderful woman? Her passion was so strong it had rubbed off on to her daughter-in-law Farzana.

Exactly due east of Valai sits Jahangira and a few kilometres southeast where the Kabul River pays tribute to the Indus, is the hamlet of Khairabad. In full view of the imposing battlements of Akbar's Attock Fort, this was the major crossing place from the sixteenth century onward. We have noted already that the other fords in this neighbourhood were downstream at Bagh Nilab another upstream at Hund.[5]

In Khairabad, Momina and I ended up at the house of Ghulam Nabi Khattak. If he believed the Grand Trunk Road was built by the Suri king, his seventy-year-old mother Dilshad Bibi, speaking with Momina, said Sher Shah had nothing to do with the old road because it 'had always been there, long before his time'. The fort was of course Akbar's handiwork and its gateways are named after the cities they face, she said.

From Momina's narration, it was clear that Dilshad and Ambiya Bibi, about half her age who had married into Khattak's family from Swat, were more informed than the men I met outside. Ambiya was indignant that Hinduano Mohalla of pre-partition days had been renamed Islamabad Mohalla. Why, she asked, did they have to change history like that?

Zahid Malik sauntered into the men's area and by way of introduction my host said he 'fancied himself a writer'. And nowadays everyone was writing official history, not the real one for that takes too much research, he said. Despite these put downs, Malik remained unfazed. He offered to send me his recent book and asked for my address. I said I would write it down as soon as I was done with the tea and biscuits. Then I steered him away from the subject

---

5) Curiously, the Mughals knew the Kabul River as the Kama. Both Babur and Jahangir in their diaries refer to it as such

After the building of Attock Fort by Akbar, the Grand Trunk Road having passed through Nowshera swung southeast to make a beeline for the Attock ferry. En route it passed through the broken, hilly country of Valai. Sometime during the reign of Shah Jahan this delightful baradari was laid out. The legendary pond that older people know from tradition would have been in the depression hidden behind the building. The area in front and not visible in this image, now covered by cultivation was once a garden, very likely the quadrangle or chaharbagh as favoured by the Mughals. Today no sign remains of that garden

The spandrel of the main entrance still carries four hundred year old paint. However, total disregard for historical monuments has added ugly graffiti all around this heritage site.

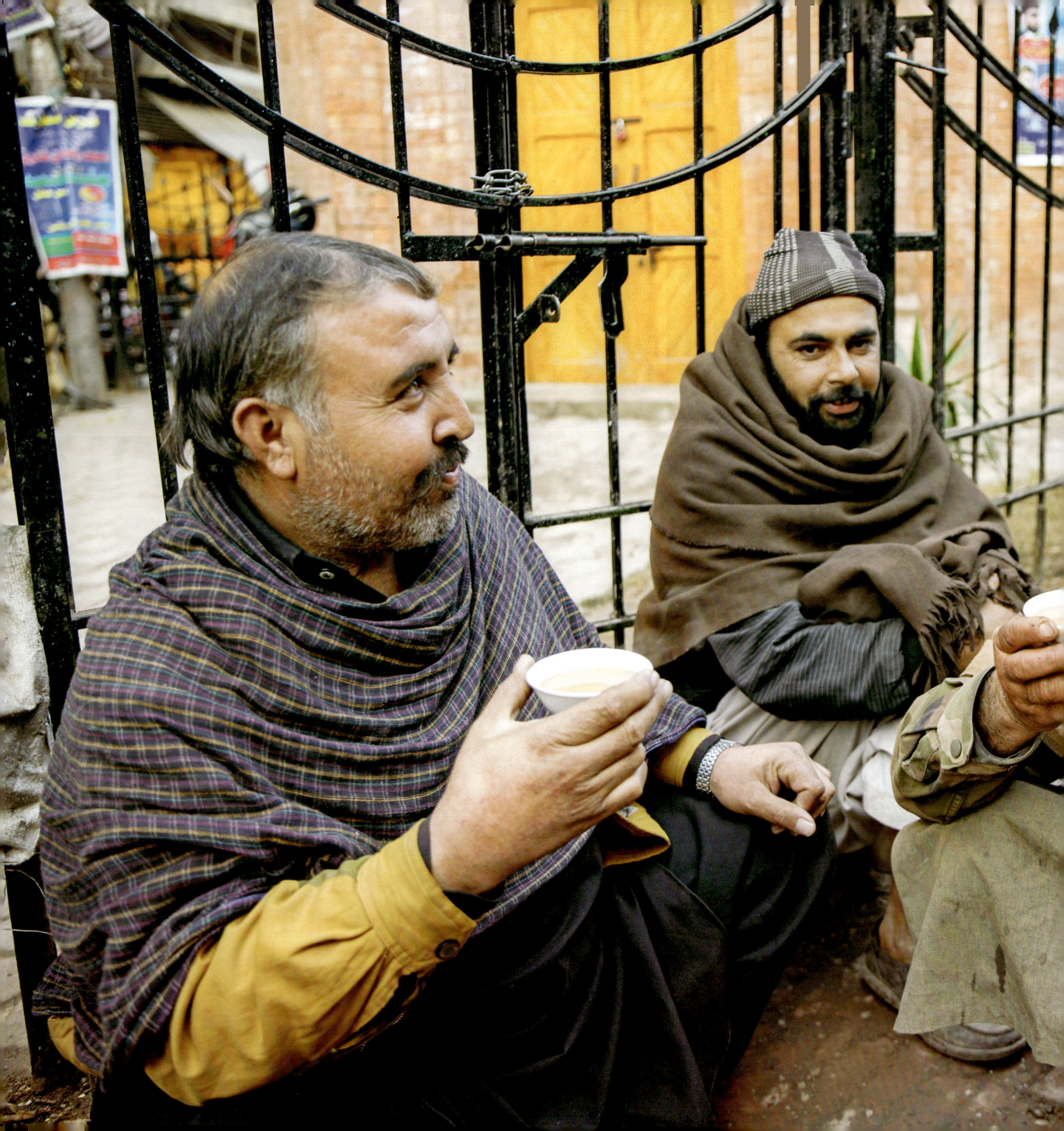

until we departed.

Back in Peshawar, I went to the Gorkhatri dig again. The archaeologists at hand said there were layers below the bottom and boasted that Peshawar was the oldest living city of Pakistan. I knew it was no empty brag. No matter what they said about Lahore, those of us who have read their ancient geography and history know that Lahore became a city only when Peshawar was already two thousand years old.

If Peshawar could live through all the upheavals that the layers of cultural remains show in the Gorkhatri excavation, surely it can come out of the damage inflicted upon its soul in recent decades. Call it what you will: Pushpapura, Kaspatyrus, Purushapura (from which our pious Chinese called it Po-lu-sha-pu-lo), Parshawar or Peshawar, its flowers still bloom and scatter their fragrance.

Peshawar will come through for it is still the City of Flowers.

Located some ways off the main cluster of the Taxila complex, Bhamala, tucked away in the upper reach of the Haro River, can rightly be called the Hidden Monastery. Like Mohra Moradu, this has a cruciform stupa (right background) rather than of the usual circular form. However, when the Huns came with fire and sword, they did not spare even remote Bhamala for signs of arson and violence have been found here. Recently, a seven-metre statue of Buddha in the Maha Pari Nirvana (demise) was discovered in these ruins. Laypersons incorrectly refer to it as the Sleeping Buddha.

3
East of the Indus

More than four thousand years ago, the Indo-Aryans, having set out of their Central Asiatic grasslands and meandered across Afghanistan, were poised to cross the Suleman Hills into the Indian subcontinent. Until then they had seen rivers that were but piddling flows. Even in spate, streams like the Syr Darya or the Waksh Ab (Oxus) generally remained confined to their beds. There were no floodplains a score or more kilometres across. When they first came down the Suleman Hills they met the mightiest river they had ever beheld.

It must have been at the height of a summer monsoon when the waters were swelled by distant glacial melt and rainwater washing down the lower hills. The red-brown swirls and the huge whirlpools gurgled and mewed like a living being as the newcomers stood in awe by its clayey banks. They would have shrunk in horror as the mighty flow reached out to swallow yet another large chunk of land not far from where they stood as it claimed a wider stream for itself.

The leap of the blind dolphin, too swift and short for them to determine its size and shape, would have intrigued them. For the first time they would have seen the slithering horror of the river crocodile as it slunk out to grab an unsuspecting sheep from their herds. What other manner of denizens peopled its dark waters, the newcomers must have wondered. And as they watched that flowing, living being, the strangers could not spot the far bank: all there was to behold was a vast eddying flow of earth-coloured water.

They were acquainted with seas like the Caspian or Aral where the far bank could not be seen. For them this stream the likes of which they had never seen became Sindhu. In their language the name signified a very large river or even the ocean. A millennium and a half was to go by before the Persians would borrow the word for this magnificent stream, the giver of life to the western part of the subcontinent, and alter its name according to their own usage.

Borrowing a Sanskrit word beginning with s, ancient Persian interpolated the initial letter with h. Thus, Sindhu became Hindu. The land where this mighty river flowed was accordingly Hindustan – Land of the Hindu [River]. We have already heard of the sea captain Skylax who undertook the exploratory voyage on the Indus on orders from Darius the Great of Persia. Borrowing outside words, the Greeks habitually dropped the initial h sound rendering the river's name as Indu. Append that with the s ending of Greek proper nouns and we have Indus from which they called its land India that spread from the Suleman Hills to the Gangetic Plain.

In the middle of the first millennium BCE, the land of India intrigued the Westerners, whether Persian or Greek. Here was a country of immense learning, art and literature; a country whose masters did not hold their erudition close to their breasts as they did in China and Persia. This was a country, where commoners thirsted for learning and masters spread it without restrain. In that long ago age, the land of the Indus River was as much the coveted centre of desire for learned Westerners as the West is today for the semi-literate who now live here. While those ancients came this way for the learning and to experience the superior culture, the westward movement now is for wealth and a better life.

At the bridge on the Indus river, in full view of the brooding battlements of Akbar's Attock Fort, we were poised to enter the heart of the Indus lands. Long years ago, before the road bridge currently in use was built, road traffic veered right (southward) to take a long detour to the railway bridge which was also used by motor traffic. In the 1960s and indeed even in the decade after, I frequently heard that the old railway bridge rested not on girders, but on the femur of the prophet Adam. 'In days of old, giants walked this earth,' the teller would end the fable with a solemn face. By advocates of this yarn, it was only about a millennium ago that mankind suddenly shrivelled to its present size.

That road skirted the entrance to Akbar's fort that has, since the late 1950s, been the home of Special Service Group of the army and out of bounds for civilians. Below the fort, by its northern rampart the fortified caravanserai of the Begum is likewise not accessible.

Not far from these off limits heritage sites, is a small Mughal *baradari* almost sequestered away from wandering eyes. One has to look hard for it to spot it on the south side of the Grand Trunk Road. Besides the now ruined water works, tanks and fountains there are two lovely little pillared cubicles. The one placed in the back sits on a high plinth, while the other on the right as one enters the complex, is at ground level. The pillars are simple, but the arches are multi-cusped and clearly late Mughal. Folks know it as Behram's Baradari and in his time the little cubicles would have been laid out with lavish spreads for the master to repose upon.

Behram was one of the several sons of Khushal Khan Khattak, the poet and warrior whose poetry raises goose bumps even today, three and a half centuries after it was penned. Starting out as a Mughal loyalist he was, in 1641, acknowledged by Shah Jahan as the chief of the Khattaks and appointed guardian of the Grand Trunk Road from Attock to Peshawar. Aurangzeb, however, failed to recognise the worth of this great and good man. The words of Olaf Caroe, the well-known historian of the Pakhtuns, should effectively cut short the long story of the falling out:

> All said, we have to judge between two men. Which voice is the more authentic, that of the King who killed his brothers and imprisoned his father to reach the throne, and, with all his genius and persistence, led an empire to corruption and decay; or that of the warrior-poet whose words still kindle fire in the hearts of his compatriots?

In 1658, Khushal Khan was imprisoned on the orders of Aurangzeb. Upon his release six years later, he spent the

The *baradari* of Behram Khan. His father, the patriotic Khushal Khan Khattak, would not have approved of his selling out to the Mughals. When Behram reposed in the cubicle in the middle (accessible by the steps), he would have seen the Indus flowing in the near distance. Today the view is blocked by the raised bed of the Grand Trunk Road.

An overview of Behram's *baradari* giving an idea of
the waterworks and the central fountain in the garden.

rest of his days on earth struggling to unite all Pakhtun tribes against the Mughals. Aurangzeb made several attempts to run the warrior to ground but failed. But where the force of arms fell short, lure of lucre became an effective weapon and for bribe whose value we do not know Khushal Khan's own son Behram turned against him. He who forsook his father was rewarded by the crown with chieftainship of the area. It was during his years of power that he built this complex in or about 1681.

Khushal Khan died in 1689. His eldest son Ashraf buried him on a quiet hill a goodly ways off the Grand Trunk Road where the 'dust of Mughal horses would not reach'. Khushal's legacy lives on and as Caroe notes, does indeed set hearts aflame not just of the Pakhtun but of anyone who values liberty and whose heart is instilled with love for the land. On the other hand, Behram is just somebody who built this pretty little pleasure house from where he would have watched the Indus whether in violent brown summer flood or in languid green winter flow roll past. Behram is forgotten; few even remember that he was one of the sons of Khushal Khan Khattak.

Less than a kilometre eastward of the baradari stands the lofty dome of Kanjri da Maqbara – Tomb of the Courtesan.[1] It has always been known as that, though never did anyone disclose who this courtesan was and why she merited this tall dome. Azeem had a mischievous smile as we stopped by it and, having crossed the road, went looking around its walled enclosure. But he said nothing regarding the identity of the courtesan. I persisted and Azeem grinning wider said something about the lifestyle of kings in those days, winked and said, 'Get the drift!'

Behram had opted against his father's life of principled resistance not without reason. He garnered wealth and status from royal patronage. Like all men of status, the man seems to have kept a mistress whose memory lingers. Surely, as he reposed in the apartment on the high plinth directly looking north to the mighty Indus, he would have had the nameless woman's company. Both lover and beloved might have kept her name secret by design for there is no tablet on the simple grave inside the mausoleum. Behram who coveted wealth and glory was likewise forgotten and we have no word on his burial.

∞

With Azeem alternating between discourses on Gandhara statuary and the work of modern makers of fakes that teem around old Gandhara sites, we weaved our way through disorderly traffic and along narrow serpentine lanes to the majestic shrine of Panja Sahib at Hasan Abdal, just below once beautiful, verdure-draped hills that now stand ravaged by decades of uncontrolled quarrying. Years before the man Hasan the Abdal who left nothing behind, nary a legend, save his name for this town, the place was called Haro after the river that having risen in the Murree hills flows nearby on to its junction with the Indus near Attock town.[2]

---

1) Kanjri is a dancing girl or a prostitute and in Punjabi carries a more pejorative sense than courtesan.
2) Abdal is the highest level of spiritual attainment in Islamic mysticism. The least being Wali followed by Ghaus and Qutb as communicated to me by my archaeologist friend Mian Attique Ahmad. Haro is pronounced Her Row with emphasis on the second syllable.

Among the important holy places connected with Baba Guru Nanak Dev, the founder of the Sikh faith, the beautiful white and gold of its dome, domelets and vaulted half domes rising above a stone foundation, this gurdwara is a fine example of the best of Sikh architecture.

The shrine is sacred to the hand print on a rock above a bubbling spring in the courtyard of the shrine. The print is said to have been miraculously left behind by Guru Nanak Dev. The story is that the guru came upon this place tired and thirsty after a long trek and found Wali Kandahari – Holy Man of Kandahar – sitting by a spring of water. It is variously believed that Wali was either sitting on the hilltop where a shrine marks his *baithak* (place of repose) or at the foot of the hill on slightly higher ground.

Taking the Muslim ascetic to be a brother in spirituality, the guru asked for a drink of water. Wali Kandahari was enraged by the presumption of a man who carried no title to show his rank. Why, how could he, a non-believer, ask a Wali for water. Secure in his own position, he tossed a stone at the guru. Again it is variously told that the stone was either one huge boulder or a small pebble that grew in size as it tumbled in the direction of Guru Nanak Dev. As it neared the guru, it was large enough to crush a man. But the guru raised his hand and without even letting it come in contact with the boulder, guided it down to the ground. Miraculously, his hand was imprinted upon the hard substance of the rock. Then he commanded the earth to give up its supply of clean drinking water. One version of the story also has it that the spring that Wali Kandahari was so proud of ran dry immediately as the guru's spring welled up. To this day the followers of Guru Nanak Dev believe the story with all their heart and long to be given the chance to visit the shrine and bathe in its holy waters.

The nameless courtesan's tomb sits right by the Grand Trunk Road, not far from the baradari. It is believed to have been built by Behram Khan for the mortal remains of his secret lover.

Now, the great Guru Nanak was born in November 1469. In 1505, when Babur first came into India, the guru was at the youthful height of his evangelical career of a syncretic religion and it is right possible the two met somewhere in Punjab. Though the *Babur Nama* (Babur's self-written diaries) contains no mention of the guru, stories abound. Sikh lore has an encounter between the two where Babur sat in awe of the holy man's wisdom with an attentive ear to his expositions. Another tale concerns the miraculous mill in Eminabad near Gujranwala. Enraged over something, so the believers relate, Babur ordered Guru Nanak Dev to be put to work a mill. When the Mughal later visited to see

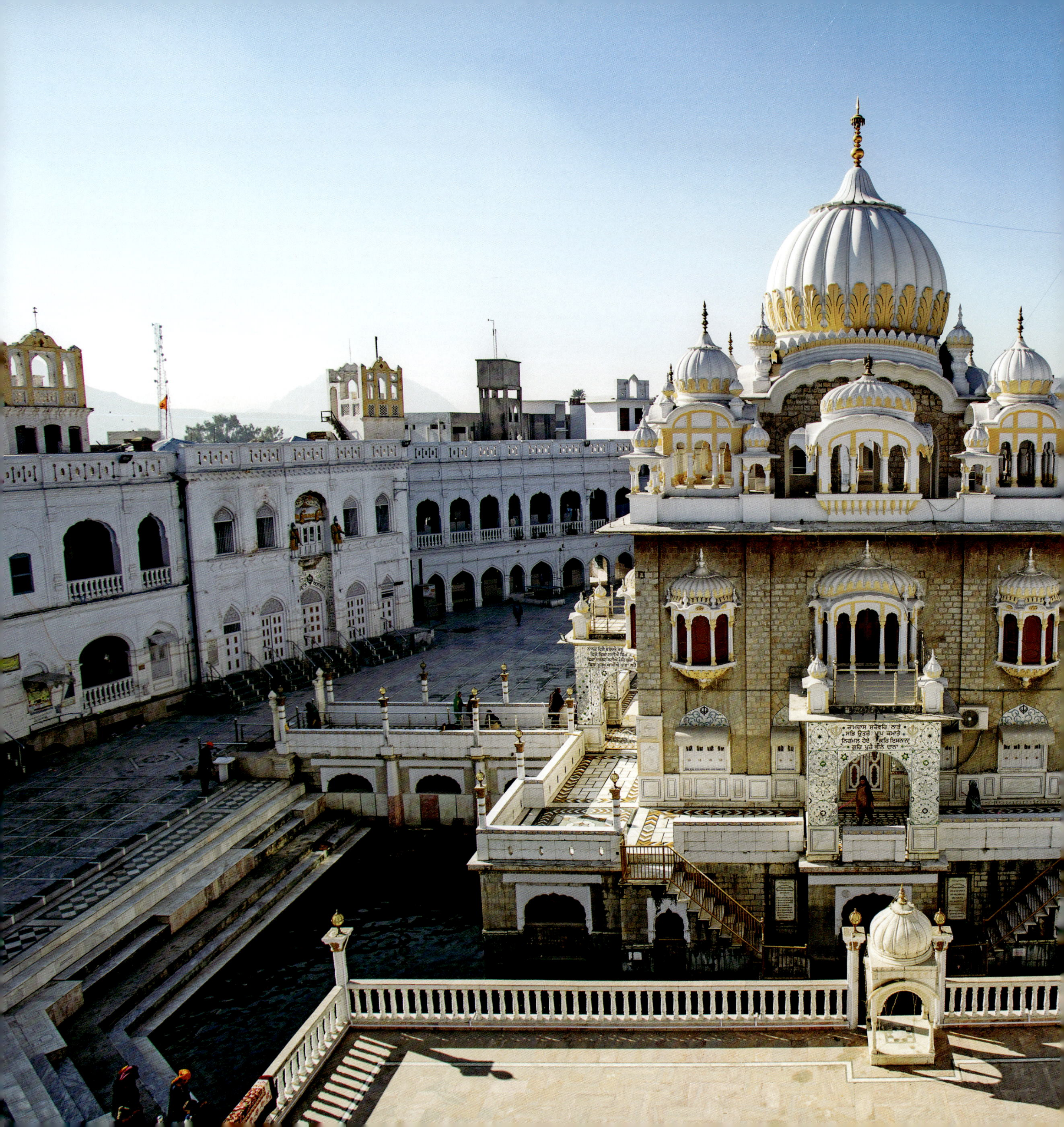

from Landi Kotal *to* Wagah | East of the Indus

The Panja Sahib gurdwara is an exquisite beauty of cupolas, bay windows, cusped arches, domes and fluted pillars. As one of the holiest of Sikh shrines, it vies for first place as architectural gem among several others in Pakistan.

how the punishment was chastising the man of God, he was surprised to see the holy man in relaxed repose even as the mill worked all by itself. And so to this day, we have a Gurdwara Chaki (mill) Sahib in Eminabad.

We hear nothing of the guru from Babur's son Humayun, but we can excuse that for the man lived in a fog of opium smoke and lacked the interest his father had in the world around him. Akbar, whose history comes to us from a faithful court diarist and one of his Nine Jewels Sheikh Abu'l Fazal, also travelled through Hasan Abdal en route to Peshawar. But the otherwise detailed compendium fails to notice either the town or the shrine. Indeed, it does not even mention the natural beauty of flowing waters and forested slopes at this place. We know that the emperor camped at this delightful spot en route to the crossing point where he later built his monumental Attock Fort, exactly a day's march away. Yet the fame of Hasan Abdal as a centre of spirituality went unnoticed.

Jahangir, the fourth Mughal emperor of India, who like his great-grandfather was a writer of diaries, notes Hasan Abdal sitting on the great highroad between India and Kabul and expresses an appreciation of its scenic beauty. In all, between the years 1607 and 1626, Jahangir passed through this town all of six times and thought it an 'enchanting place'. On the last day of April 1607 – his first ever visit here – Jahangir exulted over the waterfall east of town (it is actually south) where the stream 'rushes with great force' which he thought had no match anywhere on the road to Kabul though there were, he tells us, two or three like it on the highroad to Kashmir.

Jahangir writes in his *Tuzk* that the flowing water creates a basin in the middle of which Akbar's trusted courtier Raja Man Singh, another of his Nine Jewels, had raised a small building. This tank teemed with fish that were as much as forty-five centimetres in length that he caught with a net and after 'putting pearls into their noses', set them loose again. The *Tuzk* records that the king tarried here three days drinking wine with those who were intimate with him.

Jahangir tells us that he asked local story-tellers about the tale of Hasan Abdal who gave the town its name and not one could tell him anything. But historian Mir Masum Shah (died 1634 and author of *Tarikh e Masumi*, an authoritative history of Sindh) who served as governor of Bhakkar (Sindh) under the Mughals lists Baba Hasan Abdal among the saints buried in Kandahar from which place he originally hailed. Having travelled to Arabia for the great pilgrimage, the man returned home where he was visited by Shah Rukh Mirza, the ablest son of Tamerlane who then ruled over Afghanistan from Herat. When he died, the holy man was buried in Kandahar and his last rites were attended by the Mirza.

Shah Rukh Mirza died in 1447, twenty-two years before the birth of Baba Guru Nanak Dev. Therefore, there is no truth in the meeting of the Kandahari and the Punjabi saints in Hasan Abdal. Having said that, we have some inference to the former's journey through this part of Punjab in the final years of the fourteenth century. He may have halted a fairly long time in the town that carries his name to have become sufficiently celebrated for the name of old Haro to be altered. But this celebrity did not outlive the man for even though his name stuck to the place, it was quickly forgotten what his fame lay in and within two hundred years Jahangir's inquiries drew blanks. Apparently his prowess as a man of religion had failed to impress local folks.

The *Gazetteer of Attock District* of 1930 preserves a remarkable little story that the followers of the great guru would prefer expunged from its pages and from human memory. While memory can be obliging, the written page has a way of surviving for inordinately long and sometimes vexing periods of time. The story is told by historian and author James George Delmerick (1830-1915) who claims that it was also known to and narrated by some very devout Sikhs of Rawalpindi and Hasan Abdal.

Kamma, a Muslim stonemason, was one day idling by the spring of water right below the hill now associated with Wali Kandahari. Having nothing better to do with his hands, he carved a print of it on the rock. Several years went by and Ranjit Singh having risen to power, sent his army to raid Hasan Abdal. As the terrified populace abandoned the village and fled into the hills, one mendicant named Naju remained. This man evidently had a very sharp mind and a sharper imagination: in order to save his skin, he invented the story of the miraculous hand print during the tussle between the founder of the Sikh faith and the Muslim saint.

One wonders, however, whether the invention was instantaneous or the man had been toying with the notion for some time. It is remarkable that the man recalled the Muslim saint who had not been known just two hundred years earlier when Jahangir stopped here for a while. At just three hundred years old, Sikhism possessed the most ardent followers who believed the story of the miracle. And the rest is not just history but one of the most impressive Sikh religious monuments in Pakistan and millions of devotees who fervently believe the legend to be true, despite Delmerick's assertion that old residents of Hasan Abdal insisted that before the reign of Maharaja Ranjit Singh, there was neither a shrine nor a place of worship at Hasan Abdal.

Finally, it is intriguing that Mountstuart Elphinstone who passed through this place in the first decade of the nineteenth century, took no notice of the miracle while the East India Company's veterinary surgeon, that admirable William Moorcroft, visiting only a decade and half later, found Hasan Abdal sanctified where Sikhs came in pilgrimage. He thought the story was 'the probable invention of a very recent date' which only exemplified 'the credulity of the people'. His conclusion was that the Afghans having held Hasan Abdal until only a few decades earlier would not have tolerated a Sikh shrine and pilgrims in their area.

Muslims too have their counterpart in the hilltop shrine marking the place where Wali Kandahari is supposed to have spent forty days in worship. When I visited it in the early 1980s, it was a lovely little spot scoured by cool winds and accessible by a walking path. The little domed cubicle was shaded by a solitary *phulai* (*Acacia modesta*) tree and several eucalyptus. Nearby, perhaps to recall the nature of the tiff, was a row of earthen pitchers from where the keeper who reeked of hashish would offer unwashed tumblers of water to visitors. But all who came were not curious people like me. They all came seeking benediction from the saint who lies buried a thousand kilometres away in Kandahar. I saw women and men prostrate upon the threshold of the little room mumbling their petitions to the long dead man who was not even buried there. Question their belief and they challenge you with the assertion that people have had their heart's desires by putting their forehead in the dust of the cubicle's threshold.

In 2019, the once beautiful hill with grand vistas all around especially to Wah Gardens, just over two kilometres in a straight line to the southeast, is ugly with spikes of half a dozen microwave transmission towers. The hill itself is viciously raked with sharp vertical escarpments, the result of mindless quarrying to feed the cement factories of the rich and powerful. This is surely not the state the saint of Kandahar would approve of.

Back to Jahangir's memoir, we find the emperor so taken by this lovely place that he bequeathed nine thousand rupees apparently to build resting places where royalty could stay on subsequent visits. In 1622, on yet another outing to Hasan Abdal, Jahangir killed thirty Punjab urial (mountain goat) after they had been trapped in a circle of beaters. It needs be said that both he and his father Akbar were wanton killers of wildlife for in their respective times, they destroyed some two thousand wild goats and ravine deer in the Nandna hills of the Salt Range.

The tomb of the Hakim brothers whose acumen as medicine men was much valued by Akbar the Great. The building had earlier been raised by Khwaja Shams ud Din Khwafi, another Akbari courtier, perhaps for his own burial. It was appropriated for the brothers on royal orders.

Having done my photography, I sat alone by the tomb of the two brother hakims, physicians versed in traditional medicine. In 1985, I had been here marvelling at the fish in the water tank overseen by the tomb. Now, but for some water boatmen (*Corixidae* bugs), the water was lifeless. A couple with a small child and a teenage boy were sitting across from me taking selfies. I could hear they were talking about me. The man called out to me asking, in English, where I came from. I replied in Punjabi that I was from Lahore and the woman burst out laughing.
'Are you making a video?' Since every other person with a camera at such places now masquerades as a film-maker, my camera on the tripod never fails to fool people.

I said I was just doing still photographs and the man asked why I did not use my cell phone. From my pocket, I dug out of my simple cell phone and held it up for them to see. The woman let out a squawk of mirth again. The man asked what I proposed to do with the images.
'I am a writer, and these images will go in my book.'
'Do you also write television dramas?'
This was a question I have been asked often before.

Speaking across the now fish-less water of the pond, I asked them if they knew who was buried in the octagonal building just behind them. 'Lala Rukh?' asked the man uncertainly. 'And who was this Lala Rukh?'
I countered with my own question. 'We have no idea, but everyone says she was a princess.'

The octagonal two-storeyed building and this pond was built on the orders of Khwaja Shams ud Din Khwafi who held ministerial office during the reign of Akbar. For what purpose this squat and sturdy building was raised is not known and one can assume the Khwaja would have either used it simply as a resting place or may even have wanted to be buried in it.

There were two others that Akbar valued greatly: the hakim brothers Abu'l Fatah and Hamam. These two men were as close to Akbar as Khwaja Shams ud Din and the king greatly valued their expertise as men of medicine. In fact, Abu'l Fatah was so trusted that when Akbar had to assign the office of Keeper of Intoxicants, he chose this man. In an age when regicide was not unknown, this was an assignment of utmost trust. When Abu'l Fatah died in 1589, the emperor ordered Khwaja Shams ud Din Khwafi to conduct the body to this pleasant spot for burial in this particular building. Six years later, his brother Hamam's lifeless body was also brought to the same building for internment.

On his death bed in 1605, Akbar sorely missed Hakim Abu'l Fatah. Having roundly censured one Hakim Ali for 'his pretensions to medical knowledge' and failure to provide a cure to his ailing monarch, Akbar compared his dead medicine man with Galen of old.

The couple at the pond asked why everyone called this place the tomb of Lala Rukh. Lala Rukh whose name means Iris Face is said to have been a princess fathered either by Akbar or his son Jahangir. But we know nothing of her and I told them no one had any idea where the name Lala Rukh comes from. A hundred metres to the northeast of the tomb of the hakim brothers, Lala Rukh's simple sarcophagus sits on a high plinth within an enclosed garden whose walls and their corner turrets are clearly early Mughal. However, the histories of the purported fathers do not mention a royal daughter of this name.

If our Lala Rukh was indeed a daughter of either of the two kings she would have been dead for more than a century when the Irish poet Thomas Moore wrote his epic love poem *Lalla Rookh*. Moore makes his heroine a daughter of 'Aurangzebe' who is travelling to Kashmir to wed the local prince. Her entourage comprises among others a young bard who composes and sings to the princess four melodramatic poems en route. Unsurprisingly, Lala Rukh becomes enamoured of the young man and just when she is about to refuse to marry her intended beau, she discovers that the poet is the very man she has been sent out to wed.

Moore wrote his poem in 1817, which sets me wondering if some imaginative British traveller of that era having read *Lalla Rookh* might not have plastered the name on a tomb romantically situated in a walled garden. Two travellers of the 1820s who could possibly have had the name in mind and who passed through Wah were William Moorcroft followed by Charles Masson, the erudite deserter from the army of the East India Company. Though neither made any mention of the princess or her burial in their respective travelogues, could it be that a carelessly tossed name picked up by an attendant became legend?

Tomb of the mysterious Lala Rukh. In March 1860, Lady Charlotte Canning found it a ruined heap of bricks.

What convinces me that it was never known with certainty who was buried in the walled garden, is the fact that Lady Charlotte Canning refers to 'Noormahal's tomb' at Wah. Lying a little off the road, it was, in March 1860, 'a ruined heap of brick in an enclosure'. The two old cypresses towering above the burial told her that it was a 'cared for spot'. Nevertheless, despite the lack of identity, the tomb seems to have been an attraction of sorts for the Cannings were taken out to see it while halted at what we now know as Wah Garden.

Azeem and his sidekick Ali Raza brought me back to the present. We drove back to the Grand Trunk Road and took the turn south to Wah Gardens where the clear Jublat River brings life to verdure and fish. In 1610, three years after Jahangir's first trip to Hasan Abdal, William Finch, itinerant British trader who left behind an account of his journeys in India, tells us that Akbar was so enchanted by the beauty of this place that the appreciative exclamation 'Wah!' escaped his lips. And the place has been Wah ever since.

In 1985, I was told by an elderly man lounging on one of the benches in the garden that the 'Wah!' was, in fact, Babur's. Finch's yarn was copied and narrated by William Moorcroft who passed through this place in 1823. Moorcroft's two-volume compendium is an excellent account of Ladakh through Kashmir and northern Punjab to Afghanistan where he died under mysterious circumstances in Balkh. No one would have read the travels of Finch or Moorcroft, but somehow the 'Wah!' tradition travelled through time. From history we hear no such anecdote, however.

The pavilion that Jahangir tells us of as having been built by Raja Man Singh in the middle of a tank would once have stood in Wah Garden but is no longer extant. This is a right delightful little paradise, a very pleasure for a king. The pure waters of the gushing river fill a large stone-lined tank from where the water flows into an even larger one with a pedestal on the southeast perimeter for royal seating. From here, the best of Mughal hydraulics fed the fountains. On the far side of the pond, is the two-winged *baradari* – twelve-doored pavilion – which is not actually twelve-doored. The two halves of this edifice have a water channel with fountains running between them.

It amazes me how much of the actual construction was still extant just two hundred years ago at the time of Moorcroft's visit:

> The chambers in the southern front of the western wing ...... constitute a suite of baths, including cold, hot, and medicated baths, and apartments for servants, for dressing, and reposing, heating rooms and reservoirs: the floors of the whole have been paved with a yellow breccia, and each chamber is surmounted by a low dome with a central skylight. Fresco paintings of flowers and foliage in the compartments embellish the walls, and unless injured by mechanical violence, the colouring has lost little of its original lustre. Although possessing nothing majestic or imposing, the baths at Wah bagh must have been both commodious and elegant.

Today the frescos are damaged and the breccia flooring exchanged with a modern veneer. The plaster on the exterior too is gone exposing brick and mortar. In the mid-1980s, very little work had been done on this site. Later, archaeologist Shahid Ahmad Rajput showed what Moorcroft had described was buried beneath the accumulation of two hundred years. More than that, excavation revealed the ingenious gravity-based hydraulic system that Rajput terms 'a marvel of hydraulic engineering' that was 'very simple but amazingly perfect'.

Having determined the working of the system, Rajput was of the idea that his work would lead to restoration of the hydraulics to 'serve as a prototype', perhaps to be replicated in other places. He laments no effort has been made to revive the system.

∽

From the maddening noise and rush of the Grand Trunk Road as it nears Rawalpindi, we turned into the bazaar to make our way to the quiet of Taxila Museum. We had come by the road Babur used in the early sixteenth century; not by the one Alexander had taken from his crossing of the Indus at Hund and through the Chach Plain of Attock district. Alexander was not anticipating hard fought battles because Ambhi – Omphis or Taxiles to the Greeks, the king of Taxila – had already presented himself

---

The tank and pavilions of Wah Garden. The pavilions once looked out on water flowing in channels and playing fountains, now dead for many decades. Despite a thorough investigation into how the waterworks functioned, no effort has been made to restore them.

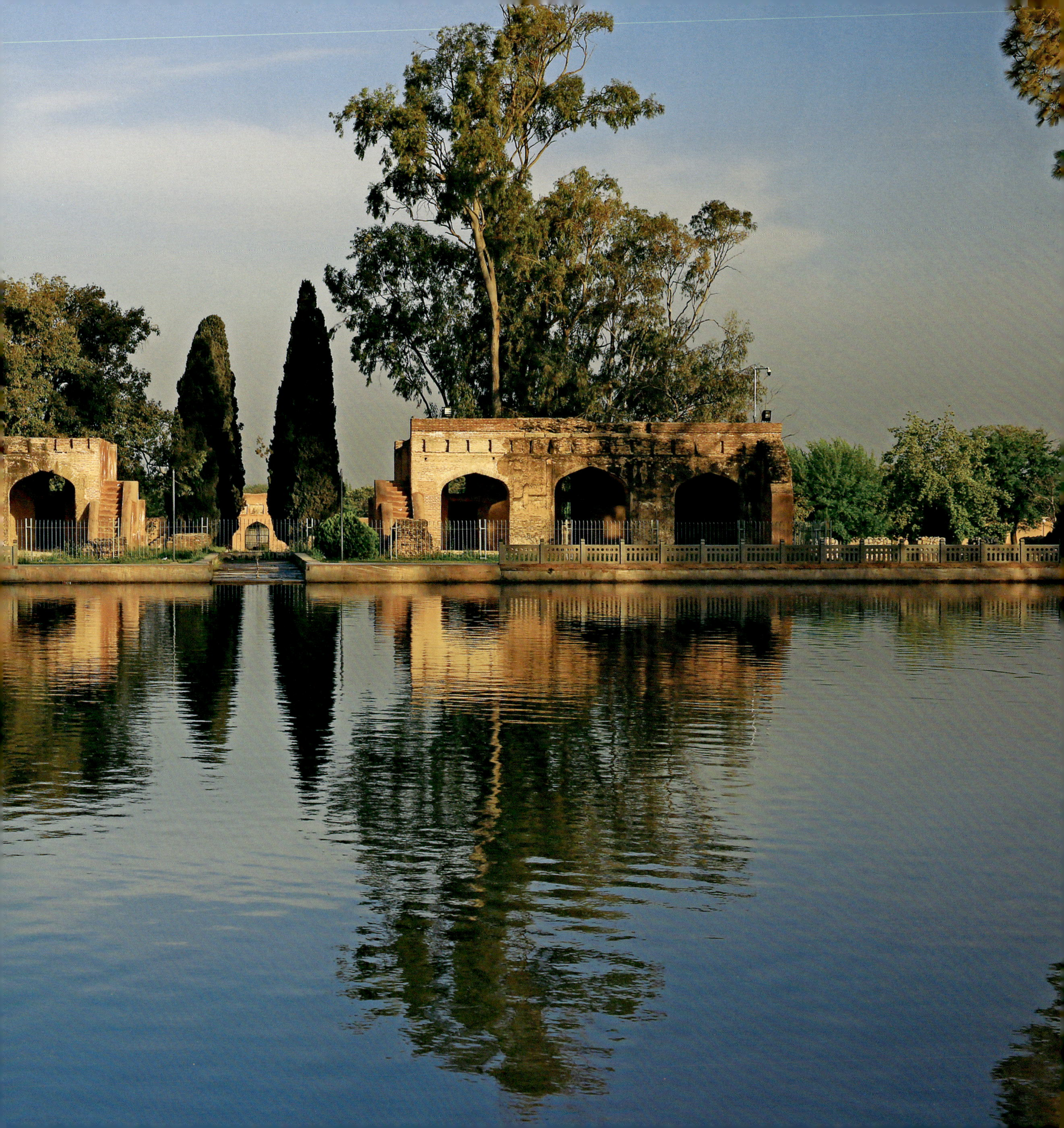

to Alexander when he was still in Nangarhar in the vicinity of modern Jalalabad (Afghanistan). There he had made a dramatic speech about why would he wish to fight Alexander. If he, Ambhi, had greater wealth, he would willingly share it with the Macedonian. But if Alexander were the richer, Ambhi would feel no indignity in asking for his largesse. Alexander just loved it. He accepted the Punjabi king as an ally.

The pavilions of Wah Garden where kings and their queens once reposed to look out on water channel and fountains.

On the far side of the Indus River, Alexander had gone up into Swat fighting as he went. He descended into the fertile Yusufzai Plain by way of the Ambela Pass and made his way south to the ford of Hund, the ancient Udabhandapura. The fighting was behind him now for he found his general Hephaestion had bridged the river and organised large boats for the troops to cross in. He also found a tribute from Ambhi: a substantial amount of silver, three thousand oxen and more than ten thousand sheep for sacrificial purpose. Beyond the fertile plain of Chach lay the city that the historian Arrian deemed 'the most considerable between the Indus and the Hydaspes'.

Alexander and his men were completely taken by Taxila. Officers in Alexander's army were writing away what they saw: a city of three different religious persuasions, namely, Buddhism, Brahmanism and Zoroastrianism, that yet lived in utter peace with itself; where theft and trickery were unknown; where the most exacting standard of rectitude was the natural way of life and where masters of erudition were held in the highest esteem and much sought after and almost worshipped. Oh, how we have converted!

Megasthenes, the Greek ambassador to the court of the great Chandragupta Maurya at Pataliputra (Patna), however, gives greater detail of Taxilian life in those distant times. Now, the Macedonian empire lasted only as long as rigor mortis had not set in on Alexander's handsome frame. In 322 BCE, encamped at Babylon and preparing future expeditions, he was struck by a fever. In the first week of June that year as his breathing became more and more laboured, his generals gathered around the deathbed to ask whom the empire would go to. 'To the strongest,' is what Alexander is reported to have whispered with some difficulty.

Then he took off his signet ring and handed it to his general Perdiccas. And there began the great struggle to determine who the strongest would be. At the end of several years of warfare between erstwhile friends, the Macedonian Empire that had stretched from Libya, through Turkey, Persia, Central Asia and Afghanistan into what is now Pakistan stood fragmented between the generals. One of those was Seleucus Nikator who took what was once the Achaemenian Empire of Persia and which had been dismantled by Alexander.

In 302 BCE, Seleucus took it into his head to pull another Alexander on India. With a large army, he marched east to meet Chandragupta Maurya at the foot of the Khyber Pass. It is moot if the Mauryan king inflicted a decisive defeat, but we do know that the Greeks were discomfited to some extent. Peace was negotiated and the European general gave either his daughter or a niece in marriage to Chandragupta. In exchange he received a number of war elephants. Also a treaty resulted in the establishment of diplomatic relations between the two kingdoms. And so it was, that Megasthenes came to the Pataliputra court in the year 300 BCE.

His ambassadorial stint lasted a full fifteen years during which Megasthenes travelled extensively around the northern part of India. Taxila, being a second capital of the Mauryan kingdom, was one place where he seems to have either spent considerable time or visited several times over the fifteen years. The result was a book titled *Indika* which he wrote upon returning home in 285 BCE. Though the book comes down to us in fragmentary form it is yet a reliable compendium of Indian life in the fourth century BCE. Of course, it contains some delightful fables as well. This *Indika* became the basis of the work on India by the Greek geographer, philosopher and historian Strabo (BCE 63–CE 23) and the soldier historian Arrian (CE 92–175).

To begin with, Megasthenes found it 'truly remarkable' that slavery was unknown to this wonderful land because it had been frowned upon by ancient philosophers. The world has learned a great deal from our forefathers for law that they held dear more than two thousand years ago belongs today to a universal charter of human rights: 'no one among them shall, under any circumstances, be a slave, but that, enjoying freedom, they shall respect the equal right to it which all possess', Megasthenes assures us. Interestingly, a strong caste system existed, even so the supposedly lowest in social standing were free people.

Coming to Taxila just twenty years after Alexander's passage, Megasthenes recorded the prevalent customs. Business was transacted not by written deeds and memorandums, but by word of mouth. Yet, he observes, the courts of Taxila did not have a single case of fraud. Theft was unknown in this city. Folks left home without securing their properties with locks. It was not that poverty was absent; he tells us that an indigent father unable to wed off a marriageable daughter would bring her to the town square where boxers would fight for her. The maiden would, understandably, go to the last man standing.

Perhaps the earliest example of punk hair styles in the world is recorded from Taxila. Gentlemen of the town had their hair dyed the whitest of white or blue, purple, green or red and as they went about their business, the better off among them with servants shielding them from the sun under wide parasols. The men wore platform shoes to seem the taller and their cotton dresses were embroidered with gold thread and studded with precious stones.

Taxila was home to three religions: the followers of the Boutta, the Brachmanes and those who put their dead out for wild beasts and birds to eat. And there was no conflict between followers of the three religions. Taxila – and indeed much of the rest of the Mauryan Empire, if we are to trust Megasthenes – was the very epitome of Utopia.

The oldest residential university of the subcontinent was in Taxila. Here men like Panini who hailed from Salatura, just across the Indus, formulated for the first time ever the rules for Sanskrit grammar. He would surely have attended this university as a young man. And Vyasa, the brilliant virtuoso, who collected the epic Mahabharata in the form of a book too passed through the corridors of the same university before sitting down in the shady glens of Taxila to execute his monumental work. Ghosha, the medical man specialising in diseases of the eye too lived and studied here. They said in those far off days that he could restore sight to the blind. A few centuries later, perhaps even as Alexander tarried at Taxila, the brilliant Chanakya Kautilya taught here. Surely it was the years of intellectual exchange and private contemplation that led this great thinker to write his unbeatable political treatise *Arthshastra*. It was from Taxila that this great mind moved on to become advisor to Chandragupta Maurya.

It is not difficult to imagine what life in the afterhours would have been. Though Taxilians frowned upon drunkenness, there would have been taverns in town. I imagine students from the university gathering there with clay tumblers of the best rice wine to lubricate the discussions on the meaning of life and history of the human race and its place in the greater scheme of things. As they spoke, crowds of laypersons gathered around to listen, rapt and awed. Perhaps even offering the learned ones a round or two.

∞

With Nasir Khan, curator Taxila Museum, expounding on the bane of the many makers of fake statuary and coinage to fool unsuspecting visitors we walked around the ruins of Bhir just outside the museum. Only partially excavated, this was a sprawling city in Alexander's time. Here he and his closest chums would have had the nightly binges they were famous for. But when he was sober, Alexander wanted to meet the philosophers of Taxila whose fame spread beyond the frontiers of their country.

With an invitation for these men of thought and learning to come to the royal dining table, Alexander sent Onesikritos, his aide, and when the king sailed, the helmsman of the ship. Beyond the clump of habitation, in a sylvan dale where a pure stream passed, the gymnosophists – naked philosophers – engaged in their business. I had always wondered where their abode would have been and one day it came to me in the days I spent cycling around Taxila in the mid-1990s. It was almost epiphany. The philosophers abode was where half a century later Asoka would build his fabulous stupa and monastery of Dharmarajika.

With his entourage, Onesikritos headed out across the clear, bubbling Tambrah rivulet and up the slight incline shaded by trees that our ancestors held sacred, trees like the *pipal* and the banyan. On the far side of this hillock he found the philosophers clad only in loincloth, sprawled out or sitting cross-legged on the rocks heated to an unbearable degree by the May sun.

A young philosopher, the first one Onesikritos came upon, mocked the foreigner. The tenderfoot wanted to learn his philosophy when he was so expensively attired. He would be well advised to undress and lie next to the sage on the stones. But an elderly man, considered the master of the philosophers whose Hellenised name we learn was Mandanis, rebuked the youngster and called the Greek over to himself. Onesikritos greeted him:

> Hail to you, oh teacher of the Brahmins. The son of Zeus, king Alexander, who is the sovereign lord of all men, asks you to go to him, and if you comply, he will reward you with great and splendid gifts, but if you refuse will cut off your head.

We must recall that Megasthenes came to our part of the world a quarter century after Alexander. Mandanis, who was already quite old when Onesikritos met him, seems to have passed away and what the ambassador records is hearsay. But the thing is that the events of that recent past, the unprecedented resistance to ultimate power by a defenceless man, were deeply ingrained in the minds of the Taxilians who must have repeated the events again and again and kept them alive.

We read that Mandanis heard Onesikritos with a 'complacent smile' without lifting his head from his pillow of leaves. The passion of Mandanis, his detachment from this worldly life and his lofty courage in resisting power is clear in his response:

> God, the supreme king, is never the author of insolent wrong, but he is the creator of light, of peace, of life, of water, of the body of man, and of souls, and these he receives when death sets them free, being in no way subject to evil desire. He alone is the god of my homage, who abhors slaughter and instigates no wars. But Alexander is not God, since he must taste of death; and how can such as he be the world's master, who has not yet reached the further shore of the river Tiberoboas, and has not yet seated himself on a throne of universal dominion? ..... Know this, however, that what Alexander offers me, and the gifts he promises, are all things to me utterly useless..... The earth supplies me with everything, even as a mother her child with milk..... Should Alexander cut off my head, he cannot also destroy my soul. My head alone, now silent, will remain, but the soul will go away to its Master, leaving the body like a torn garment upon the earth, whence it was also taken..... Let Alexander, then, terrify with these threats those who wish for gold and for wealth, and who dread death, for against us these weapons are both alike powerless, since the Brahmins neither love gold nor fear death.

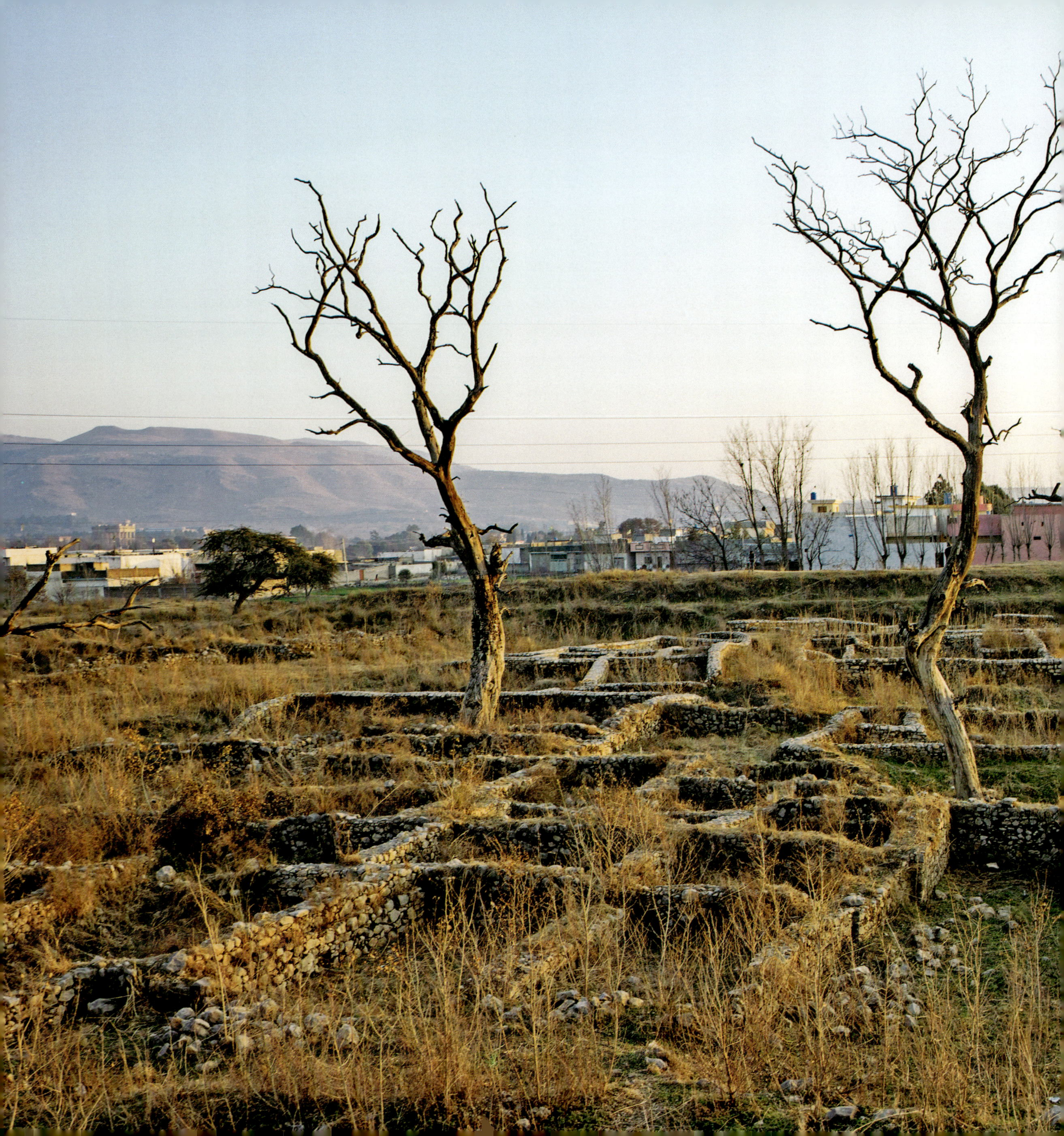

The philosopher concluded by telling the Greek to tell Alexander that there was nothing he possessed that Mandanis had either need for or desire. But if there was something Alexander sought from the sage, it would be unbecoming of the king to not go to him.

What a man Mandanis was! Now more than two thousand years since his passing we are so much the poorer for we find no Mandanis among us.

It must have been a dejected and overawed Onesikritos who returned to Alexander to recount the exchange. Megasthenes tells us that Alexander 'felt a stronger desire than ever to see Mandanis'. Here was Alexander, the subduer of so many kings, who finally met a challenger clearly more than his match, writes the Greek diplomat.

History records that two of the philosophers eventually did accept Alexander's invitation to dine with him. What we are not told is how that came to pass. But I can imagine that intrigued by Mandanis, as he clearly was, Alexander may well have gone out himself to invite the savant of Taxila to his banquet table.

We also know that Alexander requested the philosophers to travel with him to Greece so that en route when he had time, he could learn of their philosophy. Mandanis refused point blank. But another elderly man Kalanos agreed and

The Bhir mound ruins of Taxila, the city where Alexander tarried in May 326 BCE. Only this small portion of a once bustling and rather large city has been excavated. Many of its secrets still lie buried under the dust of ages.

left Taxila in the Macedonian's train.

In Taxila Megasthenes heard common people celebrating Mandanis for his supreme values and his rejection of the conqueror's overtures. Here they had a model to emulate. Even today, as I walk among the ruins of Dharmarajika, I wonder how many young men would have sought the presence of the ageing sage to learn the same higher values. Megasthenes tells us that on the other hand, Kalanos (whose name derives from Kalyan) was reviled all around for succumbing to lust for material wealth.

Alexander's historian Arrian writes in the second century CE that Kalyan having travelled with the army all the way through modern Pakistan, having suffered the scorching heat of the Makran Desert in early October, eventually fetched up in Susa (Persia). Kalyan, who had until then never suffered ill health, became unwell and one day told Alexander that his body and soul were worn out and he thought it better to mount his funeral pyre. The king protested. Why, there was so much more he wished to learn from Kalyan and Alexander had not even attained a fraction of the sage's knowledge. The self-inflicted death had to be deferred, begged the king.

But the master declined and on the appointed day, just as Kalyan was about to mount his pyre, Alexander once again approached him asking for him to relent. Arrian tells us that the sage closed the discussion with a strange utterance. He told Alexander not to worry for within the year they were destined to meet again in Babylon. And sure enough, ten months later the great conquering hero Alexander lay dying in that Mesopotamian city.

Meanwhile, in Susa Arrian records a momentous funeral procession for the Taxilian philosopher. A horse of the finest breed available, was brought for the master to ride, but all strength had left his body and he had to be borne on a litter. A solemn procession of horses, elephants and soldiers in armour followed. Kalyan's countrymen, who were also in the Macedonian army, sang hymns to praise their gods as the bier wound its way through the streets of Susa. As he mounted the pyre, the master handed the reins of his horse to Lysimachus, a Greek student of his. Among all his other friends he distributed the gold and silver goblets that had been offered to him as tribute. Having performed his last rites, Kalyan laid himself down on the pyre. As the fire was kindled, there was, by Alexander's order, an impressive salute. Bugles sounded, in unison the soldiers roared out their battle cry and, not to be left behind, the elephants joined in with shrill trumpeting. The master, Arrian informs us, sat motionless amid the leaping flames until life left him and all that remained of his mortal body was a charred coal.

However, at home in Taxila even after twenty years, Kalyan was reviled for submitting to lust and repudiating the way of life of the Indian master. This was not strange. The philosophers were highly esteemed teachers. They seldom came into town, but when they did, people thronged to them to hear them speak. Folks invited them into homes, begging them to dine there, shopkeepers offered them items from their display free of charge and others came with oil for their hair or with water to wash their feet.

Azeem and Nasir Khan were unanimous that these stories were unknown to common folks. Why, they did not even comprehend the cultural importance of Taxila. This brought us to my old lament: Pakistanis consider sites of built heritage only as picnic spots. They come with their hampers, eat their greasy food, and strew about their Styrofoam plates right next to a rubbish bin. They care nothing for the place nor do they have any desire to learn about it. 'That's because nobody ever tells a schoolchild what Taxila or Pushkalavati stand for. An understanding and appreciation of our historical heritage should be inculcated at the earliest level. And that is not happening,' said Azeem.

To find out how much the average person understood, I returned to Taxila two months later with my friend Sheherbano, Sherry to all of us. We were visiting with a relative of hers who had been requested to invite some elderly women for us to talk to. The relative, with hair dyed an uncanny black, said he had invited 'local historians' to teach me everything I needed to know about Taxila.
I protested that I needed to talk to elderly women only, but the foul deed had been done. Three men were ushered in, one of whom was a storekeeper and part-time historian. The other was a 'professor' who also wrote newspaper articles and the third one just kept to himself. The storekeeper told me there were two Alexanders or Sikanders. One was Sikander Unani (Ionian) and the other was Sikander Zulqarnain.

Zulqarnain – Two-Horned – of the Quran could either be Cyrus the Great who wore a horned helmet or Alexander who sometimes wore ram's horns with his diadem. The Quran records a short adventure of this unidentifiable Zulqarnain where he imprisoned Gog and Magog behind a rock wall steeped with molten lead before going on to the place of the setting sun. There he saw the sun setting in a dark pool.

The shopkeeper also revised some more history for me. He snickered when I said the fort of Rohtas was built by Sher Shah Suri. Why, the Pakhtun king was but yesterday. It was Shahabuddin (also known as Muizuddin) Ghori to whom the fort is attributed.

With no desire to improve my knowledge any further, I asked our host to please find us an elderly woman and presently Fatima, all of fifty-five or so but completely worn out, waddled in. She had never, neither in her youth nor after her marriage, been to Taxila Museum or the various excavated sites. Her children, even her daughters, went sometimes. Sherry asked her if she asked her children what they saw there.
'No. I've never asked and neither have they ever offered to tell me,' Fatima spoke clearly baffled by this question. It was as if she wanted to ask what was there to see in Taxila other than a few stones.

The average person with the usual government school education is simply not tutored from childhood to comprehend what would only cultivate in the mind a sense of pride in the land and its culture and of belonging to it. This has sadly become the privilege of the better off who attend good schools before ending up at universities abroad. This realisation came a couple of weeks after this interview when I was again in Taxila with Emily Macinnes, the young Scottish film maker.

In the museum we got talking to a bunch of youngsters and their parents who lived abroad. One young man said when he left the country several years ago he had no idea what he was abandoning. Now, having completed his education and on the verge of beginning work, he had returned to learn about the land of his ancestors. Now as a foreign national, he seemed to have no desire to live here permanently, yet he did not want to be ignorant of what once was in the country that we call Pakistan.

Nasir Khan, Azeem and I did a tour of the monasteries: the magnificent Dharmarajika, the quiet and peaceful Mohra Moradu before heading off for Bhamala. Sitting on an elongated spur on the right bank of the Haro River, the stupa of Bhamala is unique for its cruciform plan. The recent find here is what everyone, even newspapers and politicians, calls the Sleeping Buddha. Azeem, the Gandhara specialist, pointed out to me that it was Maha Pari Nirvana, the Passing of Buddha. A colossus at about seven metres, it is Buddha lying on his right side with a hand under his cheek, eyes half closed. This is enough for the layperson to classify this as they do.

After the passage of the Macedonians in 326 BCE, Taxila thrived under the Mauryans. It is, however, the way of all dynasties to rise and fall. Chandragupta and his grandson Asoka were brilliant administrators, but after the latter's death in 232, his kingdom passed on to weaker kings.

Within half a century, the sons of the very man that Chandragupta had defeated, having expanded their influence from distant Syria into Afghanistan, had set their eyes on the fertile land between the five rivers.

We know them as the Indo-Greeks or Bactrian Greeks for they had set up their base in Bactria (Balkh) to control most of modern day Afghanistan. History also remembers them by another name: the Euthydemids after Euthydemus who first took Bactria. By about 180 BCE they had marched across the Khyber Pass and possessed Peshawar and Pushkalavati. Within a couple of years Taxila and Sangala (Sialkot) fell to them.

Demetrius, son of Euthydemus, whose coins show a rather handsome square-jawed man, copied Alexander, erroneously regarding him an ancestor. He was the leader who carried Greek arms and influence for the third time across the Suleman Hills into the Peshawar Valley. With reference to his taking of India, the local issue of his coins represented him with the elephant scalp head-dress. If Alexander had found Taxila an agreeable place, Demetrius thought otherwise. The jumble of housing and shopping areas in winding streets was not entirely to his liking. The Greeks preferred cities aligned with the cardinal points and laid on a grid.

A kilometre and a half northeast of the old city, the Greeks laid out the foundations of a new Taxila that we today know as Sirkap. The main street, bordered by houses and shops, stretched from the north to the south with intermediary lanes intersecting it at right angles. The town was girded by a hefty masonry wall with entry from a strongly bastioned gateway facing north. Funnily, people of the very land where four thousand years before the Greeks, cities were laid in grids had forgotten that orderly town planning. Somewhere along the line, something had disrupted the link with the ancient past.

Though Hindu nationalists clamour for the world to believe that the Aryans rose from the Gangetic Plains, the truth is that they did come from elsewhere. Their home had once been the wind-scoured grasslands of Central Asia where they travelled about in horse or ox-drawn wagons in search of sustenance for themselves and their large herds. When they halted, the chief's wagon became the centre of the temporary habitation with the tents of his followers radiating outward in lines following the pecking order. Having arrived in the Indus Valley, they found its magnificent cities already decaying because of flooding. In the manner they were accustomed to, they set down their townships with the chief occupying the centre. Over the centuries, the old system of orderly cities was forgotten until it was taught to us again by the Greeks in the second century BCE.

Greek rule lasted a mere seven decades when, once more, fierce horse-riding nomads burst out of their home on the Central Asian grasslands and came to possess the Indus Valley. Enriched with Siberian gold, these Scythians, or Sakas as they were known locally, were no savages, however. Years of interaction with their old kinsmen the Parthians had taught them to respect and take advantage of superior cultures. Ruling from Taxila, their king

Buddha in a typical preaching pose at Bhamala. This monastery is home to the recently discovered seven-metre statue of Buddha in Maha Pari Nirvana, that is, demise. By many it is erroneously referred to as 'Sleeping Buddha'. Remote as this monastery was from the rest of Taxila, it was yet not spared by Hunnic savagery. Here too archaeologists found signs of arson and violence.

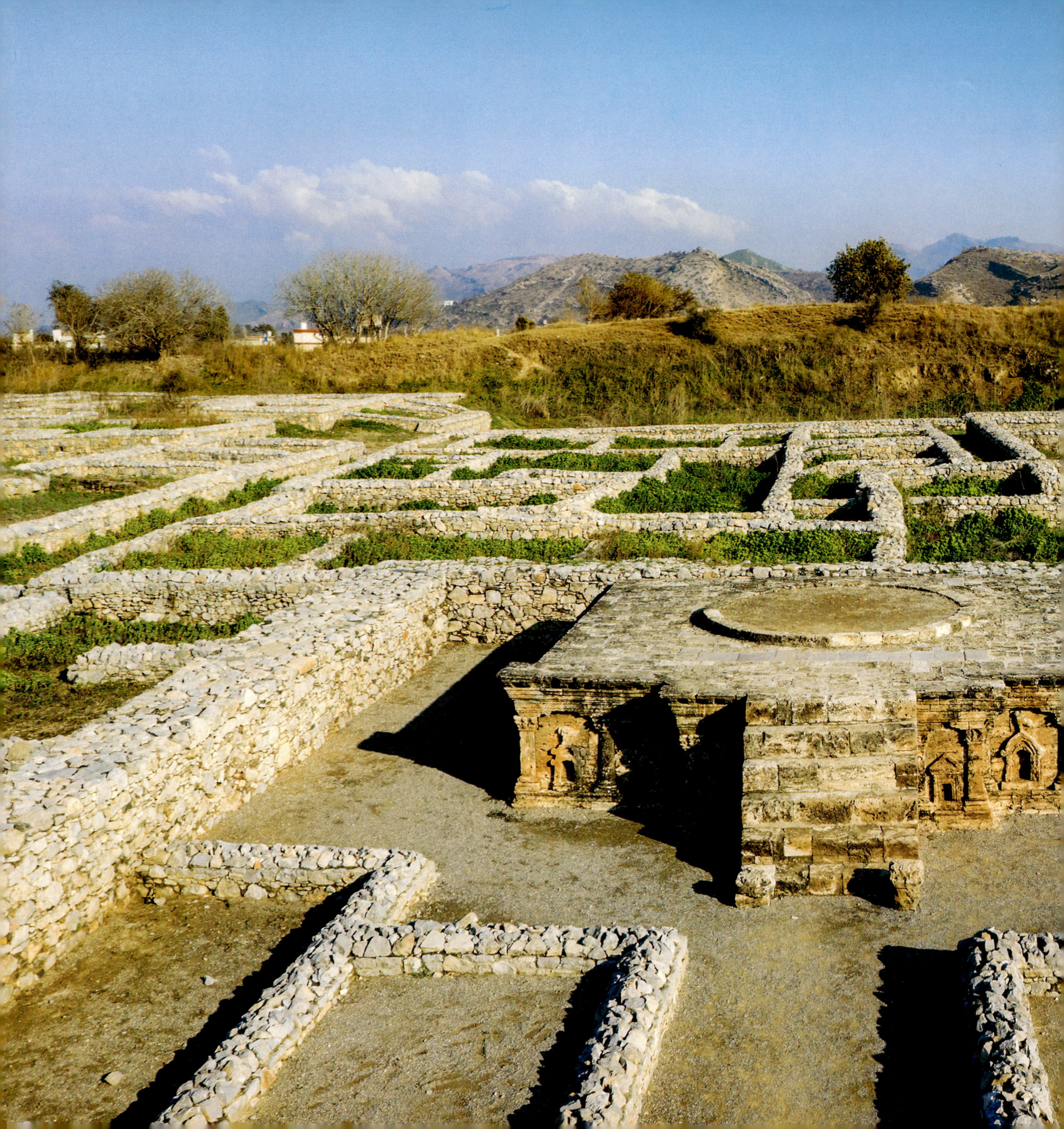

Maues (Moga in the local dialect) blatantly followed the Euthydemid design of coins, even calling himself Basileos Maues or King Maues in Greek.

The death of Maues in about 53 BCE, was followed by a flurry of quick regnal changes over three decades. Gondophares the Parthian king brought stability in 19 CE when he took over Taxila whose fame he certainly would have heard even before he left his homeland on the shores of the Caspian Sea. Six years later, in the year 25, the city was laid low by a devastating earthquake. Gondophares quickly set to rebuilding the city The ashlar masonry employed by the Greeks in place of the coarse undressed rubble used in old Taxila was discarded in favour of the finer diaper style: the interstices between the dressed blocks were neatly filled in with chips for greater stability.

All around the main city, schools and monasteries thrived. If Asoka's Dharmarajika Stupa – Stupa of the King of the Faith – and its monastery were humming with murmured prayer, newer places of worship were coming up on the outskirts of the city. If there was a cosmopolitan city in Punjab, it was Taxila. Here one heard a babble of languages and met travellers and traders from distant lands as one walked the streets of the city.

If Buddhism was the predominant religion of the period, the fire-worshipping Gondophares gave a boost to Zoroastrianism. Across the green fields and just a kilometre due north of the north gate of the city that Gondophares

The ruins of Sirkap housing with the Stupa of Double-Headed Eagle in the foreground.

Detail of stone carving from the plinth of the stupa of the Double-Headed Eagle. Notice the Greek influence of a work rendered in the first century CE.

Top Left/Bottom Left: Imagery from the Dharmarajika stupa.

Top Right: Imagery for Votive Stupa, Mohra Moradu monastery.
Bottom Right: Imagery from the Dharmarajika stupa.

raised from the rubble, sat on slightly raised ground a beautiful Greek style temple of Jandial. With massive pillars resting on large bases to support a high roof, the temple is believed to have been built about the middle of the first century BCE. This was a time when Taxila was held by the Zoroastrian Scythians. Consequently, archaeologists favour the theory that it was a fire temple.

Amateur historians as well as some archaeologists believe Jandial to be the temple that features in the story of Apollonius of Tyana who visited Taxila in or about the year 44 CE. Having travelled from his hometown in central Turkey, this Greek philosopher fetched up in Taxila to meet with the city's philosophers. These, he knew, were the very ones whose ancestors had astounded Alexander with their wisdom.

King Gondophares had instituted that no foreigner may enter the city without permission from the administration. The rank and status of the permission-giver was commensurate with the stature of the visitor. Common traders would have to petition someone perhaps from the municipality. But important persons like teachers and diplomats were admitted only after the king himself granted permission.

And so, in the course of the few days waiting for his petition to enter Taxila to reach the top of the pile on the king's desk, Apollonius and the young prodigy Damis who accompanied him as diarist, waited outside the city in a temple. Damis describes the temple as built of marble whose external walls were adorned with large copper plate murals showing vivid scenes of battle. In these, Alexander was the victor and Raja Paurava in defeat.[3]

What remains of Jandial temple is sufficient to show that it was constructed of limestone blocks and not marble. To my mind it, therefore, cannot be the one where Apollonius and Damis would have tarried. The eminent archaeologist Dr Saifur Rahman Dar points out that back in the early 1960s, he had seen the remains of a temple outside the village of Mohra Maliarañ, a little way off from Jandial. He believes this and not Jandial was the visiting philosopher's temporary abode. Today not even a vestige of that ancient

Jandial Temple at Taxila. The massive pedestals in the foreground are the bases of pillars that once held up its roof. Their size recalls the impressive building that it once was.

---

3) Paurava, a dynastic name, was the learned person's pronunciation. On the tongue of commoners it was Pora which the Greeks transliterated to Porus.

temple remains for the land is now under cultivation.

Royal permission granted, an escort was sent out to bring the man of learning to the presence of the king. As they neared town, Apollonius would surely have remarked upon the city's protective wall with its massive turrets and the houses rising above in the background. Entering through a wicket gate, the escort would have asked his charge to notice how new the city looked. It was true, he would have said, that in his few decades of life he had never experienced an earthquake the likes of which ruined his beautiful city only a quarter century earlier. In a way, he might even have added, this was for the better because the ramshackle old houses of half a century earlier had now been replaced.

As they walked along, the garrulous escort would have asked the visitors to notice the wares on display in the stores fronting the houses on either side of the street. He would have boasted of the trade Taxila had with distant lands and especially remarked on the fine gold jewellery worked by second generation Scythian Taxilians. About halfway to the king's palace, the escort paused in front of the temple of red marble on the right side of the road. Damis once again writes of its outer walls decorated with large copper plate murals showing scenes of battle between Paurava and Alexander where again the latter was the winner. He remarked on the exactness of colour and drawing for it seemed one beheld an actual scene instead of a painting.

The visitors were told that these murals were ordered by Raja Paurava when he received word of Alexander's death in Babylon in June 322 BCE. Now, we have seen that in the year Alexander died, the city of Taxila was what we today call Bhir. The murals would initially have been installed on some building in that city. A century and a half later Demetrius built New Taxila leaving the old to the working class and artisans. It seems he ordered the murals to be removed to the new site. To have done that, he must surely have admired them greatly for had he left them in the old city the would have been eventually vandalised and forgotten.

The ruins of the Taxila of Demetrius sit six metres below the surface of the one Apollonius visited. In those two hundred years between the two, the city was destroyed several times and rebuilt on its own rubble raising its level to the Taxila of Gondophares. Each time that happened, the murals were faithfully removed and perhaps even restored with colour to be installed afresh on some newer building. Clearly, these murals were held in such great esteem by Taxila's kings and commoners that three and a half centuries after Raja Paurava had them installed, they were still there in very good fettle.

To my mind this indicates two things. For one, as the diary of Damis tells us, the artistry of the murals was very true to life which would have made them admirable for the public and the kings. Secondly, the message conveyed by the murals was worthy of being remembered and followed. We are told that Raja Paurava, upon receiving word of Alexander's death, ordered the murals so that history may never be subverted.

Consider: Alexander was dead in far off Babylon, his Greek governor and the army left behind in this part of the world had bolted to take part in the War of Succession. Ambhi was dead; Paurava was now the master of the land between the Indus and the Ravi. He could have ordered anything and within the space of twenty years, he would have been celebrated, wrongly, as the only man in history to vanquish Alexander. But here was a man browned by the Punjabi sun, of character far loftier than his towering physical self. He did not wish for history to be undermined even if that truth did not flatter him.

Sadly, modern day faux historians fall over themselves to 'prove' the crushing defeat inflicted by Paurava on his Macedonian rival. In their crude attempts they take away so much from the greatest monarch of the early history of the Punjab.

We had empire-building kings among the Greeks, Scythians, Parthians and Sassanians who, even when they had to fight over Taxila to win her, built her with feeling. We also had aberrations like the Huns who only destroyed. Afghanistan fell to Tor Aman in the last quarter of the fifth century CE and, as if the vicious monster had not had enough of rape and slaughter in the highlands, he moved east. As word of his ruthlessness preceded him, the populace would have rejoiced when in 502 they heard of his death.

But the sense of relief was short-lived for he was succeeded by his son Mehr Gul who was twice as cruel and blood-thirsty as the father. Coins show them both to be of exceeding physical ugliness: large, bulbous nose, fleshy jaws and chin, bull neck and narrow head. Mehr Gul with his frightful grimace has a particularly demonic look. What we know from history is that both father and son had only one ambition: to destroy civilisation as it was then known and it seems they killed humans for sport.

Humans were not all the Huns enjoyed massacring, however. In Kashmir, Mehr Gul saw a military elephant accidentally slipping over a sharp verge into a deep ravine. The terrified scream of the poor beast so delighted that barbarian that he ordered several more elephants to be forced into the abyss. The exact spot of this cruel sport is to this day known as Hastinavanj – Elephant Went.

The most chilling account of Hunnic barbarity we read of in the *Rajatarangni* – Chronicle of Kings. Written in the middle of the twelfth century, six hundred years after the event, this was the master work of the Kashmiri Pundit Kalhana. The eight-volume work covers the rule of Kashmiri kings from the early Middle Ages down to the time of the writer. Though the chronology of the book is sometime out of kilter, it is still a great read not only for the historian but for the novice appreciative of the literary hyperbole employed by writers of that age. Writing six centuries after the event, Kalhana relied on existing local sources that no longer exist and much real history is to be gleaned from the effusive prose.

Kalhana tells us that the killing was so wanton and thoughtless and the count of bodies in the wake of the advancing Hunnic army was so huge that a dark cloud of crows and vultures followed the horde to feed on the dead. Those that were not killed by the sword, were drowned in the rivers as if for sport. Rape and plunder were without measure.

In Taxila, as indeed in the fabulous cities of Pushkalavati and Peshawar, a record of arson dating to the first decade of the sixth century is clearly seen. The stupas and monasteries of Dharmarajika, Mohra Moradu, Jaulian were laid low. Even the outlying Bhamala monastery revealed a layer of ash and charcoal when first investigated.

I can imagine an early morning with thin skeins of mist swirling around the open fields amid the low hills topped by the stupa and the monastery of Bhamala. Done with their early morning ritual of ablution and prayer, the monks would have been preparing to set out for town, begging bowl in hand, to secure their day's sustenance. In the distance they might have seen the dark cloud of carrion-feeding birds so easy to be mistaken for a raincloud. But then the din of the advancing horde would have drawn nearer and nearer until the clash of armoury and the cries of the victims would have reached the monks.

Some would have panicked and escaped into the hills. The more devout would have stayed, not to fight for that went against their creed, but to die for their belief. They may even have attempted to hide the most valued images of Buddha, but that was futile for there was no time. And then the bloodthirsty host was upon them. Within hours, with scores of bodies littering the once quiet and peaceful precincts of the monasteries, raging fires were licking through the buildings.

The savages moved on and the centuries of the sound of murmured prayer was overtaken by a hush that was to last fifteen hundred years. It was broken again by the clank of metal in 1913 when John Marshall began his investigation. This time it was not the sword of the barbarian, but the spade of the archaeologist. From the glens of modern day Khyber Pakhtunkhwa to the narrow valleys of Taxila, ruins of the monasteries show a layer of ash and charcoal dating to the first decade of the sixth century CE. The rusted arrowheads and spear points recovered from the dust and ash of centuries are the accusing finger pointing at the Huns.

Having undertaken a long and arduous journey, Xuanzang, the Buddhist master from the seminary of Chang'an (Xian), arrived in Taxila. The mission he followed with single-minded conviction was to procure the true word of his Lord Buddha so that the corrupted texts in China could be set right again. The year was 631, only a hundred and twenty years since the savagery of the Huns had swept through the land. In Taxila, Xuanzang saw many monasteries in ruins and deserted and the city had only a few priests. The only consolation was that the masters still followed the Mahayana code of Buddhism. Mehr Gul was still remembered as was his defeat at the hands of the Rajputs in the south.

What the Huns wrought had a long lasting effect on Taxila. It went into decline whose speed was only added to by another event. Xuanzang noted that the ruling family was

The massive drum of Dharmarajika stupa that is, to this day, Asoka's greatest gift to Taxila. The monastery surrounding the stupa was once the largest and busiest in the city. Signs of arson remind us of the barbaric attack of the Huns in the early years of the sixth century CE.

Mohra Moradu monastery.

Votive Stupa, Mohra Moradu monastery.

dead and Taxila was in the throes of political squabbling. From the *Rajatarangni* we know that the king at the time of the pilgrim's visit, Narendraditya Khinkhila, a pious follower of Lord Shiva, focussed his attention on feeding the clergy and establishing newer places of Vedic worship. There was little focus on governing the vast kingdom stretching all the way from Kashmir across the Suleman Hills into Afghanistan. This lack of oversight led to a time of anarchy speeding up the decay of the city that had once been the finest between the Indus and the Jhelum rivers.

In 631, when he came down the western hills and again in 646 as he headed home to China, Xuanzang was the last person in history to know the city by its old name: Takshasila whose name scholars tell us meant Rock of the Takas, or Takshas after a tribe living in the area. In 1017 or the year after, Abu Rehan Al Beruni, the polymath from Uzbekistan, was in a moribund Taxila. The city was called Babarkan or Babar Khana – House of the Tiger. Rendering the name Babrahan, Al Beruni added that lying halfway between the 'rivers Sindh and Jailam', it was the 'best known entrance to Kashmir'. The new name for the city stemmed from the legend of Buddha feeding a starving tigress with his own flesh. The city was all but dead.

The Takshasila that had drawn men of learning and wealth to its gates, died without so much as a whimper. The empire builders of old, kings like Chandragupta Maurya, Demetrius or Gondophares, who had built this city with so much love were long gone. Five hundred years of unbroken peace since the passing of the Huns had ended with the repeated incursions of Mahmud the Turk who ruled over Afghanistan from his capital at Ghazni. Those who lived within the city's walls moved away and slowly but inexorably silence and the dust of time began to settle over housing and worship place alike.

Within a few centuries all that remained were high clayey mounds, some scattered with finely dressed stones, others perhaps spiked by the upper part of the umbrella topping a stupa. If the grandeur of Taxila was dead and buried along with its name, its splendour remained alive in the collective memory for they called the several mounds Dheri Shahan: Mounds of Kings. Robbers moved in to dig and plunder the supposed treasures buried with the city.

A full millennium after Al Beruni, British archaeologist Alexander Cunningham who had read his Alexander in detail came following up on the ancient conqueror. At the Mounds of Kings he paused to ask. But Taxila had faded from human memory. Cunningham's cursory exploration in the 1860s confirmed what he had suspected: this vast sprinkling of mounds was indeed the very Taxila where Alexander had tarried. Within two decades after him engineers of the Raj laid their railway line past the Mounds of Kings. They named the station Taxila, surely much to the bafflement of the locals who had never heard the name. Another couple of decades passed and John Marshall's men in tweed jackets and thick-shelled solar hats came with teams of labourers to carefully peel away the veneer of dust and for the first time in a thousand years let the masonry walls of Taxila resound with human voices. Curious locals came to ask what the excavation revealed.

It was Taxila, they were told. Over the years and for nearly a full century 'Taxila' was a synonym for ancient ruin or archaeological excavation for locals. Only they could not pronounce the name right. They called every ruin Tuskla. In the 1990s I repeatedly heard the phrase, 'So, you want to see the Tuskla of Mohra Moradu or the Tuskla of Jaulian?'

Today even that is passé.

The Margalla is said to mean Cut (Mar) Throat (Galla) Pass. Tradition has it that brigands hiding in its bends would fall upon passing caravans to kill and plunder. The lofty obelisk known to one and all as Nicholson's Memorial celebrates the general who died aged thirty-five. History remembers him as a bully and a psychopath, but for his followers, Punjabis and Pakhtuns alike, he was a hero for his unflinching courage in battle.

4
Over the Cut Throat Pass

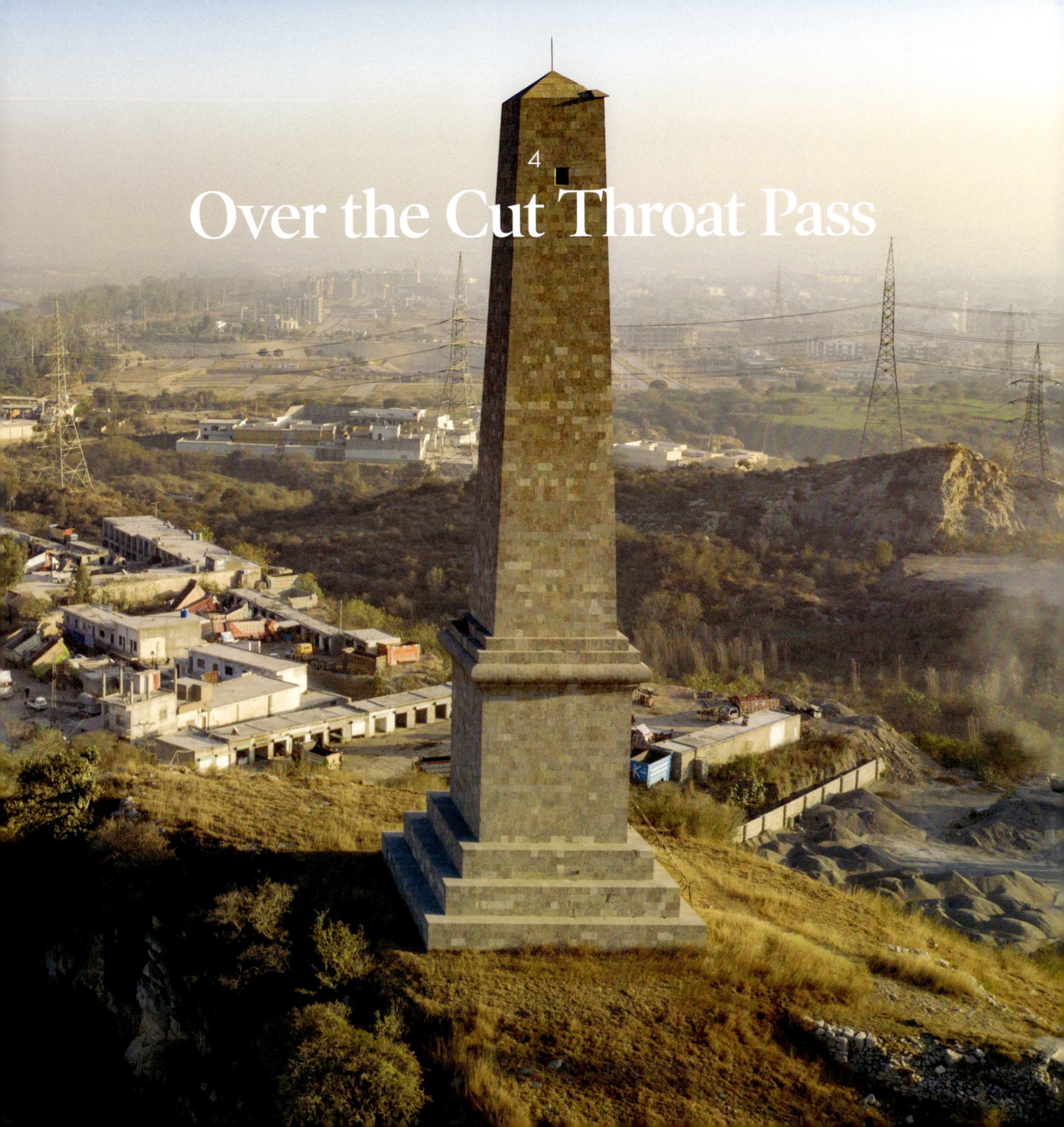

Azeem, his archaeologist's instinct in full flow, did not want me to miss the famous Lohsar *baoli* (stepped well) in the cantonment of Wah. We had to go through a military security check and one of us had to leave his identity card with the guards against which we were given a pass. Larger than most others I have seen, this Mughal monument was the one that no alien or even a passing local tourist would be permitted to visit without a protracted and frustrating song and dance.

The gateway of the steps leading down to the water had been restored, and rather nicely too, in the last years of the past century. The brickwork, after more than three centuries, is still in good fettle and the cross-spans in the stairwell are beautifully crenulated. However, the sad thing is that without proper expert oversight, the left side (as one descends the stairs) has collapsed sending down a huge amount of debris blocking the way to the water. Immediate restoration by those who have the right expertise is urgently needed. But the nightmare that authorities will employ local 'engineers' to 'renovate' this historical building with modern cement and bricks is a real possibility.

And so we passed into the Margalla Pass. Tradition has it that the narrow, twisting road through this low pass was the haunt of ruthless brigands. Not satisfied by the plunder alone, these bloodthirsty thugs were never averse to killing their helpless victims. Since they cut (*mar*) the throats (*galla*), so the name. To our right (as we proceeded in a southerly direction), atop a hill towered the granite spire of Nicholson's Memorial. On our side of the road was the little drinking fountain housed in a beautiful little Greek stoa.

I have been seeing the stoa since my childhood when the Grand Trunk Road was single-lane two-way. Then it stood smack by the berm of the highroad. Now we have a two-lane double track and the stoa still stands a little off the berm. Azeem had the answer: in the 1980s, with government coffers fattened with the aid received for fighting the war in Afghanistan, road widening was at a frenzied pitch all across Pakistan. A bureaucratic mind worked somewhere and the lovely little building, instead of being torn down, was dismantled, its granite blocks numbered and the whole reassembled at the present spot.

We climbed up to Nicholson's memorial obelisk. The door leading into the little cubicle at the bottom was open and there on the front wall was a black plaque with the dedication to John Nicholson, Brigadier General. However, the iron ladder leading to the lighthouse like upper chambers was fixed in such a way cutting diagonally across the tablet so as to prevent photography. It reads:

> This column is erected by friends, British and Native to the memory of Brigadier General John Nicholson, taking a hero's part in four great wars for the defence of British India. Kabul 1840, First Sikh War 1845, Second Sikh War 1848, Sepoy Mutiny 1857.

Nicholson, who died during the War of Independence

(Mutiny to the British[1]) of 1857, barely five months shy of his thirty-sixth birthday was a man whom history looks at in varying colours. For some, he was a hero of the First Anglo-Afghan War; of battles against the Sikhs and of the mutiny of 1857. For one historian he was an 'imperial psychopath', while his own sister had termed him a 'bully'. The fact is that this tall, imposing man of reportedly great physical strength was courageous to the point of being completely mad. We hear of what sort of a man was this John Nicholson from Charles Allen's *Soldier Sahibs*.

In July 1848, Akbar's great fort of Attock was securely in Sikh hands. And the British wanted it to keep an eye on an Afghanistan they so coveted. Nicholson, then all of twenty-seven, rode out of Peshawar with a band of sixty Pakhtun irregular cavalrymen and two companies of recruits. After a day and night of hard riding when he arrived at the ferry of Attock, the recruits had fallen way back while of the hardy Pakhtuns only thirty had been able to keep up with the gruelling pace. They forded the Indus at daybreak and at an hour when the Sikh guards at the gate did not expect such company, Nicholson rode up.

In a remarkable show of derring-do as he passed through the first gate, Nicholson shouted for the guards to gather their weapons and follow him. In the enceinte, the startled Sikh troopers raised their weapons to the intruder. Nicholson dismounted, walked up to the nearest man and wrested his musket from his grasp. In a loud voice he ordered the soldiers to arrest their own guard commander. Half asleep and unable to grasp what really was going on, the Sikhs obeyed and Attock was taken by a mere thirty men without firing a shot.

A day later in the Margalla Pass, Nicholson rode into the Sikh garrison and told the commandant that he had one hour to submit failing which the entire garrison would be eliminated. For the duration of the allocated time, the Sikhs argued among themselves as Nicholson sat motionless on his horse. When the hour was done, the commandant came up and surrendered.

Thereafter, in his administrative assignments Nicholson won fame and the respect of Pakhtun and Punjabi alike for his fair dealings and sense of justice. Indeed, even today we hear of the Nikkalsenis, a Sikh cult that reveres Nicholson as a saint. Unsurprisingly, when his admiring countrymen began the granite obelisk commemorating John Nicholson, there was no resistance. Completed in 1886, it is to this day, a monument – and a rare one – that has suffered no vandalism.

Just below the obelisk, right across the road from the drinking fountain, but caught behind a truckers' stand and sure to be missed by the casual tourist is a stretch of flagstoned road. It was a quiet early morning when I

---

1) The difference is a matter of perspective. For the East India Company, their soldiers had risen up on the perceived view that the bullets for the new rifles were coated either with cow or pig fat. The former unacceptable to Hindus and Sikhs in the service and the latter to their Muslims colleagues. For the rebels, however, it was an attempt to rid India of British dominion.

The old flagstoned Grand Trunk Road and the two obelisks that mark the beginning of its ascent into the Margalla. This paving is from Jahangir's period.

Four centuries of countless feet passing over it, the paving is still in perfect fettle. Today only two hundred metres of the old paving remains.

went there alone. The mechanic who had just opened his nearby workshop came around to chat.

'You've come to see Sher Shah Suri's road,' it was more a statement than a question.

'No. I've come to see the road that Sher Shah had nothing to do with.'

The man smiled an uncertain smile as if to say, 'you're kidding me'. I reeled out my spiel done so many times before. Despite all his admirable qualities, the Suri king could not have made the road, built inns and dug stepped wells in his five years as king before being killed by a mining device gone wrong. The mechanic had been told by 'professor sahib from Taxila' that Sher Shah had ruled for close to fifty years.

I told him that the Gakkhars who had sworn allegiance to Babur and his family had not permitted the Pakhtuns to advance any further west than Rohtas.

'So who built the grand *baoli* in Wah, the one they call Lohsar?'

'Consider Akbar or his son Jahangir,' I suggested. 'You know, we wrongly attribute every stepped well to the Pakhtun king and if we find one on Mars, we'll be convinced even that was built by him.' The man guffawed and slapped his thigh.

This brought us back to the two hundred-metre stretch of flagstoned road. I told him what I had learned on the earlier trip a month before from my archaeologist friend Azeem: that this surviving bit could be attributed to Jahangir. I could see he was perplexed. He could easily have discredit a layman like me, but that an archaeologist had said something seemed to make sense.

∽

Southward lay the city of Rawalpindi. I had been on the road for days that I had lost count of and I was not yet half way between Landi Kotal and Wagah. For that I blamed more winter rains than we had known in recent years. They had hounded me and destroyed the wheat fields of many sorry farmers. It was on another rainy afternoon when Azeem and I turned north from the Grand Trunk Road at the sign saying 'Serai Kharbuza'. About three kilometres off the highway we stood under the massive but now completely ruined walls of the serai mentioned by Jahangir in his memoirs.

Jahangir says it was built in 'earlier times' by the Gakkhars who used it as an octroi station. The name, he tells us, is because a dome here was shaped like a melon. Melon Inn, if I may call it that, sits fifteen kilometres from Taxila, a leisurely day's march. In 1994, having read Jahangir's diary for the second time, I stopped here. Two sides of the enclosing wall and its turrets were gone and inside the compound were a number of houses jumbled close together. Flush with the west wall was a ruinous mosque whose dome was indeed shaped like a melon.

This time around, the decay was even greater with only a bit of the wall and two corner turrets remaining. The melon dome was gone; the mosque forgotten.

∽

Ammad Ali is the living encyclopaedia of Rawalpindi. A native of Kahuta, a little ways northeast of town, he has spent years walking around the streets, exploring the rugged ravines outside town, discovering crumbling ruins and writing very interesting articles for a weekly newspaper. He is an incessant talker who segues from subject to subject and one has to keep one's ears and mind open so as to not miss anything. With him it is easy to lose the thread of his conversation. When asked, he had readily agreed to lead me to the fifteenth century mosque built by the Gakkhars just outside their grand fort of Pharwala.

We drove out on the road to Kahuta and at one point turned in the direction of the little village of Bhimber Trar. Ammad said next to the mosque, in an overgrown area there was a small domed building that kept the remains of Sultan Mukarab Khan, who lived in the middle of the eighteenth century and was the last independent chief of the Gakkhars. He was, if anything, a remarkably opportunistic man. Having fought against the Yusufzais and defeated them, Mukarab teamed with Ahmed Shah Abdali, the first king of independent Afghanistan. During Mukarab's chieftainship, Gakkhar influence expanded east of Gujrat to the vicinity of Eminabad for the first time.

Mukarab Khan's star set when Gujar Singh Bhangi trounced him in battle and he sought refuge with his kinsman Himmat Khan of Domeli who had a keen eye on events and foresaw the rise of the Sikhs: he treacherously slew Mukarab and flaunted his heroic deed for the Sikhs to notice. Not long afterward, even Himmat got the short end of the stick from the Sikhs.

With a young talkative man as our guide, Ammad and I climbed across a rocky spur and descended into and overgrown area known as Bagh Jogian – Garden of the Jogis. It was thick with *bhekar* (*Adhatoda vasica*) and *phulai* (*Acacia modesta*) where spider webs brushed our faces and jujube thorns caught on our clothing. The interior of the tiny domed building was thickly overgrown, but it was clearly from the late eighteenth century. Fearing snakes, I did not enter to see if there was a sarcophagus. Behind this tomb was a roofless rectangular room with a banyan tree growing from its stone wall. It seems that there was a time when Mukarab Khan's sons resorted here, then a garden of sorts. Here passing yogis may have found a few moments of solace for it to be named after them.

I was returning to the ruinous and abandoned fifteenth century mosque after twenty-four years. A building that had withstood the ravages of over five centuries had changed little in the past quarter century. Only the wild growth had encroached closer upon it. The three-domed worship house has three small bays and a courtyard in front whose wall has collapsed, its stones cannibalised for other buildings. The left dome is cracked and all the plaster inside and on the exterior has peeled away to reveal coarsely dressed stones beneath. The call of the muezzin has not echoed out of its prayer chamber perhaps since the time of Mukarab Khan's passing.

Across the clear bluish water of the Soan River, here an ankle-deep trickle when it is not raining, stood the bulky ramparts of Pharwala Fort. In February 1519, Babur was camped on the banks of the Soan River in the vicinity of

Rawalpindi when an emissary from the Salt Range Janjuas sought audience. The envoy was well received and presently the chief of the Janjuas had a hearing with the Mughal.

A month later, Babur having journeyed to Bhera across the Jhelum River was back in Janjua country where the chief, Malik Asad, saw his chance to set Babur against his old enemy. Chief of the Gakkhars, Hathi was the bad man in the area who gave no man peace; he robbed on the roads and brought everyone to ruin and he ought to be severely punished, pleaded Asad the Janjua.

With a guide provided by the Janjua chieftain, Babur made a forced day and night march through rough, broken ground until 'the blackness of Parhala (sic) showed itself from two miles off', so the *Baburnama* tells us. Babur put his army in battle order and stormed the walls of the fort. Behind the rampart attacked by the Mughals, waited Hathi Gakkhar, a man of gigantic stature and phenomenal strength. It is said that when he stood on the ground in his bare feet, he yet towered above a mounted warrior. With him rallying his forces, the Mughals were soon routed. The way Babur glossed over the failure in his diary, it is clear the retreat was rather undignified.

Babur called in the reserve and a resolute attack was mounted a second time. This time the Gakkhars were beaten. As the Mughal force poured into the fort from Hathi Gate named after the chieftain himself, Hathi dissolved into the forested gully beyond Bohri vala Darwaza (Banyan Gate), on the far side of his fort. But a fortnight later, he sued for peace and made friends with Babur. However, he did not get to live long after that. His nephews, Sarang and Adam whose father he had slain only a few years, earlier had been waiting for the chance to get even. Finding the opening, they dispatched Hathi and in his stead submitted to Babur. Later, when Babur returned again to possess India, the brothers Sarang and Adam joined his victorious train to Delhi.

In 2015, returning to Pharwala after a gap of eighteen years, I was sorry to see the deterioration in its state. Since most educated Pharwala men go to work in Rawalpindi or Islamabad, the village inside the walls is mostly deserted during the day. On this occasion we met a man who told us that those who lived in the fort, including himself, had

Pharwala Fort, the medieval redoubt of the Gakkhars stands above the Soan River. On the right Begum Darwaza (Gate) can be seen.

been cannibalising material from the fort walls to enlarge their own homes.

Appalled, I rebuked him for being a Gakkhar and destroying Sarang Khan's legacy, whose descendent he and all others in Pharwala claim to be. The man looked at me blankly. The fort, whose battlements first went up perhaps as early as the thirteenth century to be repaired and improved periodically, has always been a Gakkhar home, yet it was of no significance to the illiterate man. Though he lived within its walls, he did not seem to belong to Pharwala.

Babur may have been an astute ruler, his son Humayun was an utter failure. Within years of the father's death, the son who forever lived befuddled by opium, had fought two disastrous wars against an ambitious and energetic Sher Shah Suri and lost them both. In 1539, the first battle was fought at Chausa in Bengal and carried by the master tactician Sher Shah in a lightning strike. The second, fought a year later near Kanauj, once again spelled ignominious defeat for Humayun who made off from the field on a lame nag.

Sher Shah Suri pursued Humayun through Rajasthan whence the Mughal fled through Sindh and Balochistan to seek refuge with his friend Tahmasp I, the Safvi king of Persia. At home, the brilliant and tireless Pakhtun became king of India and set about consolidating his hold. But fortune gave him a mere five years. In 1545, overseeing the mining of the walls of Kalinjer fort in Rajasthan, Sher Shah got in the way of an explosive charge rebounding of the fortification. He was badly burnt and only stayed alive until word came to him that the fort was taken.

The old mosque outside Pharwala Fort. So completely abandoned that not even rock pigeons and owls roost under its domes.

However, during his lifetime, he tried to bring the Gakkhars of the Potohar Plateau to terms. But Sarang and his brother Adam Khan were men true to their salt: years earlier they had sworn allegiance to Babur. It was not their way now to abandon Babur's son, not even when he was a fugitive in a distant land with scant hope of ever regaining his father's kingdom. Guarding the roads through their territory, the Gakkhars harried Pakhtun troopers passing through.

This could not go on. Encamped at Bhera on the east bank of the Jhelum River, Sher Shah sent a message to the defiant brothers to present themselves in his camp. Sarang Khan replied with a pair of maces and a couple of arrow-filled quivers. Gakkhar lore has it that he also sent a pair of lion cubs with the taunt, 'You call yourself "Sher", so I send you these cubs that you try to imbibe the qualities of these noble creatures. It is doubtful, but you may yet acquire some of their character.'

The Gakkhars, inured to war and hardship, kept to harassing travellers on the Grand Trunk Road passing by their stronghold. Meanwhile, Sher Shah's advisor who knew these hill men better advised against open all-out war. They had to be contained by a strong permanent garrison on the borders of their country. A survey showed a low, broken hill on the banks of the Kahan River as an ideal place for the cantonment. And so, in 1541, work began on the building of Rohtas.

Sher Shah died in 1545. It took Humayun ten years to muster the courage and strength to attempt to regain India. When he came down through Afghanistan, the Gakkhars were there to greet him at Pharwala. A year later, in 1556, in a wet and humid August, Humayun's rebellious brother Mirza Kamran was arrested by the Gakkhars faithful to the Mughal crown. On his brother's orders the prince was promptly blinded by a heated lancet and despatched on a pilgrimage to Arabia.

∞

In Rawalpindi Ammad Ali walked me in the narrow lanes off Raja Bazaar showing me one building after another that would have once been home to rich Hindus and Sikhs. All of them are now homes to those whose parents migrated from India in 1947. Through Bhabhra Bazaar, he led the way into narrow alleys with literally no room to swing the proverbial cat. Constantly dreading some leaky drain dumping sewage on my head (which thankfully did not occur), we wound our way to the *haveli* of Sujan Singh.

It would once have stood in an open piazza, but was now encroached upon from all sides and had a dark aura of aggressive abandonment. Its tastefully carved door was padlocked and dusty. After years of occupation by the police which had left it in a poor state of upkeep, in 2006 the government ceremonially handed over the building to the Fatima Jinnah Women University. Subsequently, there were plans for it to become the Rawalpindi campus of the National College of Arts, Lahore. But when or indeed if ever anything will happen is not known.

I did not know of Sardar Sujan Singh, the master of this tasteful house; Ammad pointed me in the direction of Lepel Griffith's *Punjab Chiefs*. We are told that this son of viceregal courtier Sardar Nand Singh was a 'successful man of business' from an old moneyed family. He made a living by securing large contracts and farming leases and was a very prominent and public-spirited gentleman of the city. During the Afghan Campaign of 1880, Sujan Singh supplied fodder, grain and fuel to the British army. Griffith tells us that this responsibility he fulfilled sometimes under great difficulty for which he received official commendation. The man's crowning glory came in 1889 when he received the title of Rai Bahadar. The family continued to live in Rawalpindi until Partition in 1947 when they were forced to move to India.

The house, built about the closing years of the nineteenth century, is a beautiful amalgam of wrought iron, cut brick, intricately carved doors and arches within arches. The first floor windows are designed to create trefoil arches, a throwback to the shape of the entrance in Hindu Shahya temples built in the Kashmiri style during the Middle Ages. Sadly, however, the years of neglect has caused much of the timber work of the fine lattice and the balconies on the first floor to rot away and the ledges of the old balconies are sagging. Ammad, who had seen the interior, said there were some fine frescos waiting to be restored to their original glory.

An Urdu newspaper article forwarded me by Dr Abdul Azeem says that in 1947 after Sujan Singh's sons had fled to India, the forty-five-room *haveli* spread over 2230 square metres was allotted to forty families of refugees from Kashmir. That is, the mansion where an aristocrat lived with his wife, two sons and two daughters, was crammed with perhaps as many as three hundred persons! In 1982, the building, then in a poor state of upkeep, was vacated to be restored. However, after several years of half-hearted non-starters, it was recently handed over to the National College of Arts and locked away. The article also tells us that many years ago Sardar Gurbachan Singh, a grandson of Sujan Singh, served as the Indian ambassador to Pakistan. One wonders if during his tenure he ever visited the premises where he spent his childhood or if he petitioned the government of Pakistan to preserve his grandsire's legacy.

Regardless of his religion, Sardar Sujan Singh was a son of Rawalpindi, a son that the city was once proud of. His old and crumbling *haveli* is a priceless piece of our built heritage that needs to be preserved. If the will can be found, this forlorn piece of heritage can yet be brought back from the brink of oblivion.

The haveli of Sardar Sujan Singh, one of the richest gentlemen of Rawalpindi town in the early twentieth century.

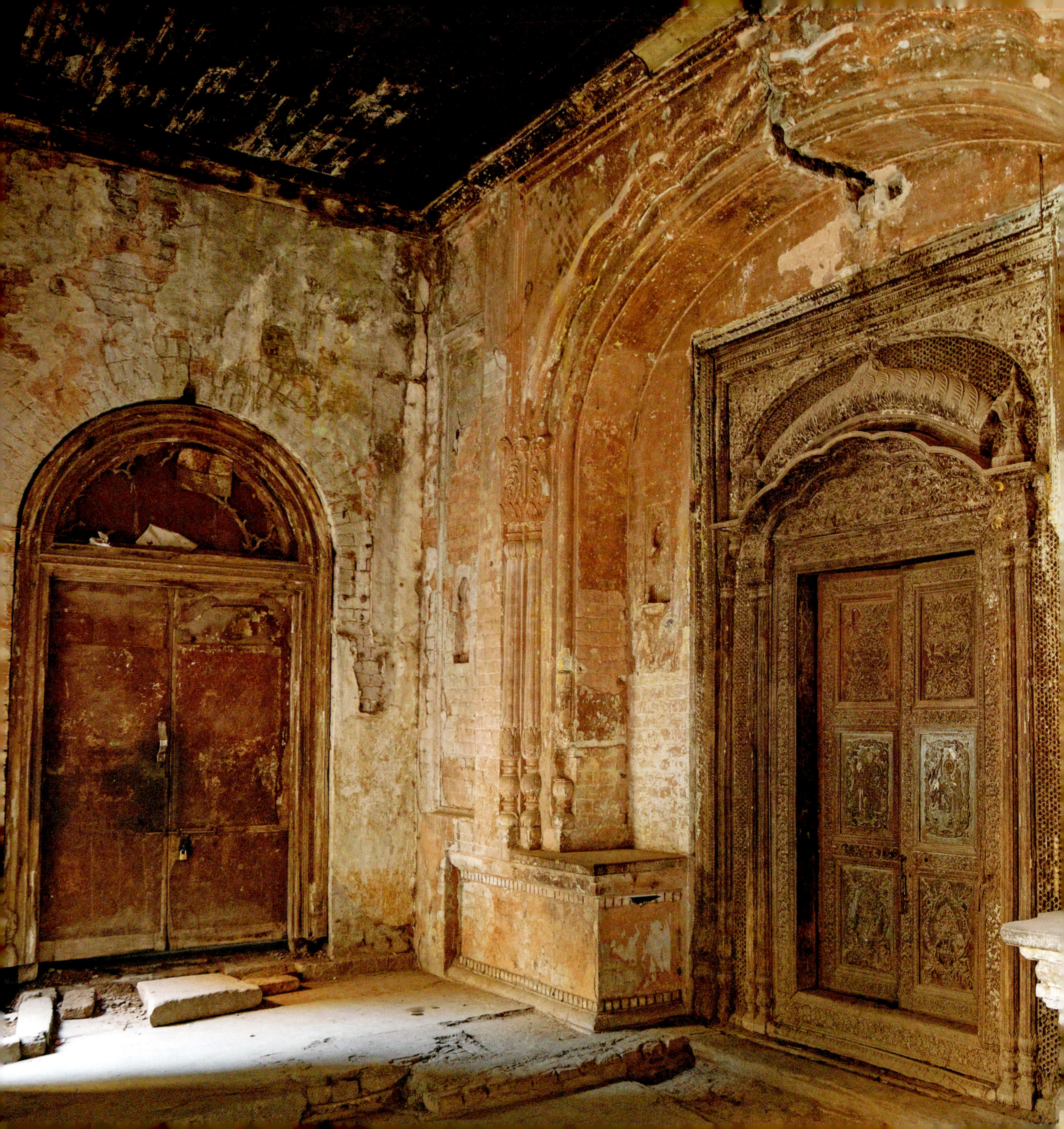

Main entrance of Sujan Singh's *haveli*

As we exited back into the main bazaar, we were followed by two pre-teenage girls who pestered me to photograph them. Having done their bidding, I took out my notebook and asked them for an address to send the images to. Address? Puzzled, they looked at each other and giggled.

'What address?' one of them asked.

'An address where I can post your pictures to you,' I explained.

'We don't have an address,' said the girl who had spoken before.

'Doesn't the postman ever come to your home?' I asked using the Urdu word *dakia*.

'What's a *dakia*?' The girls' bafflement was complete and genuine.

I explained that the *dakia* was the man in the khaki uniform who rode a bicycle and brought letters from loved ones living in other cities or even in other countries. The girls looked at each other and back at me. But the light of recognition was missing from their eyes. Both of them shrugged.

I turned to the man standing nearby enjoying our exchange.

'These girls don't know what a *dakia* is,' I remarked.

'Who would? Especially when everyone now uses this,' he smiled holding up his smartphone.

That was the twenty-first century for me.

∽

The girls who had never heard of a *dakia* or postman

We headed for Kohati Bazaar where Ammad had another heritage piece to show me. I asked if he knew who the city was named after and he said Jahangir, the fourth Mughal king, had mentioned Rawalpindi in his memoir. The *Tuzk e Jahangiri* tells us that in April 1607 the emperor halted at Rawalpindi which was 'founded by a Hindu named Rawal, and *pindi* in the Gakkhar tongue means a village'. He tells us of a 'stream' flowing nearby which is the Lei, now nothing more than the main sewer of the city. Back then, it formed a pool about two hundred and fifty metres across, the depth of which, the king's Gakkhar attendants said, was never measured because it was believed to be alive with crocodiles.

Ever the curious man and with a mean streak to boot, Jahangir ordered a sheep to be thrown into the pond.

It swam clear across to the other side. Then the king ordered a servant to get in. With faltering heart and on his lips many breathless prayers and surely a few curses for his king, would the man have stepped into the murky water. But even he, having swum around, came out unmolested. 'There was no foundation for what the Gakkhars had said,' concluded the king. However, long before it was turned into a sewer, it was a clear water stream that would surely have teemed with all kinds of aquatic life.

A few weeks later, Jahangir was back in Rawal's village. Here he ordered a *qamargah* – hunting ring from which hapless animals had no escape – where he so proudly killed twenty-nine antelopes. His sons killed several more. As well as that, twenty-seven 'red deer' and sixty-eight 'white deer' were also killed. Today, if we do not find any ungulates in the hills around Rawalpindi, we know who to blame for the most part!

In Kohati Bazaar Ammad knew of the Kalyan Das temple. He said it once possessed grounds spreading over seven acres which were all now built over. Most of the land was taken over for housing in 1947 when refugees from East Punjab ended up in Rawalpindi. Even the land directly around the temple was now occupied by a school for blind pupils built in the early 1980s. Named after a rich businessman of the area, the temple was consecrated in the 1880s.

We entered the school through the open gate and as I was volubly admiring the fine stucco artistry on the façade and the frescos in the veranda, I was hailed by someone just behind me. With his face right up close to mine, the bearded man demanded to know with whose permission we had entered the premises. His eyes seemed to focus

Kalyan Das temple in Kohati Bazaar, Rawalpindi

Frescos in the veranda of the temple.

Frescos in the veranda of the temple.

Top Left: The main entrance of Rawat serai The façade criss-crossed by all sorts of cable, however, shows how not to do things.

Bottom Left: The interior of the serai with the mosque in the background. The name Rawat is a corruption of Rabat, the Arabic word for caravanserai. However, its tall gateway and crenulated walls have led people to believe it is a fortress rather than a serai.

Top Right: Graves of those Gakkhars who lost their lives in the struggle against Sher Shah Suri. The lofty dome in the background is believed to be the tomb of Sarang Khan, the chief. There is no cenotaph in the building, however.

Bottom Right: Mankiala stupa built in the second century CE during the reign of the great Kushan ruler Kanishka was believed by Buddhists to have been the site where Buddha fed his body to a hungry tigress. The redness of the earth (likely from the presence of subsoil salt) was pointed as proof of Buddha's largesse. The stupa and accompanying monastery (no sign of the latter remains today) were destroyed by fire and over the centuries the stupa was damaged by treasure hunters. Jean-Baptiste Ventura, a general in the army of Maharaja Ranjit Singh, investigated this site and removed some artefacts that are today part of the British Museum collection.

Top Left: Detail of decoration on the capital of mock pillars adorning the drum of Mankiala stupa with the date of restoration during the British Raj.

Bottom Left: The west gateway of the fortified Pakka Serai. In the early years of the seventeenth century, both emperor Jahangir and the travelling English merchant William Finch stopped here on their respective journeys. The wide interior of this fort too is a growing village.

Right: Corner turret of Pakka Serai

Top Left: Exterior of Bedi Mahal, Kallar Syedan.
Bottom Left: Detail of woodwork on the front entrance.

Top Right: View of first floor rooms.
Bottom Right: The atrium of Bedi Mahal is resplendent with frescos whose richness has not faded in a century.

Right/Left: Detail of frescos from Bedi Mahal.

on something just above my head and behind me. And then I realised the school for visually impaired children had, appropriately enough, a visually impaired watchman. If that was not a contradiction in terms, I cannot say what can be.

I fibbed that I was a director from the Department of Archaeology (though I did not sound half as convincing as my archaeologist friend Azeem) doing government work and threatened to put him through to the joint secretary in Islamabad. The watchman asked his sidekick to call the principal of the school who upon hearing that I was an officer of the government at once permitted me to proceed with my work. The watchman who said his name was Mubashir then ordered tea for Ammad and me.

The exterior ripples with fine stucco work, bay windows, mock pilasters and arches. Frescos on the exterior have all been washed away, but in the veranda they are still in colourful glory. Gods of the Vedic pantheon and worshipful humans fill the spaces between forests of flowers, vines and leaves. But now the sound of prayer does not hum through the temple, said Mubashir's assistant, because the locked idol chamber contained old and broken school equipment.

As we were leaving, I looked back and felt it was just as well the temple was now inside a walled government property. Any other way and it would have been torn down to raise an ugly shopping mall.

With few sunny days between rainy interludes Ammad and I found one overcast afternoon threatening to let loose and hurried out to Gulyana, ten kilometres south of Gujar Khan. Ammad said a certain Baba Gulla, octogenarian Gulzar Ahmad, lived near a lovely little temple and told tales of the village. Asking for directions in the village, we were pointed to a drain running along the middle of the alley and told to follow its flow to the very end and we would end up at the temple. The modest little temple with a Samadhi next to it is used as a storage room by local farmers. The exterior is plain, but the interior still blazes with frescoes that have preserved their bright colours.

The painting in the middle of the vaulted alcove on the wall opposite the entrance was resplendent in blues, reds and greens. The figures were partially defaced and I had no idea what I was looking at. My anthropologist friend Zulfiqar Kalhoro revealed the secret: the crowned male figure was Lord Rama attended by his consort Sita. The flanking figures were Laxman on the right and Hanuman on the left. Hanuman's extended right hand probably held some offering which might have particularly offended some modern day iconoclast for the hand is scratched off.

Ammad sent word out for Baba Gulla and presently we had the talkative old man telling us of the several rich Hindus and Sikhs he remembered from the years before Partition. The striking ruins of the large *haveli* we had passed on our way to the temple was the property of Tara Singh, the lawyer, said Gulla. He said Gulyana was home to some of the richest people of the district. They all left in 1947 and local poor people moved in to occupy their agricultural lands.

'Only two or three people died in the riots. Here the thugs focussed on looting instead of killing,' he said without emotion.

∽

I made the fatal error of mentioning the 'Buddha Caves' outside Islamabad by the little hamlet of Shah Allah Ditta. 'Rubbish!' said Azeem. 'There is absolutely no proof of Buddha ever having come to what is now Pakistan. Zero!'

Having said that, he confirmed that the place was known as Sadhu da Bagh – Garden of the Sadhu. Until 1947, with a large Hindu and Sikh population, the place was a favourite haunt of sadhus, Hindu religious ascetics who spend their life wandering God's earth and practicing a strict mystical discipline. Then there was a large mural with paintings which lasted until a couple of decades ago. It is not known if it fell victim to natural decay or the maleficence of humans, but today there is neither a mural nor a Sadhu.

But long before humans mastered speech, our early ancestors would certainly have sheltered under these overhangs. Here they would have crafted their stone tools, butchered and perhaps cooked their hunt and here they would have procreated and died for tens of thousands of years. But if those early residents left any sign of their presence, it has never been found.

We rolled past sector D-12 of Islamabad through the village of Shah Allah Ditta to what was once a pristine and wild little garden of mango and mulberry trees at the closed end of a rocky limestone gorge. Water spilling down the sharp verge had beautifully festooned the rock with creepers. On the crest grew a few banyan trees whose roots were suspended nearly to the bottom of the gorge like some prehistoric giant snakes.

The temple of Gulyana

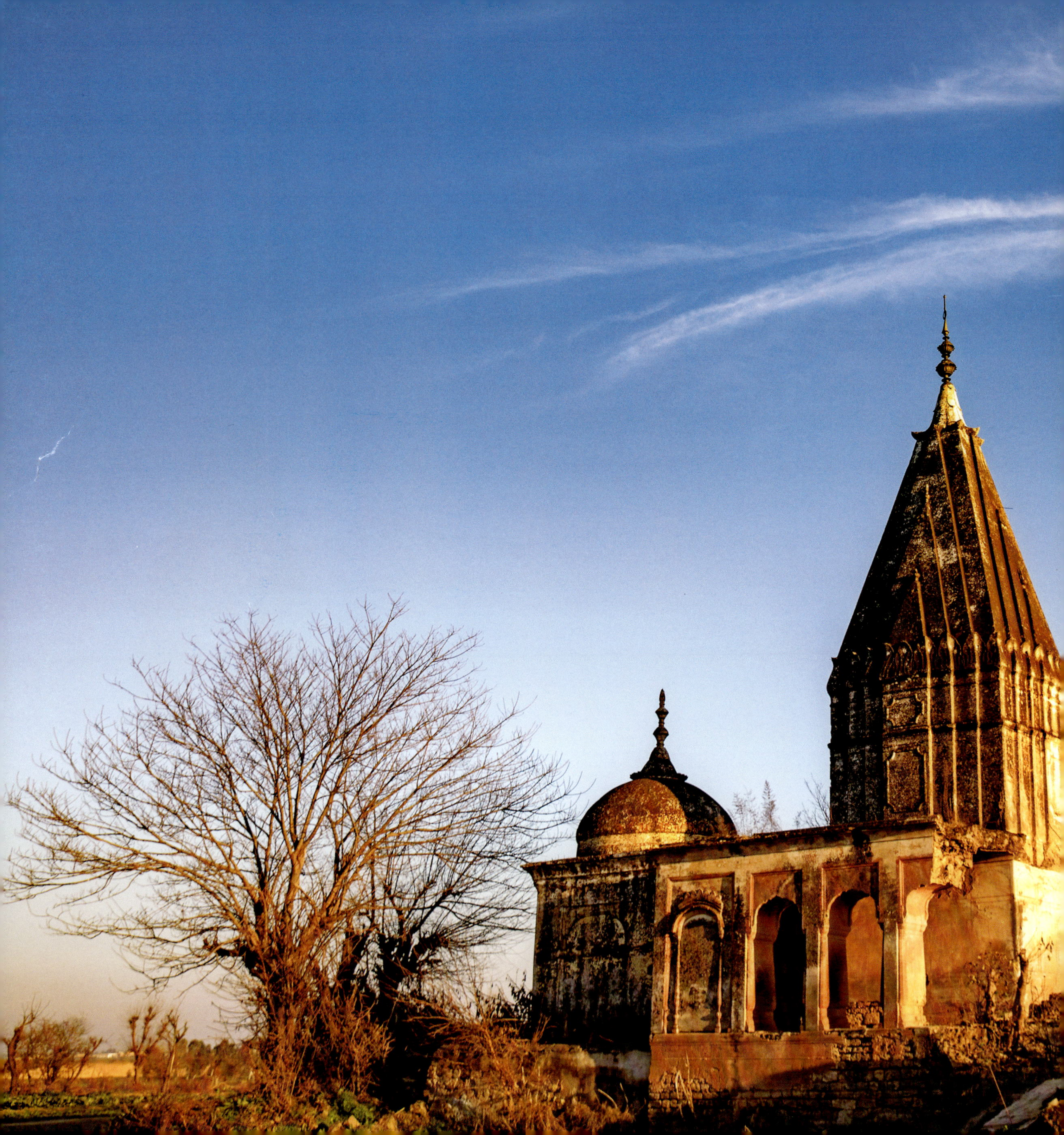

from Landi Kotal *to* Wagah

125 | Over the Cut Throat Pass

The temple of Gulyana

Here the porous rock, having eroded over millions of years, had created a couple of overhangs. They were just that: overhangs. Some mind wild with imagination but unlettered on the life of Buddha had turned the shallow overhangs into caves and supplanted Buddha in them a long way off from where he ever was. By and by folks began to resort here to glean some of the residual, but spurious, two millennium-old piety. Once deserted, in time the place acquired a resident ascetic who had no fables to relate.

By 2018, the so-called Buddha caves had turned into a picnic spot. Then it was only a matter of time for the mushroom growth of cheap eateries to forever kill the aura of the place. Today freshly bulldozed dirt roads snake up the hill on which cross country vehicles zoom up and down to remove what little atmosphere the place had . A spot of solace, peace and beauty has been destroyed forever.

However, there is one little side trip up a recently prepared trail to the so-called Buddhist stupa on the direct and shortest path from Bhir and Dharmarajika Stupa to Islamabad. At the highest point on this trail from where one can see the villages around Taxila there lay amid pine trees and *bhekar* bushes a tumble down heap of dressed stones. Years ago Dr Ahmad Hasan Dani designated it a stupa and for everyone it was that. The pile has received a recent makeover and in keeping with what the late professor had said, they have given it the shape of a stupa.

The truth is that this is not a stupa at all. Archaeological investigation back in 1963 revealed some iron arrowheads and coins from the third century BCE. Recently a few coins of the Mughal era have also been found. The one thing that is missing is Buddhist religious iconography. Now experts view this relic as a way station on the shortest route from the various monasteries and townships of ancient Taxila to the city of Rawal.

In 1823, the vetrinary doctor William Moorcroft passed this way. He mentioned 'the pass between Shaladatta [Shah Allah Ditta] and Khanpur'. As he was travelling westward, he could espy the Tamrah rivulet of Taxila in the valley in front and referred to it as the Dhamrai.

Carrying on westward, en route to Taxila, a short descent brings one to the spacious pond of Ban Fakirañ – Pond of the Fakirs. Once stone-lined and perhaps much deeper, it is now ruinous. Most of the stone lining is lost, cannibalised for modern housing and centuries of rains have washed down soil from the surrounding hills to fill up the pond almost to its brink. Near its western corner there stands a small ruined hulk. The *mihrab* facing west indicates this was once a mosque.

A good walker could carry on and in an hour and half fetch up in the shadow of magnificent Dharmarajika. If there is a trail in Islamabad yet not polluted and crowded with walkers, it is this pleasant walk from Sadhu da Bagh through the way station on the top of the pass and the old pond.

∞

The *Tuzk e Jahangiri* brought the story-telling Jahangir from Lahore to Peshawar whereas we were travelling in the opposite direction. His journey from Rohtas to Rawalpindi was a pleasant one on a cloudy April day along a road bordered by an abundance of *dhak* (*Butea monosperma*) trees in flaming blossom. In a rapture, Jahangir describes their beauty and concludes that the day being so beautiful he felt like setting up camp for a drinking party. Though he does not explicitly describe the party, he hints that it did take place for he concludes: 'In short, this road was traversed with great enjoyment and pleasure'.

The halting places en route he tells us were Hatya and Pakka before his procession reached Rawalpindi. Incidentally, William Finch, the peripatetic English trader, also mentions the same places. These establishments mark that branch of the old Utra Rajapatha that Babur called the sub-montane road between Wah and the ferry on Jhelum River near the town of the same name. In the Middle Ages, this was an alternate branch of the Grand Trunk Road. From Pakka, Jahangir skirted the fortified caravanserai of Rawat on the main axis of the highway and made straight for Rawalpindi.

Pakka, Jahangir tells us, is so called because of the burnt bricks it is made of as opposed to dressed stone blocks used in other serais in the area. Like all serais in our part of the world, this too is strongly fortified. However, its broad and spacious enceinte is now a village. Hatya, on the other hand, has lost all traces of the old hostelry.

On a fine sunny morning, Azeem and I went in the direction opposite to Jahangir's, making Rawat our first stop. Until about twenty years ago, the crenelated walls of the serai were visible as one drove through Rawat village, but now the unplanned jumble of housing blocks the view. The serai is now visible only after one has left the road and driven up the narrow street to its front gate. Scaffolding covered the bastions flanking the gateway across the façade of which passed a very maze of electric and telephone cables. Even when the restoration work is over and the scaffolding removed, the ugly wires that typify the ad hoc, unplanned manner of doing things will continue to mar the prospect.

Inside the wide compound sit the grim reminders of the bloody tussle between the Gakkhars led by Sarang Khan and the troops of Sher Shah Suri under Haibat Khan Niazi stationed at Rohtas, the brand new fort of that time. A number of graves under the open sky are said to be the last resting place of the several sons of Sarang Khan who were used up by the battles. By the northwest wall towers a domed building that I had always believed to be a resting place. Azeem said the still empty building was raised as a mausoleum for Sarang Khan.

We have moved a good deal forward from the time when 'restoration' meant either demolition and rebuilding a historic edifice any which way authorities pleased or plastering up with modern cement to stop further deterioration even if it created an ugly blemish. Of the former we see the classic case of pulling down of the *baradari* of Kamran Mirza in Ravi River outside Lahore to be rebuilt any which way the rulers desired *circa* 1990. Examples of

Octagonal and circular turrets and crenulated walls with musketry loopholes tell us that Sangni fort was built in nineteenth century.

Interior of Sangni fort with the tomb of Abdul Hakim where newly-weds come to seek the dead saint's blessing.

such thoughtless destruction of our built heritage can be seen across the country.

The restoration work at Rawat – which derives from *rabat*, caravanserai in Arabic – is done under the watchful eye of trained archaeologists. The material used is the same lime plaster as would have first joined the masonry five hundred years ago. Thankfully, this is another rare conservation effort being done right.

On an overcast afternoon, we drove down to Gujar Khan and took the road northeast to Sui Cheemian, just missing Serai Pakka and headed for Sangni Fort which stands on a slight eminence and is visible from some ways off. We parked the car just as rain began pattering down and as we were walking through the wheat fields, Azeem collected shards of terra cotta strewn among the crops and along the pathway. He commented on what he had: rim of a cooking vessel or jar here, base of a large pot or a small drinking cup there. The larger pieces bore black geometrical designs.

'These bits come to us from the second century BCE,' Azeem said, handing over the pieces to me.

There were other bits that he said were from the early Middle Ages. He said several years ago, Dr Ashraf Khan, the soft-spoken and kindly-faced gentleman archaeologist who I knew from his time as curator of Taxila, had led a survey in this area. In a paper for the *Journal of Asian Civilizations* (Vol 33, No 2 of December 2010) Dr Khan described his collection from Sangni as a large number of rims and bases. The rims were mostly decorated with black paint or incised lines. Besides these, grinding stones and terra cotta figurines had also been unearthed. Dr Khan had dated the site from second century BCE to eighth century CE.

The city, spread over more than ten acres, would have been a few decades old when the horse-riding Scythians made it their home. Under them it would have come of age and then lived through the upheavals of time. Situated so far off the main axis through the land, it may have escaped the savagery of the Huns in the early sixth century, and it would have thrived during the peace after the Hindu Shahya kings of Kashmir extended their rule to Afghanistan in the following years. Then, for reasons that we cannot know until a proper investigation is carried out, it was snuffed out of existence in the eighth century.

On that same site, a thousand years later the Dogra rulers of Kashmir raised the octagonal turrets and sharply edged crenulations of Sangni Fort to protect their route down the Poonch River to the Grand Trunk Road. Later, the fort became the last resting place of Abdul Hakim, a supposed miracle working saint. The whitewashed dome of his recently built tomb rises above the denticulate walls of the fort.

Those who believe the man to be a saint relate that he chose this spot as his place of penance and worship. But the Dogras arrived to uproot him and raise their fort. Abdul Hakim admonished them for booting him out and is believed to have said that long after they were dead, he would continue to be there. Hakim left the place and when he died he was buried in a nearby village. But after the Dogras ceded this area to the British, so the fable goes, the man's followers dug up his grave to bring his body to the fort. They found it empty for the casket had miraculously flown to the fort. The story conveniently disregards the fact that Muslims are traditionally not interred in caskets. Over the past fifteen years, whenever I hear this story, it is embellished with new fabrications.

On a clear sunny day I returned alone to photograph Sangni and found the enceinte of the fort and the veranda of the tomb littered with ornate little pitchers and turbans. These latter are the kind bridegrooms wear. A chat with three men working in the wheat field outside the fort revealed that newly-wed couples come to pray at the tomb. The brides leave behind the pitchers and their husbands the turbans in the belief that the saint will bless them with a happy married life. But surely sometimes old Abdul Hakim would be remiss. What of the divorces, the devil in me asked.
'Once blessed by the saint, there can be no divorce,' said one of the men.
'Is there a protocol here for divorcees to return seeking back their donation of pitcher or turban?' I asked even as I feared treading dangerous ground.

The trio looked aghast. But they admitted there was nothing of the sort. I assured them there were divorces even after the blessing and that none of those unhappy ones returned to remonstrate with dead saint. Leaving them to chew over the new notion, I quickly changed the subject.

One of the men said the water of the stream that passes below the western wall of Sangni is blessed. The turret on that side has a square hole and pulley looking down to the blue water of the stream about twenty-five metres below. If drawn up through this hole, and only through here, it is a certified cure for whooping cough, said the man.

I asked them who collected the money from the collection box by the door of the burial chamber. With one voice they named Hussain, or his sons. Of a sudden the story of the miraculous flying casket was clear. Retired and without any skill, Hussain had little else to do. He built upon a vague earlier tale of piety and raised the tomb with his pension and set up the collection box to rake in the dividends. All is going well for him, but only as long as the tomb has only meagre gleanings. Once the earning grows, there will be other more powerful takers.

Sangni Fort is a beautiful monument. But what catches my imagination are Dr Ashraf Khan's words regarding the surrounding area: 'Suitable for archaeological excavations and investigations.' What wonders and what secrets the mound of Sangni will reveal is beyond imagination. Until then, the dust of two thousand years keeps the secrets in its bosom.

On Babur's sub-montane road sits an ancient caravan stop known then and now as Dhamiak. In the spring of 1206, the Turkish ruler of Ghazni Muizuddin Ghori (otherwise known as Shahabuddin Mohammad) was returning from yet another depredatory raid on India. Stalking him was a band of Khokhar Rajputs who had taken his success against their brother Rajputs as personal affront. At the halting place of Dhamiak the Ghorid king halted for a night and the Khokhars found the chance they had been seeking.[2]

Silently stealing into his camp, the Rajput warriors despatched the king's guards before mortally stabbing the sleeping king several times. Even before the camp could react to the cries of his dying bodyguards, the Khokhars had evaporated into the night and Muizuddin was dead. It was already the month of March and the Punjabi heat was making itself felt. The king's attendants carried out the usual practice of disembowelling the corpse to keep it for the journey back to Ghazni. The royal entrails and the three dead bodyguards were interred where the Dhamiak camp stood and the long march west began.

The shortest route to Ghazni lay through the Kurrum Valley to Sankuran and over Peiwar Kotal. Sankuran, lying just outside Parachinar town, is modern Shalozan, that delightful sylvan spot whose orchards are watered by crystal clear rills and shadowed by the towering mountain known to the Pakhtuns as Spinghar and to Persian speakers as Safed Koh. Now, in those long ago days, Sankuran together with outlying districts of Ghazni was governed by Tajuddin Yalduz, the trusted and very loyal servant of Muizuddin.

---

2) A very common misconception, even among some scholars, is that men like Mahmud and Muizuddin, and much later, Nadir Kuli aka Nadir Shah of Persia were Pakhtuns. All these men were Turks who had conquered Afghanistan and established themselves over it.

The *Tabakat i Nasiri* of Minhajuddin Siraj completed in 1260, tells us that Yalduz rode out to receive the funerary procession and when he saw the bier drawing up, he dismounted from his horse to receive 'it with the utmost veneration, and he wept to such a degree, that others were quite overcome and wept also'. Yalduz escorted the grim procession to Ghazni and there buried his master in the seminary founded by Muizuddin in the name of his daughter, his only child.

The question arising is why would some Khokhar adventurers imperil their lives to slay the Ghorid king? Only thirteen years before this deed, in 1192, the Ghorid adventurer had defeated Prithviraj Chauhan in the second battle of Tarain. The year before Muizuddin had been routed by the same army led by the same king. This revenge attack may never have taken place if the Rajputs had not fought the usual way permitting the Turks to make away with their lives.

Ghori may not have known it but since times immemorial battles even to the death were like sport to the Rajputs of the subcontinent. Before they went into the fray they prepared their families at home to perform *jauhar* – the act of self-immolation – in case word of defeat reached them. But on the field, when their enemy faltered, it was below the Rajput to close in and slay wantonly. They held back – waiting to see if the enemy would rally around for further engagement. In the first battle of Tarain, as the Ghorid rout began headlong, the drum and horn for cessation of engagement were sounded. As he watched the fleeing Ghorids disappear in the dust raised by their own mounts,

Prithviraj turned homeward to be celebrated. That was 1191.

The following year, the Turks returned not just better equipped and numerically stronger but with an understanding of Rajput tactics. On the same battlefield of Tarain, Prithviraj was defeated and captured. Some sources say the proud Rajput was poorly treated by his foe before being blinded by heated lancet. My source, the *Tabakat i Nasiri*, only records that he was captured and executed.

Emboldened by the victory of 1192, Muizuddin returned again and again to cause more downfall. For thirteen years the Khokhars smarted under the ignominy of the rout and slaying of their king Prithviraj Chauhan and kept alive their thirst for revenge. One wonders how many times Khokhar raiding parties would have stalked the Turkish army as it withdrew to the safety of Ghazni without gaining the chance to strike. Their opportunity arose finally. On the Ides of March 1206, a party of Khokhars stole into Ghori's camp and despatched Muizuddin in his sleep.

In July 2019, my wife Shabnam and I were at Dhamiak after a gap of a quarter century. The three tombs that had been with their original limestone topping slabs and under the sky a quarter century ago were now all marble and under a shed. These would be the burials of Ghori's bodyguards killed by the Khokhars in their attempt to reach the king.

Across the lawns, on the other side of the marble tomb,

The supposed tomb of Muizuddin Ghori. History tells us that the body was taken to Ghazni for burial. Only his intestines would have been interred at this site of Dhamiak.

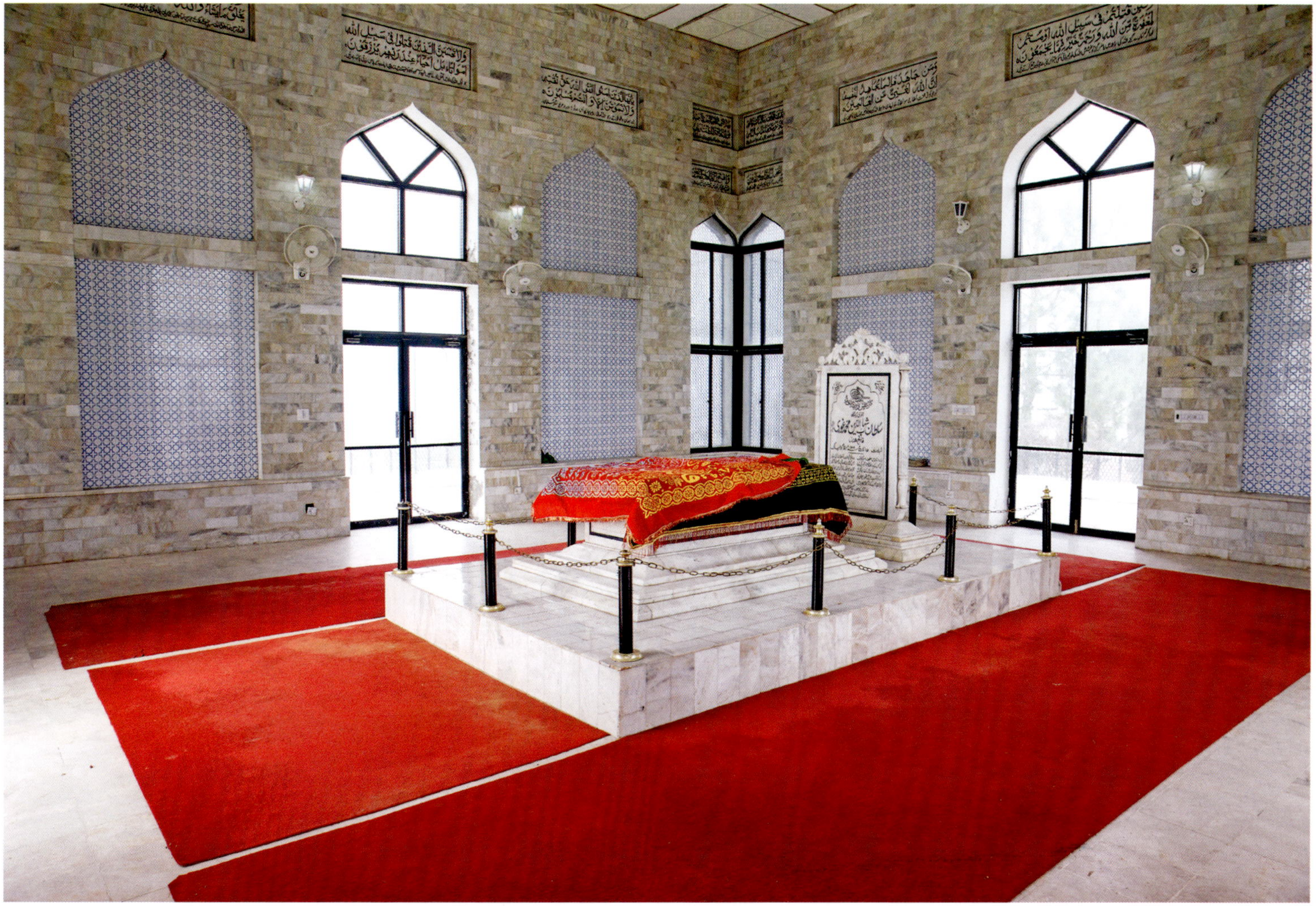

an old woman and a young man sat with their heads together in solemn discourse. Shabnam spoke with the septuagenarian Mukhtaran. She lived nearby and said she had escaped the clamour of a joint family home to discuss some private issue with her son.

In the beginning there were just four graves. All in a single group on raised ground under the blue sky, she said. All were shaded by a lovely copse of *phulai* (*Acacia modesta*) trees. Under one tree, there rested a large pot of water for passers-by. That was when she was a child and the road was but a dirt track and the traffic was mostly pedestrians passing between the villages. Mukhtaran said since her childhood some seventy years ago, she frequently walked by the burial site. Never had she seen it revered or heard any stories about it.

Shabnam asked Mukhtaran if word had always been about one of the graves being the burial of Muizuddin Ghori. 'No, no! They had another name for the grave, something like Moda,' she said. 'I am not certain about it and do not wish to mislead you. You will be better off asking someone else.' Clearly, Mukhtaran was a very cautious woman.

A couple of kilometres away, back the way we had come, we met Dr Ansar standing outside his homeopathic clinic and paused to ask. He very kindly invited us in. While we waited for tea, the doctor made a phone call telling us this elderly friend of his from a neighbouring village was very well informed. And this is what we learned: until the early 1990s, when the unknown grave was declared to be that of the Ghorid king, it went by the title Babay Mohnday dee Qabr – Grave of the Old Man Mohnda. But it was never known who this strangely named person was. Today, someone would have us believe that Muizuddin aka Shahabuddin Ghori lies buried under the shining white marble tomb. But the *Tabakat i Nasiri* tells us that the body of the Sultan was taken to Ghazni.

∞

Looking at a large scale contour map or Google Earth, one sees a series of folded rocky hillocks on a north-south alignment. The terrain between Dhamiak and the Grand Trunk Road is seemingly impassable even for pedestrians. But there is a veritable web of footpaths and one blacktop road connecting the villages. The blacktop road that Azeem, his assistant Ali and I were now following to reach Rohtas Fort sits on the ancient alignment of the Utra Rajapatha for the upkeep of which Chandragupta Maurya had assigned an entire department of engineers and technicians. Sprinkled like milestones along this line are serais each at the distance of a day's easy journey for a rider and a somewhat harder journey for one on shank's mare.

Twenty kilometres northwest of Dhamiak sits the serai known since the Middle Ages as Pakka for its burnt bricks. Its name now retained by the village that has sprouted up in the compound. A little over three kilometres southward of Dhamiak, not far from the village of Karonta, is the large tree-shaded pond of Sar Jalal. On its bank stands a single stone wall that was once part of a large and elaborate structure.

Nearby is a small mosque which, on my first visit in 2005, had been 'renovated' – as they like to say – with modern cement plaster. This time around it had a newish coat of paint. Unlike other mosques, it has no dome, but a pitched roof. The west wall is reinforced with three tapering turrets. Since these look somewhat like the tapering buttresses of a fourteenth century tomb in Multan and also because of the brickwork in the building, I had wrongly thought it to be six or seven hundred years old. Azeem disabused me of my dilettante's knowledge. The mosque was of a more recent date, he said, perhaps late seventeenth century.

Had we been intrepid walkers, we could have trekked twenty-five kilometres cross country, past the *baoli* of Khukha to the 'jail house of Sher Shah Suri'. But our lot was to brave the 'racing' trucks in the bends of the Grand Trunk Road between Sohawa and Dina where one turns for Rohtas. Loaded well beyond the capacity their engines are designed to haul, the eighteen-wheelers groan and wheeze at twenty-five kilometres an hour at which speed one attempts to overtake the other going only marginally slower. On the upward incline they worm on alongside taking up the entire width of the blacktop blocking all other traffic. Yet the one being overtaken will not slow down even by a kilometre to let the other go and clear the road. This is, however, one game in which the Grand Trunk Road holds no monopoly; it is played all over the country on every intercity highway.

From my earliest visits to Rohtas in the early 1970s, I had been told of the famous jail house and gallows where the Suri king hanged the contumacious Gakkhars. It was in 2005, that I first saw the supposed jail house better known as Rajo Pind. Here they tell vague tales of the woman Rajo who ruled over the village. Some say she, being of the Arain caste, was famed for her green thumb; others would have her as a sort of a queen lording over her fief.

As I entered the high, imposing gateway, I knew immediately that this was no jail house. It was yet another fortified serai dating to early Mughal times. Here was yet another marker on the Rajapatha of old and the Grand Trunk Road of our times that only fell into disuse when British engineers realigned the old highway a little to the north to suit wheeled, and later, motor vehicle traffic. And like all abandoned serais, it too had been taken over and turned into a village.

Inside, only a few travellers' cubicles remain along the north wall. The rest have been pulled down and their stones used up for newer construction. It is said there were two mosques in the compound. The larger one has been demolished and replaced by a modern structure complete with tube lights and loudspeakers. The other one, flush with the west wall, fortunately remains intact but only because locals seem not to realise it is a mosque. In 2005 it served as a byre as indeed it does to this day.

Back then I met the lady of the house making cow dung patties for fuel and plastering them on the wall of the mosque. Her little house was built in such a way that it had incorporated the mosque. Keeping my voice down so that the neighbours did not hear and cause her any trouble for desecrating a mosque, I told her what the structure really was. She looked at me open-mouthed and incredulous. 'All our lives we've lived here and no one ever told us what you are now saying,' she replied a little cautiously. I could see she was worried that if I were a government man, I could get her evicted. I reassured her of my harmlessness and tactfully guided her away to Rajo who had made the village famous. She had no idea who Rajo was but in the finest tradition of hospitality she said since I had taken the trouble of coming out from Lahore, I could at least have a cup of tea.

As she brought the dying embers back to life with her steel *phoonkni* (the tube used to blow on fire), I told her the place was actually a caravanserai established not by Sher Shah Suri but by Jahangir if not by his father Akbar. She turned around, studied my face blankly for a bit before reverting to her fire. I told her what I had long believed: Rajo was the innkeeper here. We know from history that inns were traditionally kept by women. Having seen scores of ruined serais, some turned into villages, I have never heard of any other connected with a woman. I suspect this Rajo was a rather dynamic and impressive woman whose fame outlived her by all these centuries. Long after the hostelry fell into disuse, which would be about a century and a half ago, and the village established within its walls, the memory of Rajo was preserved in the name of the village.

On his journey from Lahore to Kabul in 1608, English trader William Finch wrote of reaching 'Loure Rotas ... a citie with a strong castle on a mountaine, the frontier of the Potan kingdome'. While there is a village within the walls of Rohtas Fort, early in the seventeenth century, it was strictly a military station. The city that Finch mentions is the caravanserai on the far side of the Kahan River, the one where it is right possible that Rajo kept a watchful eye on her guests. Finch's time overlaps with Rajo's and one wonders why the Englishman made no mention of the woman innkeeper.

The brand new Rohtas Fort, then just about sixty years old, would have been a sight imposing and impressive. Inside the towering gateways the even higher mansion of Raja Man Singh Kashvaha would have risen higher than anything else. As Finch squinted up, he would have seen Mughal soldiery in armour and helmet patrolling the massive crenelated walls. But the English merchant would not have been allowed to pass into Rohtas garrison. He rode his horse across the brown waters of the Kahan stream to the caravanserai.

In the 1820s, when Rohtas was in the hands of the Sikhs, veterinary surgeon William Moorcroft with traveller's curiosity also sought entry. The commander of the garrison rudely told his party to make themselves scarce. As they rode along the west side, he noticed 'several practicable breaches in the walls'. Naughtily, he and his party climbed up and entered 'an abandoned outwork' that he thought was built to protect a *baoli*. This can be no other than the Langar Khani Darwaza which does indeed have a stepped well. The doctor was impressed by the massive stonework and the quality of mortar, noticing that the walls were as thick as 'thirty feet'.

Apparently the Sikh garrison was napping on duty for Moorcroft and his men 'ascended the highest part of the parapet without attracting observation'. He then goes on to describe the extent of the fort and its strategic location. But he errs on the subject of Rajo's caravanserai which he says was ordered by Aurangzeb.

In late December 1835, the prima donna among fellow travellers, the Austrian Baron Carl von Hügel, was briefly in Rohtas of 'Shir Shah Lodi Patan' as he came down from the snowy hills of Kashmir en route to Lahore. Like the very rich adventurer of his time, the Baron was travelling in luxury with a large entourage of cooks, bearers and orderlies, and coolies to carry his sedan chair. He was amazed by the scale of Rohtas but was concerned that it had fallen into disrepair. Surprisingly, he thought the fort had only three instead of the actual twelve gateways. As they have always done and continue to do to this day, the remains of Raja Man Singh's palace caught his attention. Von Hügel describes the building unmistakably:

> The angular pillars yet standing; the one window in each direction, still traced in the solitary fragment of the ruined palace, struck me forcibly. It seemed unaccountable how, it could have survived the ravages which have laid all waste beside it.

Back in 1541 when Sher Shah ordered his fort as protection against the raiding Gakkhars, he placed his most trusted financial wizard Raja Todar Mal in charge of works. To assist and protect his project were two of his generals Khwas Khan and Haibat Khan Niazi. Yet the doughty Gakkhars remained undeterred. They mounted daily raids forcing the workers away until the builders were hard put to procure labour.

Meanwhile, in 1543, Sher Shah came to inspect his border garrison and found it not to his liking. It was too cramped for the number of soldiers he wanted stationed at Rohtas. He ordered an enlargement.

In 1974, fooling around in Rohtas as two crass and unread young men, a friend and I were accosted by a tall, rail-thin, sun-browned man who wanted to know what mischief we were up to. A resident of Rohtas village, he was a retired corporal of the army who had fought in Europe in the First World War. He told us Rohtas stories, three of which remain etched on my mind.

The gateway everyone today knows as Sohail Darwaza after a nearby grave of someone called Sohail was in 1974 called Zohal (Saturn) Darwaza. The old man said when the gateway was being built Saturn stood right overhead in the night sky. He walked us to the southwest side and led us in through the portal that he called Darwaza Under Kot – Gateway of the Inner Fort. This is now known as Chand Wali Darwaza after another saint who never was. 'Sher Shah initially ordered this fort,' said the old man with a sweeping gesture taking in everything between the gateway and the north and west fortification wall. He was not certain why the fort's enlargement was ordered but knew that the extension began in Sher Shah's lifetime.

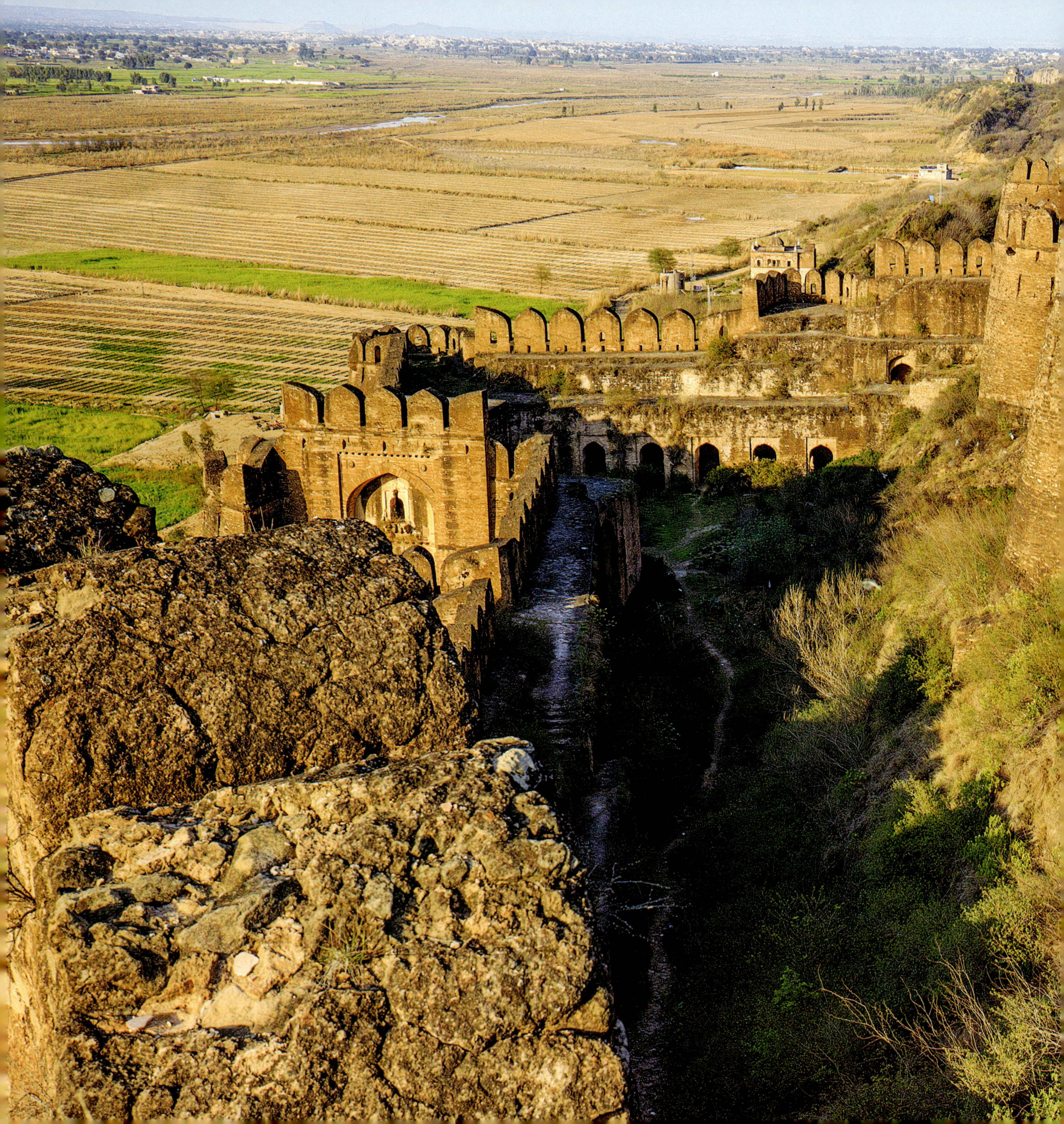

Looking north along the western ramparts with the Kahan River flowing in the middle distance. In March 1860, Lady Charlotte Canning spent a couple of days in Rohtas. Among her paintings is this exact view.

He led us to the towering domed structure where Akbar's trusted general Raja Man Singh once lived. Turning around he pointed to the broken arch of Darwaza Under Kot. The man whose name I never asked, was clearly no admirer of the milksop Humayun.

'The gutless Humayun returned to India ten years after Sher Shah's death. He was still a good ways off when he fired a single cannon ball at Rohtas. The ball took the top off the gateway,' he said speaking like the artilleryman that he had said he was.

Reading history many years later, I learned that Humayun did indeed let loose a single cannon shot. Though the damage done is not recorded, we are told that just that one shot and the entire Pakhtun garrison deserted the fort. Humayun led his army into Rohtas to find it completely empty. We also know that the original fort was ordered to be enlarged so that it actually became the Inner Fort. The gateway would logically have been called what the old man told us. As for the assertion of Saturn being overhead, I have no way of calculating its position, but I trust my teller of the tale and I can only lament how silly superstition has corrupted history.

The graves of the two supposed saints with their flat topping stones seem to be about four hundred years old. That was a time when Rohtas was a military garrison held on the order of royalty and no wandering so-called holy person would have been permitted to enter it. These burials could just be of some important military personnel killed perhaps in any of the several engagements with the Gakkhars during that period. When superstition became the way of life in Pakistan, Zohal was easily converted to Sohail and Chand Wali could have been that or any other name from Persian or Arabic.

With the Gakkhars having driven away every stone cutter and mason on pain of death, Todar Mal wrote to Sher Shah that things were in a bad way and it seemed the fort would not be completed. Sher Shah responded like a true administrator. He wrote saying he had appointed Todar Mal from among many for he considered him a man of perspicacity and had placed at his disposal a large sum of money to complete the job. If it was to be more expensive than the estimate, money was of no consequence and he was to go ahead at all cost.

And so it is said that each stone was laid at a cost of one gold *ashrafi*.[3] Sher Shah's monumental fort with its twelve gates and nearly a hundred garrets punctuating its massive walls thus cost more than three and a half million rupees in those far off times. The king whose rise to mastery of India was swift and phenomenal could not see his monument completed, however. He was the administrator whose bureaucracy gifted us a land management system that we use to this day and in whose day, we are told, the long arm of his law reached everyone and everywhere.

Humayun entered a deserted Rohtas, installed a garrison in it and advanced to Delhi to reclaim the kingdom his father had established. That was 1555. Within the year, he was dead, having tripped from the stairs of a build-

---

3) In the sixteenth century, the gold ashrafi was of about ten grams.

ing raised by his erstwhile adversary Sher Shah Suri. A teenage Akbar took the reins of power, the Gakkhars who had pledged loyalty to Babur and to guard against whom Rohtas was built, were still in the Mughal camp. Rohtas was no longer important, but far away on the east bank of the Indus River, a fort was of greater imperative. Work began on Attock Fort, even as Rohtas was not completely abandoned.

Raja Man Singh Kashvaha, one of the Nine Jewels of Akbar, was stationed at Rohtas where he built his fabulous palace. The main building was topped by a domed tower open to breezes from all sides. The tower was accessible from the roof of the main house, but when that collapsed, access was cut off. In the early years of the twentieth century, British archaeologists built a bannisterless flight of stairs which was a right terror for those suffering from vertigo. The palace was very tastefully adorned with frescoes, faded traces of which can be seen to this day.

A little to the north of this palace, is a large paved floor where once another palatial house stood. On its east side, stands a solitary domed building, the last remnant of what once was. This room, square in plan and meagre of dimension, is what remains of the residence of Roop Mati, the widowed sister of Man Singh who lived and travelled with him.

Khalid Mehmood Sarwar, the conservator and curator of Rohtas, is a spirited talker and a man of immense energy. From his several years of service in the fort, he knows things about Rohtas that were perhaps known only to its original builders. Taking me walkabout outside the castle, he pointed out slabs in the stonework etched with different patterns; some with human forms, others geometrical. He claimed there were scores of them and he had gone complete around the battlements to photographically document them all. A recent triumph was his discovery of two inscribed slabs high up on the fortification at Langar Khani gateway.

Khalid led me up the stairs of Man Singh's private room as he spoke of the master story-teller Raza Ali Abidi who once worked for BBC Urdu Service and who beat me to this story of the Grand Trunk Road by some three decades. His masterful work in Urdu delights and pulls tears at the same time. Abidi sahib, as his countless admirers know him, too had been in Rohtas and though that was when Khalid was much younger and still in high school, he knew something very interesting. This had slipped my mind despite my reading of Abidi sahib's *Jarnaili Sarak*.

The excitement of that discovery so evident in Abidi sahib's words had leached into Khalid. Breathless from the climb and from his talking, he took me to the south window to point out faded script in very fine hand in the intrados of its arch. The language was Persian and the variation in writing showed the graffiti was the work of different persons. Abidi sahib lamented that modern vandals had not just covered some of the older writing with their own but had even attempted to rub it out. He nevertheless photographed it and back in London had it deciphered by the well-known researcher Dr Ziauddin Ahmed Shakaib.

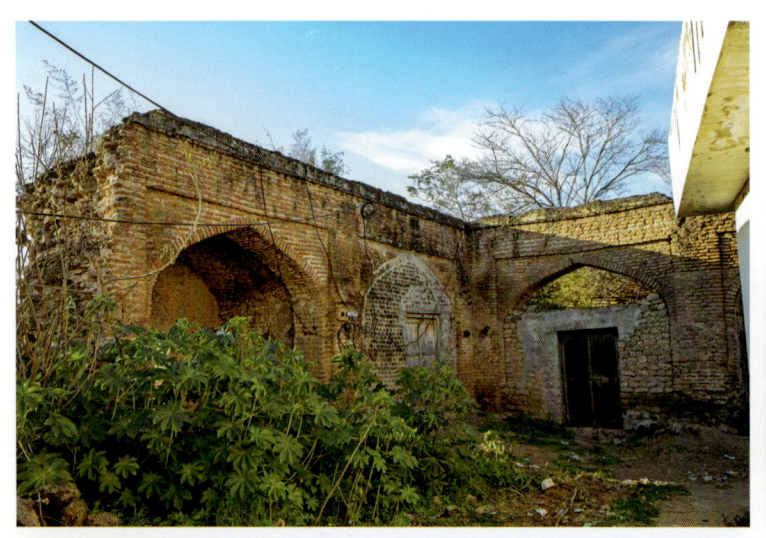

Top/Bottom Left: The ruined interior of the caravanserai of Rajo Pind. Because of its strong fortification it is wrongly believed to have been Sher Shah Suri's jailhouse.

Bottom Right: Khwas Khan, Sher Shah Suri's good and trusted general was administrator during the construction of Rohtas. This northern gateway of the twelve-gated fort bears his name. Upon succeeding to the throne, Islam Shah treated his father's loyal courtiers most shabbily. Khwas Khan and his family suffered much at the hands of the spiteful man.

Top Right: Lying just outside Rohtas Fort, this impressive though neglected mid-sixteenth century building is devoid of any ornamentation. It once contained the mortal remains of Khair un Nisa, the young daughter of Qadir Buksh who served Sher Shah Suri as his food minister. In charge of the commissariat during the construction of Rohtas, he evidently lived on site with his family during which time Khair un Nisa died. Sher Shah's vindictive son Islam Shah humiliated his late father's courtiers every which way he could. One nasty act was to order Qadir Buksh to disinter the body of his daughter. Today this handsome building is empty while Khair un Nisa's remains rest in Sirsaram where Sher Shah Suri is also buried.

Top Left: Haveli of Raja Man Singh in the inner fort of Rohtas.

Bottom Left: The large *baoli* or stepped well in Rohtas.

Top Right: Temple, Rohtas Fort

Bottom Right: Detail of the exquisite stonework of the balcony cantilever at Zohal Gate.

Phrases like 'we weep blood and the world too with us' speak of some profound grief. Then there is 'human heads were flung as if stones from a ballista'. Dr Shakaib found reference to a return from Kandahar in the year 1060 of the Hijra corresponding with 1650. Here Abidi sahib goes into an astute bit of historical sleuthing to tell us that was the year Kandahar reverted to the Persian king.

Shah Abbas II of Persia had begun operations against Kandahar as early as 1648. As he closed in, a fifty thousand strong force was despatched by Shah Jahan to prevent the fall of Kandahar. The *Shah Jahan Nama* records a long drawn out and bloody operation in which a large number of soldiery from both sides was killed. Heads did indeed fall like stones from a ballista before the fort of Kandahar fell to the Persian king in February 1649. The routed Mughal army made its weary way back to India via Kabul and passed through Rohtas early the next year to leave behind an unofficial record of history.

Khalid pointed out the Persian writing, its spidery flow all but lost under the crude graffiti of modern vandals. Since Abidi sahib's time it had suffered so much more that I could not even photograph it. If those seventeenth century 'vandals' had crafted poetry to preserve their sense of loss and the history of an ignominious defeat, the intellectual height of our yahoos was to inscribe their names and perhaps add an initial of the person they supposedly loved, nothing poetic or edifying here. Another few years and the old record, written in the intrados so that it would not be damaged by handling or passing feet, would be lost forever.

Time flew and from the Mughals Rohtas passed into Sikh hands in the early nineteenth century, forever remaining of secondary importance, a mere camping ground for royalty on the passage this way and that. It was here, perhaps in the palace of the Kashvaha prince, that in early May 1837 Maharaja Ranjit Singh got word from distant Jamrud at the mouth of the Khyber Pass of the death of his favourite general Hari Singh Nalwa. History tells us that the one-eyed Maharaja broke into uncontrolled tears. The country beyond Peshawar that he so coveted and which Nalwa had said he would secure, now ebbed out of Punjabi hands. Soon even the Maharaja was gone from this life and then Rohtas, a monument to wasted labour, faded into uselessness.

In Charlotte Canning's time (March 1860), the Grand Trunk Road had abandoned Rohtas and lay on the alignment through Dina to Jhelum town. She took a detour and stood outside the towering ramparts gazing up in awe. She went wild with paper and brush for her diary tells us she found twenty subjects to paint. Of these, F. S. Aijazuddin's *Sketches from a Howdah* holds five depictions of such accuracy of portrayal that it is not difficult to see where her easel was set up. She wrote that Rohtas was an ogre's castle from a fairy tale book which had, in an obvious reference to the west side of the Under Kot area, 'walls within walls'.

One of Canning's water colours shows the pink-tinted east wall of the lofty domed room in the house of Raja Man Singh. The lower portion of the building is still intact. This means the lost part of that sixteenth century edifice collapsed sometime after 1860 when the viceregal procession passed this way. Surely some of the earliest private housing raised inside Rohtas contains the rubble from the lost building.

With Azeem discussing how, by some peculiar mechanism, Gandhara art stopped short of the line of Soan River outside Rawalpindi, we exited Rohtas and drove south to Jhelum town. Indeed, it is strange that we find no evidence in this part of Punjab of the exquisite statuary created by Pakhtun craftsmen more than two thousand years ago. To my mind it seems, those ancient sculptors kept their skill very closely guarded. I wonder if the master taught only his own sons so that the fine art may not be vulgarised by overuse at the hands of common artists.

We passed into Jhelum town. St John's Church standing on our left side as we approached the bridge on the river, is now all but hidden behind modern housing. Back in the early 1960s, the road journey from Lahore northward passed over the old road-rail bridge. As we came over the river, away to the left we saw the church surrounded by tall trees and an odd house or two with buffalos grazing in the meadow. The sky in those days had so much more cumulus that the whole was a very John Constable vista.

With growing traffic, the new bridge was built a little downstream and as one approached Jhelum, the church fell on the right hand. It was still so beautiful to behold. But with more and more buildings, the church seems to have gone into seclusion. Today one sees only the tall spire rising above the accretion of modern times.

The priest was away and we were denied entry. From my earlier excursions I could describe the several plaques commemorating the many who died far away from their home of dales and glens of mist and rain. I retain an old image that tells us that St John's Church was consecrated on the seventh day of February 1857 by the Bishop of Madras.

We stood on the old Jhelum Bridge to look at a view that once was the prettiest in town: Masjid Afghanan – Mosque of the Afghans – broken to a million little bits and reconstructed again in the ripples of Jhelum's waters. But that view was now a thing of the past. A brand new flood protection embankment kept the river from washing the foundations of the mosque. Its façade once washed a beautiful deep green shade, with boats moored near its steps, this was surely the most picturesque house of worship. But officialdom in Pakistan works in crude and non-mysterious ways to destroy every bit of beauty in the country.

Of all the smaller district towns, Jhelum has always been my favourite. It is more cosmopolitan than, say, Faisalabad or Sahiwal; its citizens way more sophisticated and cultured. Many years ago a friend suggested the reason was the pounds sterling sent back home by the city's sons settled in Britain. That may be part of the reason. I had always believed the more significant reason was that Jhelum became a garrison town shortly after the uprising of 1857. This interaction between locals and persons from Britain and all over India brought on a distinct sophistication seen to this day.

There is more to the city and its people than just that. Carl von Hügel found it a city of 'some importance' and its people the most friendly and hospitable who insisted he spend a night there. The shopkeepers invited him to take whatever pleased him without a concern for payment. The streets 'were clean, though narrow'. He declined the kind offers, taking instead the ferry comprising 'twenty large boats, excellently built and managed' that conveyed him across the river to the serai of 'Narangabad'.[4] The crossing was free of charge for all travellers, wrote von Hügel. This indicates that even in 1835, the municipality of Jhelum was way ahead of its time providing travellers something like toll-free bridges in our time.

A quarter century after the Baron's passage, the establishment of the British cantonment brought in moneyed traders from the big cities. Some of these were Hindus, but a considerable number was also educated Parsis. The latter dealt in wines and spirits for the officers' club in the cantonment. Older natives of Jhelum remember several of those establishments were still doing business in the early 1970s. But then things changed. The old way of life went out of fashion, at least in public places, and the Parsis packed up and left. The Hindus had already gone three decades earlier, now the Parsis departed taking with them the pluralistic, colourful ambience of the city. A hangover of those earlier times persists, however, as a walk around the main commercial area in the city still shows.

In Khairabad, on the far side of the Indus, a gentleman had

St John's Church, Jhelum that still keeps its idyllic setting despite encroaching housing and a jumble of electric pylons and cabling.

4) Apparently Serai Alamgir of today was once called Serai Aurangabad.

introduced a friend of his as, 'he likes to think of himself as an historian'. The meaning was clear: the friend was grossly in error. In Jhelum town people under such illusions are a dime a dozen. Every government clerk, every other coolie at the railway station and a few rickshaw drivers dapple in 'history' and they take it upon themselves to enlighten outsiders.

And so, Jhelum has several avatars. It is the name of Alexander's horse. Or it is a compound of the Greek words for 'water' and 'cool'. Or it is the name of a daughter of Raja Paurava (the Porus of Greek annals). The men who tell these yarns have never been near any source material, nor do they have any knowledge of Greek, but if you counter them you are likely to be drummed out of town.

The horse, the very one that would permit no other but Alexander to mount it, was called Bucephalus – Ox Head – by its young master. The Greek words for water and cool are nowhere near the two syllables of Jhelum and as for the offspring of the valiant Raja Paurava, history is silent.

On the subject of Alexander's horse, Charlotte Canning has something interesting to say: 'We crossed the Jhelum [River] at Jhelum and saw the raised mound said to be the tomb of Bucephalus'. Since the viceregal entourage was heading to Rawalpindi, this mound would be on the west bank of the river. That is historically correct for the horse died of old age before going into battle, as the Greek historian Arrian tells us. He also tells us that this occurred at the spot where Alexander eventually crossed the river for his epic battle against the Punjabis.

Though the exact spot of the crossing is still moot, I tend to agree with historian Robin Lane Fox that it happened outside the modern village of Jalalpur, some forty-five kilometres downstream of Jhelum town. We also know from the sources that the ornate tomb built for the king's horse was smack on the banks of the river. That was May 326 BCE. In August, the army having revolted on the banks of the Beas, Alexander returned to Paurava's kingdom (with whom peace had been made after the battle) and was grieved to see that the tomb had been washed away by monsoon floods.

What Lady Canning saw was just a mound that had on conjecture been designated tomb of Bucephalus by some passing Raj official. It is from there that ignorant local 'historians' have woven their own histories giving the horse any name they pleased. One such person even insists that the Greeks could have called the horse anything they wished, we Punjabis knew it as Jhelum and so the city came to be known after it.

The first time ever we hear the place name Jhelum is from that remarkable Central Asian polymath Abu Rehan Al Beruni who came to India seeking to enrich his intellect. The year was 1017 and only a couple of years earlier he had been forcibly plucked from his native Uzbekistan by the Turk Mahmud of Ghazni. Unhappy in the academic sterility of Ghazni, he repeatedly requested permission for a journey into the culturally superior country of India. Finally being let off, Al Beruni passed this way and recorded: 'the river Biyatta, [is] known as Jailam, from the city of this name on its western banks'.

Lying outside the western Langar Khani gateway of Rohtas, Gurdwara Choa Sahib celebrates the visit of Guru Nanak Dev to this premises during his years of tirthayatra in search of self and God. Abandoned for years, this holy site is now again on the Sikh pilgrimage circuit. Here the Sikh period building is burnished by the setting sun as picnickers prepare to leave.

This shows that the city was established well enough a thousand years ago to lend its name to the river that flowed by. But what of the name Biyatta? History shows that the name Jhelum for the river was a local name, confined to the Punjab alone. Since times immemorial it is known in Kashmir as Vitasta and the legend of its creation is one of immense beauty and passion. After Kashmir was created, the great sage Kashyapa whose name is borne by Kashmir, prayed to Lord Shiva to purify the land. In turn, the god requested his wife Parvati to take the form of a river and flow through the land to cleanse it.

Deep inside the earth Parvati stirred in her requested avatar and Shiva struck the ground with his *trishul* – trident – to let the waters flow. Now, the width of the *trishul* was one *vitasti*, an ancient unit of linear measure. And so it was that Parvati's river avatar came to be known as Vitasta, a name that also suggests its width. In the early nineteenth century when this land was crawling with European adventurers, we hear of the river ranging here at the ford of Jhelum town from three hundred metres in winter to just over two kilometres in summer. The Sanskrit Vitasta was transliterated into the Greek as Hydaspes from which the Persians would call it Vehat or Behat; a name that the Mughals also used.

One would have thought the ford of Jhelum town became popular only after the building of Rohtas about the middle of the sixteenth century. In reality, Jhelum is repeatedly noticed in histories dealing with the period from the closing years of the tenth century when Mahmud of Ghazni began his forays into the subcontinent. This takes me back to the caravanserai of Rajo across the Kahan River from Rohtas Fort: although the present ruinous structure is only about four hundred years old, I suspect it was raised above a much older ruin that was perhaps even then known as Rajo's Inn.

While the Jhelum ferry was famous in the Middle Ages, it seems to have passed out of notice in the early seventeenth century. This was the time when European cartographers were busy putting our part of the world on paper. Among the many maps produced from the middle of the seventeenth century until the early nineteenth century, we find no notice of Jhelum. It was only when traders and travellers of the British East India Company began to pound up and down the road that Jhelum once again regained its glory.

We stood on the Jhelum River bridge. Behind us the setting sun enhanced the purple silhouette of Tilla Jogian, the hilltop monastery established by the great Guru Goraknath in the first century BCE. Beyond, across the languid waters of the Jhelum, lay the country of Raja Paurava, the only king who won Alexander's unremitting admiration for his valour in combat and his lofty character in peace.

It was country such as this where Raja Paurava stood tall at the head of his army to face Alexander of Macedon. On that fateful morning in May 326 BCE, the field was sodden with heavy overnight rain. In the month of May when the battle was fought, the land would have been fallow after the wheat harvest.

5
In the Land of Raja Paurava

My friend Muhammad Majid of Serai Alamgir is a successful homeopathic doctor. I suspect he would have done even better as an archaeologist. I met him in 2005 and the first thing he asked was if experts had discovered the fabled capital city of Raja Paurava. He had heard the lore of it being called Patta Kothi and that it was somewhere on the left or east bank of the Jhelum River. Sadly, no work had ever been done in this area and the location of that city was unknown.

Majid had done his own sleuthing, however. And one warm August day we went walking along the left bank of the Upper Jhelum Canal near Sarai Alamgir. Between neatly parcelled fields of maize and vegetables there were mounds one after the other in no particular alignment. They were just distributed randomly upon the land. Since increasing agriculture to feed a galloping population was encroaching upon ancient sites, most of them had been cut and bulldozed leaving behind vertical verges. Majid said such mounds extended several kilometres southward.

From these verges Majid had been extracting coins and terracotta pottery. I did not find any coins, but there was pottery aplenty and I obtained two wide-mouthed drinking cups with flat narrow bottoms. In Lahore, my mentor the eminent archaeologist Dr Saifur Rahman Dar confirmed that these were very common utensils about BCE 400-100. I have since imagined that after the great battle when Raja Paurava had won Alexander over with his grace in defeat and peace was made, the Macedonian would have supped wine out of such cups.

Some who pretend to be Punjabi chauvinists assert that Alexander was roundly beaten in battle by the towering Raja Paurava. They say because history is always written by the victor it is subverted. However, what we do hear from history of these two adversaries-turned-allies, the modification, if there was any, is yet complimentary for Raja Paurava.

Basing his history on extant material, Arrian, the Greek general, wrote two centuries after the event. He tells us that the Greeks outdid the Punjabis with superior tactics and by the dastardly and inhuman act of shooting the war elephants. The animals, maddened by pain, trampled their own army until all Punjabi units were in complete disarray. Arrian, however, waxes all praise for Paurava who, remaining on the battlefield even when all his units had dispersed, continued to let loose arrows into Greek lines. He himself was shot in the right shoulder, the only part of his body unencumbered by armour to permit him to draw the bow to its fullest. At last he turned his elephant around to leave the battlefield.

Arrian compares the Punjabi king with Darius in glowing terms. Whereas in the battles the Persian fought against Alexander, he fled the minute engagement began, leaving his army to its own devices. Paurava, on the other hand, 'did not lead the scramble to save his own skin, but so long as a single unit of his men held together, fought bravely on'.

Alexander, 'anxious to save the life of this great and gallant soldier', sent Ambhi, the king of Taxila, to bring Paurava to him. But the two Punjabis had long opposed each other and as Ambhi's chariot drew up, Paurava sent a well-aimed javelin in his direction. Ambhi fled. Alexander then asked the philosopher whose name we are told was Meroes to the task.

Seeing his old friend and teacher, Paurava got off his elephant and Meroes delivered Alexander's invitation. Arrian says the wounded king asked for a drink of water before mounting his friend's chariot. In the Greek camp, the chariot stopped near Alexander and his generals and Raja Paurava dismounted. A giant among men, he towered well over two metres in height, we are told by Arrian. There then occurred that epic dialogue that everyone seems to have heard of.
'What do you wish that I should do with you?' asked Alexander.
'Treat me as a king ought,' came the reply. Arrian tells us Alexander was immensely pleased by this dignified response. 'For my part, your request shall be granted. But is there not something you would wish for yourself? Ask it,' Alexander persisted. Now Raja Paurava, who Punjabis do not cherish as their own, a true hero and a man of character and integrity, bowled over the invader.
'Everything is contained in this one request.'

The majestic grace of his giant adversary was admirable and Alexander made peace with Paurava, returning his kingdom to him. Later, the Punjabi king accompanied Alexander on his eastward march all the way to the Beas River.

There an agent provocateur drifted through the camp telling the foreigners of the immense power of the Nanda kingdom that they were going to soon face. Thousands of war elephants, tens of thousands of chariots, immense cavalry and two hundred thousand infantry were all there waiting for them. For the foreigners there would be no return from the battlefield, warned the man. Many believe this prophet of doom was the dynamic Chandragupta Maurya who was to rule the country only a few short years later.

Alexander's soldiers refused to go on. Alexander sought the word from Paurava who confirmed that the Nanda kingdom was indeed very powerful. And so, the foreigner returned to the capital on the Jhelum River to sail down to other battles. Had the Macedonian been defeated, he would never have marched on any farther east. He would have fled back the way he came. Rather than portray Paurava as a fictitious victor, he should be celebrated for his honour and integrity as revealed by Apollonius the Greek philosopher we met in the year 44 in Taxila. The raja's kind of character is what we so badly need today to imbibe and build upon.

∽

To Serai Alamgir – the Inn of (Aurangzeb) Alamgir – Azeem and I went. I recounted for him my earliest memories of passing through what was then a little village in the early 1960s. On the western end of its straggle of houses there was a large yellow-washed building that in later years

Hidden away from view amid a thick growth of trees in the folds of the Pabbi Hills between Jhelum and Kharian is a little gem forgotten from the Mughal period. Local tradition attributes the water tank to Babur, the first Mughal king of India. It was once accessible by the dirt road leading up to the now demolished Banni Rest House. Now it can be reached by a short walk from Pabbi Nature Park.

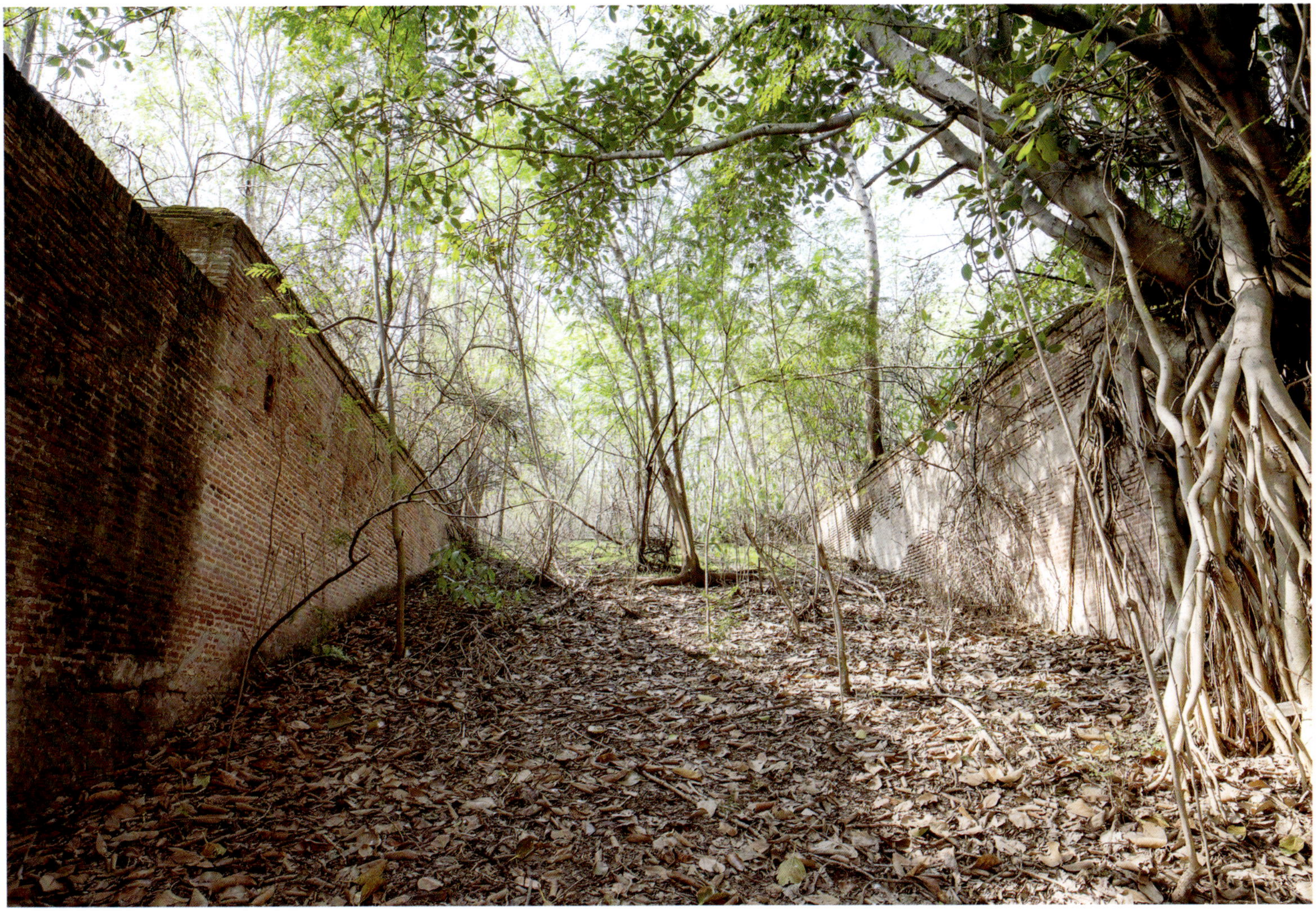

became the serai of my young imagination when I spent five years in nearby Kharian in the 1970s. Later I was told by an archaeologist that no signs of the serai ordered by Aurangzeb had been found. It was certain, however, that this place, just short of the ferry on the Jhelum River, was the logical spot for a caravanserai. Surely one would have existed earlier even before the Mughal king ordered it to be revamped with the patch of his own name.

In 1608, William Finch did not notice the caravanserai that was later to be named after Aurangzeb. Nor did the veterinary surgeon William Moorcroft two hundred years later. Neither man made any mention of the ruined mounds that could possibly have pointed in the direction of Paurava's capital. It seems as if after the rise of the Mauryan dynasty, with power centred about Pataliputra in the east and Taxila in the west, the principality between the rivers Jhelum and Ravi once ruled over by the Paurava family was amalgamated within the kingdom. The old capital lost its importance and then it was only a matter of time for it to be forgotten and the dust of time to move in and smother its glory.

Meanwhile, Finch pointed our little caravan in the direction of Khwaspur. He calls it Howaspore and mentions it as the halting place before Rohtas. At Rohtas we today have a lofty gateway looking north and called Khwas Khani Darwaza. Inside this gateway there is a tiny dome within which is a pint-sized grave with the legend Hazrat Syed Sakhi Khwas Khan Shah sahib. For a grave that size, that is a mighty long title, and myth has converted a red-blooded, valorous and principled Pakhtun into an Arab!

Recall that this man, one of Sher Shah Suri's favoured generals, was the administrator when Rohtas was under construction. History tells us that upon the death of the Suri king, Khwas Khan and his colleague Haibat Khan Niazi who commanded the Rohtas garrison, favoured the crowning of Sher Shah's elder son Adil. Islam Shah, the younger and cannier son, instead took the mantle of kingship by trickery. The men at Rohtas objected to the usurpation which led to a series of battles.

The two men rode out to fight their erstwhile master's son in the east. But the small garrison meant to contain the headstrong Gakkhars of Potohar was no match for the imperial army. A few routs in quick succession and the army was in tatters. Haibat Khan fled to Afghanistan for his life while Khwas Khan sought refuge in the Kashmiri state of Sambhal. He thought he would be safe in the custody of a fellow Pakhtun whose life he had once saved. But Taj Khan was made of baser stuff. As Khwas Khan slept one night, he stole into his guest's apartment and stabbed him to death.

To win favour, Taj Khan sent Khwas Khan's head to Islam Shah. But that was not the end of the story. The dead man obviously had a retinue that packed up the corpse and set out for Sarsaram where Sher Shah lies buried. The route they took from the hills of Kashmir was by way of Bhimber to Gujrat and then eastward. But as they neared the caravanserai of Khwaspur that the dead man had ordered only a few years earlier, the body began to rot. The corpse was cleaned out, the innards buried and the sombre caravan prepared to resume journey. What I write next is my own conjecture.

Ever curious idlers present near the serai wanted to know which important personage was being carried away for burial. It was Khwas Khan, they were told. The very man who had during his governorship of Rohtas endowed this little outpost with a fine serai and a stepped well. Why, he was a good man. And may they see his face for the last time, they asked. Sorry, said the men of the cortege. The head had been cut off. Surely the story of the dastardly murder would have been narrated, condolences accepted and prayers for the man's place in Paradise whispered before the journey to Sarsaram resumed.

From the little we know of him we can infer that Khwas Khan was a public service minded administrator and a man of sense and good judgement. He was a man well-respected. And so with the death of a good man, a legend was born; a legend of the flying headless corpse. I first heard it in the early 1990s. Khwas Khan was a holy personage titled Sakhi – Generous – who gave away whatever was his and asked for.

The tale then extant was that in a battle between Sikhs and Muslims carried by the former, the vanquished adversary was brought to the Sikh commander in chains. The man taunted Khwas Khan.
'You call yourself generous. What is it that you can give your enemy?'
'Ask and you shall have whatever it is,' replied Generous.
'I want your head,' said the Sikh commander.

History does not tell us if the good man routinely lost his head on every trivial matter, but this time he did. He lopped it off and even as it fell into the dust, the body took off and flew away. It landed outside the caravanserai Khwas Khan had ordered and there a surprised lot of people buried the headless person.

That was in the early 1990s. In those days the story was that both the head and the torso are worshipped in their respective places for supplication to them answered prayers. A recently published sham history of Rohtas tells another story equally silly and devoid of fact but does not say how the head and the torso got to be buried separately. Surely in a few more years, the myth will have altered but believers will never doubt that neither is the head buried inside the gateway of Khwas Khan at Rohtas nor his body in Khwaspur.

Back in 2005, Majid brought me from Sarai Alamgir down the Grand Trunk Road, a little southeast of Choa Kariala village. We made a u-turn and headed back towards Jhelum but halted within a couple of hundred metres. There, right by the side of the road, was a well. No stepped well this time, just an ordinary shaft with water about ten metres below the rim. It was made of burnt bricks that were used by the Mughals. But there was no other architectural feature nor tablet giving a date.

Before we drove on I grimly observed that a rashly driven sedan or a motorcycle could go straight down the shaft without even being noticed. Then a year or so later, Majid called to say that someone had filled up the well leaving no trace of it. A short way further along, about a hundred metres from the road, Majid had pointed out what appeared to be a brick structure like a wide staircase. Majid had seen it up close and said there were other affiliated structures too that made no sense to him. All that was constructed with the same brick as the well, he added. But it was August, the height of the monsoon season, and the stretch between the road and the structures was thickly overgrown. This was the season of the snake and dreading walking in sandals through the vegetation, I did not get to see the site.

Shortly after Majid gave me word of the filling of the well, he also told me that large earth-moving machinery had dismantled the old structures. Within days, roads were laid out and plots designated to turn an historical monument into a residential estate. This crime scene, for it is nothing short of crime, sits at North 32°-51', East 72°-48'.

That was the past. In January 2019, with cold rain pelting down, Azeem, his assistant Ali Raza and I were driven through the jumble of Lala Musa northeast across the Bhimber River to Khwaspur. In 1998, the so-called tomb of Khwas Khan was open to the sky. This time around a fat green dome covered it. Ali got off and ambled up to the man at the door of the cubicle of the grave. All he asked was, 'Is this the tomb of Khwas Khan?' and the attendant went livid.
'You take his name with reverence!' the man warned. 'This is Hazrat Syed Sakhi Khwas Khan Shah sahib, the giver of health and the worker of miracles.'

A month later, I returned to photograph the shrine. I was forewarned to be hypocritically respectful. The same keeper was at the shrine. After uttering sugary nonsense about the demi-god, I told him I was sent by a family in London who had visited the shrine some months earlier for the cure of their son bitten by a rabid dog. Since he was allergic to the anti-rabies injection, it was certain that the boy would die. The family flew their son to Pakistan and bringing the boy here laid his head on the threshold of the great saint. Miraculously, the boy was healed.

This or a similarly nonsensical yarn was what the illiterate man wanted to hear and he beamed with the proprietary pleasure that parents have for a prodigal child. For my edification he added a couple of equally silly anecdotes about someone's cancer being cured just by being at the shrine. He also said Khwas Khan came to our part of the world with the victorious armies of Mahmud of Ghazni. I asked him if there was ever a caravanserai here named after the holy person. There was none, said he. This brought me to the tricky question of the head supposedly buried in Rohtas Fort.

He reeled out the story of the battle between Khwas Khan and the Sikhs and the man cutting of his own head and letting his body fly to Khwaspur.
'Were there Sikhs in the time of Mahmud of Ghazni?' I asked, ignorance writ large on my face.
'Sikhs have been around for thousands of years. And they have always fought against the Muslims.' This was like the man in distant Gandava (Balochistan) who told me that his ancestor had converted heathen Baloch to Islam in the year 400 BCE!

My education went more places in that one day than it had in all the years before. One thing was certain: there was no dearth of devotees willing to part with hard earned wealth for in the two decades between my two visits, a nice mausoleum had been built for the innards of a public service minded man. Other than the irrational yarn of the flying torso nothing was known of Khwas Khan. A perfectly worldly person was turned into a demi-god who years after his death could grant people wishes.

I felt I would be challenging the man if I told him that in April 1607, on his way up the country Jahangir had spent a night at the caravanserai of Khwaspur. He knew the place had been established by Khwas Khan, a follower of Sher Shah Suri. It would have been nothing less than blasphemy if I were to tell him that the king did not hear of any miracles connected with the general who was treacherously slain. Instead, I asked him if there were any historical or cultural sites in the village. He shook his head dumbly.

That there should be no trace of the old serai was very peculiar. In January 1836, Baron Carl von Hügel remarked on the high walls surrounding the inn and that the whole was built rather like a fort. What struck him was that every wall and roof was covered with cow dung patties drying in the sun and a huge quantity of dried and ready to burn patties heaped in the central open square. Strangely enough, the Austrian used the Hindi word *upla* for the fuel cakes.

∽

Back in January, Azeem, Ali Raza and I walked through the drizzle to find the fort that I had seen in 1993. Even then the historical building had been taken over and was a residential complex. With his archaeologist's instinct, Azeem led us up some narrow alleys pointing out that a height in a city was always the nucleus of the oldest habitation repeatedly built upon. We asked a shopkeeper for the fort. He looked at us somewhat confused.
'What fort?'

It is bizarre how the story of the heartless murder of Khwas Khan turned him into a saint. His headless torso arriving from Kashmir and his connection with Rohtas were, over time, confused together to produce the miraculous story whereby he bequeaths health especially to young children who bathe from the two hand pumps installed near the shrine.

Why, the fort of Gujrat built on Emperor Akbar's orders, I said. There was no fort, replied the man flatly. Completely taken over by those to whom it serves as a residence, it seems to have been altered to the point where it cannot be recognised. One would be hard put to see so much as a scrap of wall dating to the time of Akbar. The famed royal bath adjacent to the fort and from the same period has gone the same way.

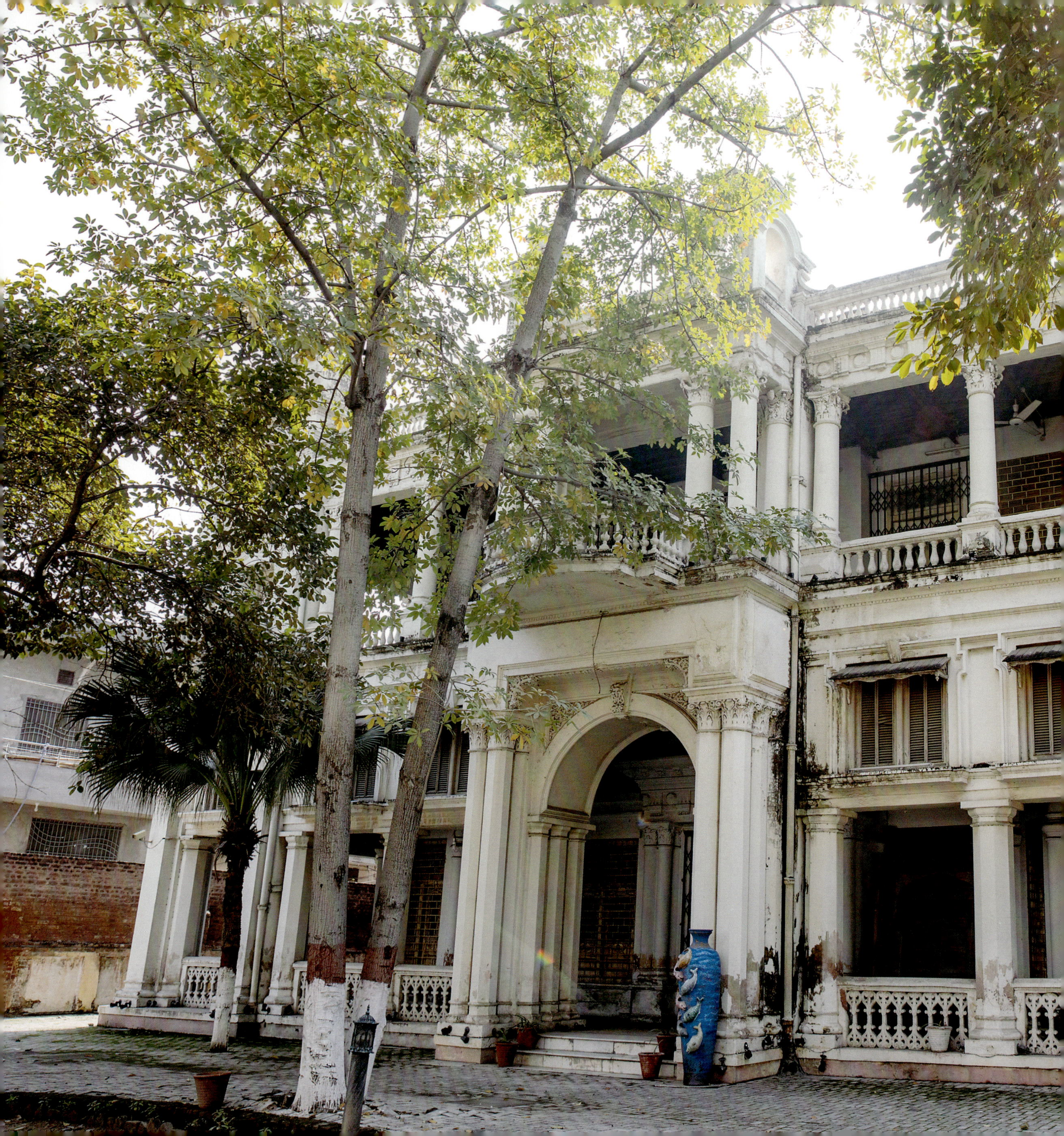

Ram Peyari Mehal, one of the few remaining iconic buildings of Gujrat. Owned by an affluent Hindu family, it became refugee property after the great migration of 1947. It has served as a school, a girls college, girls hostel and now finally is in the use of the University of Gujrat. Several other such signature buildings of the rich families who inhabited the city have been pulled down and replaced. It seems a matter of time before Ram Peyari Mehal too goes under the demolishing sledge hammer.

Detail of one of the doors of Ram Peyari Mehal.

With little official oversight on our cultural heritage, I have seen several historical sites taken over by the public and altered according to their needs. Having done their ugly deed, people yet have a sense of guilt and go into denial about the existence of the heritage piece. Outside Lahore, near the village of Lakho Dehar, there was once an octagonal – and therefore rare – *baoli* dating to Jahangir's time. The water in the well was clear and pure and the local landlord had installed a pump on it to irrigate his fields.

I photographed it on film in 2003. Two years later, having gone digital, I returned for another session. Only the pavilion of the *baoli* remained. The pipes of the pump went into cement concrete: the old well had been completely covered up by a cement concrete lintel. The attendant, a servant of the landlord, said I was mistaken. There had never been a well at the place! The fort of Gujrat has sadly gone the same way.

In his *Tuzk*, Jahangir tells us that having built this fort, Akbar brought 'a body of Gujars who had passed their time in the neighbourhood in thieving and highway robbery', and established them here. It was after them that the fort got its name. *The Ancient Geography of India* (written *circa* 1865) of Alexander Cunningham, general-turned-archaeologist, says that nothing really is known of the early history of the district except that a Rajput prince Bachan Pal founded it at an indeterminate time in the past. Traditions recorded by Raj civil servants tell us that the city here may have been called Udainagri.

Now, the Gujars whose name stems from the Sanskrit

gau char – Cow Grazer – were the lords of the land long before farming moved from subsistence to money making business. They ranged across the riverine forests with their herds from the Indus delta country in the deep south through Punjab all the way up into the Himalayas. The *Rajatarangni* of Pundit Kalhana, on the history of the several dynasties of Kashmiri kings, tells us that the all-conquering king Shankar Varma (reigned CE 883-902) defeated Alakhana the king of Gurjara.

What happened thereafter is obscured by the fog of centuries. At some point a Gujar leader called Ali Khan is said to have rebuilt Gujrat. This name is an echo of the old pre-Islamic Alakhana and, therefore, clearly a fiction. What we do gather from the *Tuzk e Jahangiri* is that there was nothing significant at the site of Gujrat until Akbar ordered the fort.

There was, however, once a story which now seems to have gone out of fashion. It was told me by an elderly gentleman in 1993.

The Jats, land-owning rich families and the Gujars, whose livestock made them wealthy, had an argument about who owned this nameless city. After much altercation that came to nothing, a delegation comprising the elders of both sides presented itself at the court of Akbar. Having heard them out, the king decreed that any party who could within one night produce eight hundred gold ashrafis would be granted the right to name the city after themselves.

The Jats thinking it an impossibility, slept over the matter. But the Gujars, lords of moveable properties in the shape of livestock, raised the required sum overnight and in the morning laid out the gold at the emperor's feet. And so it was that the city became Gujrat – the suffix *raat* signifying night.

'Had the Jats mustered the required sum, the city would have been Jatrat,' said the simple-minded teller of this rather cute tale.

The one story the old gent knew was that of Sohni, the stunningly beautiful daughter of the potter Tula. As the master craftsman of town, his wares were famous across the land, more so because of the designs Sohni painted on them. Izzat Baig, a merchant from distant Bokhara across the mountains, arrived in Gujrat to procure the famous pottery. Inside the store, the merchant caught sight of Sohni in deep concentration on a pot with brush and paint in her hands. Izzat Baig was stricken. Why, such beauty he had never seen in his native country of the Uzbeks.

He asked to purchase the one being painted. Since it had to be baked, Tula told him to return the next day. The purchase done, Izzat Baig now made daily visits to the workshop on one pretext or the other, only to see the woman he had fallen madly in love with. When it came time for his party to return to Bokhara, Izzat Baig remained behind for by now he was getting positive signals from the dazzling Sohni. Soon, the man ran out of money and destitute for the sake of his love, he offered to mind Tula's buffalos. And so Izzat Baig, the rich merchant of Bokhara became Mahiwal – Buffalo Man.

Meanwhile, Sohni too was soon besotted and the lovers began to meet secretly. But the world would sooner hurt lovers than see them happily together and Sohni was wedded off to another potter. Since the husband travelled to sell his wares, Sohni managed to continue with the secret trysts. Now, Mahiwal minded the livestock on the far bank of the Chenab, and Sohni used a baked earthen water pot turned upside down to serve as a float to paddle across. One evening, her sister in law suspecting some funny business, surreptitiously followed Sohni to the river and saw her retrieve her pot from its hiding place and ride it to the other bank of the river where she knew Mahiwal kept the buffalos.

For two or three days, the sister-in-law watched the proceedings. Then one day she quietly replaced the ringing terra cotta pot with an unbaked piece. The unsuspecting Sohni did not notice the difference in the dark and in the fast flowing waters, the pot began to erode bit by bit. In midstream, Sohni was on her own, the clay having all melted away into the water. Seeing her foundering, Mahiwal leaped into the river to save her. But the current was too fast for untrained swimmers and the two were carried away, never to be seen again.

Far away in Shahdadpur town of Sanghar district in Sindh there is a tomb of the two lovers. Some say the bodies were found in an embrace from the Indus River. Others would like to believe the love tale is of Sindhi origin and because of its attractive tragedy and melodrama it was adopted by the Punjabis.

Many years ago, the late Punjabi writer and poet, Sharif Kunjahi of Gujrat, told me what he thought of the story: Punjab has traditionally been attacked and plundered throughout history. All these brigands, now erroneously thought of as Pakhtuns were Turks, who came down from Central Asia. The Punjabi mind wishing to prevail just one time, crafted an Uzbek, no mean beggar but a rich merchant, who lost everything to a beauty of Gujrat. In a way, he said, it was a Punjabi victory.

Of the five rivers of Punjab, the Chenab is said to be the river of love and romance. The ancient Sanskrit speakers called it Asikni – The Dark One. But at a very remote time it was also known as Chandra Bhaga or Moon River. It is from this name that we get our modern Chenab. When Alexander's legions arrived here, the name Chandra Bhaga became an ominous Sandrophagos in their language. Now, Sandros or Sandro is a diminutive version of Alexander and phagos in Greek is 'to eat'.

Already chastened by the hard fought contest with the Punjabis under Raja Paurava, the word Sandrophagos unnerved the foreigners. Was this a sign from the gods above that this would be the end of Alexander? Would the Chandra Bhaga be the killer of their king and general? So far from home and without a leader, they would all be lost. The army resolved not to use the colloquial name but the classical Sanskrit one turning it into Acesines.

We did not pause at the Chenab bridge because of the rain. Two weeks later I returned to the railway bridge to check out something I had first become acquainted with three decades ago. Raj engineers who spanned the river in the 1870s to take the railway into the Khyber Pass, named the bridge Alexandra after a princess at home. A century later, when British royalty was nothing more than a few pictures in local newspapers, a very senior railwayman, someone called A A Qureshi, had a sign installed at the bridge to give out its history.

It said the bridge was named after 'Alexandra the Great, the then Chief Engineer of North Western Railway'! Even thirty years ago the paint was badly peeling and could be read with some difficulty. Also, the sign was large and the lettering so small that a readable photograph was impossible. Now there was nothing. The remarkable brainchild of Mr Qureshi has forever been lost.

Across the bridge, the Grand Trunk Road crossed into Gujranwala district, the hometown of Ranjit Singh, the only other monarch, after Raja Paurava, that Punjabis can truly be proud of. Time now was the first week of January 1836 and we were travelling in the company of Baron Carl von Hügel.

Gateway of gurdwara Rori Sahib, Eminabad (Gujranwala) is a rhapsody of plastic forms and shapes in cut and moulded bricks baked to perfection. Built in the second decade of the twentieth century, it follows the architectural style of the Spanish architect Antoni Gaudi. The nearer white and yellow dome houses the main gurdwara with the Granth Sahib. Notice the empty ablution tank on the right and the free standing arches at its corners.

6
Maharaja Ranjit Singh Ruled Here

Carl von Hügel from Austria whose name in English would be Charles from the Hills, passed through Gujrat which was 'inclosed by mud walls'. Such weak defences would be strange for a fort ordered by Akbar. But I presume, hastening as he was to reach Wazirabad, von Hügel did not pay much attention to Gujrat. And why would he? He was in a hurry to be in Wazirabad and there be entertained in a fortified palace he tells us was built by Maharaja Ranjit Singh.

In the early Middle Ages, coming up from the east, the Rajapatha made for a city they say is more than a thousand years old: Sodhra that lies about eight kilometres northeast of Wazirabad. It was a large, fortified settlement and a great trading emporium whose name signifies its vastness: Sodhra, they relate, is actually *sau-darra*, or Hundred Gated from the number of portals that punctuated its massive encircling walls. Where once passing caravans tarried is now an insignificant little agricultural town off the main road. In the sixteenth century, it may already have been slipping into oblivion for when Sher Shah Suri was building his monumental Rohtas Fort, he shifted the axis of the ancient road a little south of Sodhra.

Here on the left bank of the meandering Palkhu rivulet, once a lovely freshet and today nothing more than a sewer tainted with domestic and industrial waste, Sher Shah ordered a post station and, very likely, a serai. On my wanderings in the 1980s I was told by elders that there were foundations of a stable near the ruinous, roofless building that archaeologists say is the post station. Today not a sign of the stable remains. On recent visits, I found a pair of junkies doped to their eyeballs and drowsing against the wall that offered some shade. From the clutter surrounding them, it was clear they had taken up permanent abode inside the building.

Our guide, the Austrian nobleman, crossed the Chenab River and when Wazirabad was yet an hour's march away found a four-horse carriage waiting for him. The transport had been sent on the order of Maharaja Ranjit Singh, and seated in its luxury felt 'like a dream' to von Hügel. He proceeded to the 'palace in the midst of a garden' where he was to spend a couple of nights. He does not say that the building was called Musamman or Saman Burj, meaning eight towers or octagonal tower. But he describes the place well as it stood in 1836:

> [It] is a singular edifice, both in its exterior form and its internal decorations. It has two storeys, and in the centre is a sort of tower which divides the wings, while the outside walls, as well as the apartments within, are adorned with fresco paintings illustrative of the religion of the Sikhs. Among them are the portraits of the ten Gurus from Nanak the first to Govind the last, the size of life; the chief painter of Ranjit's court is certainly not a Raphael.

In 1991, I ended up in that palace in the midst of a garden. The property was, and still is, held by the Raja family. I met Ejazullah who very kindly took me in and up the stairs of the very tower that von Hügel mentions. I was amazed to see the freshness of colour in paintings that were then nearly two hundred years old and even if the artist was no Raphael, the work was first-class.

The Raja family of Wazirabad were chiefs of Rajaori in Kashmir whence they migrated about the middle of the nineteenth century to Wazirabad. Ejazullah said his family purchased Musamman Burj in 1855 and since that time has been resident in it. Over time, the family grew and the property was parcelled out between the various brothers and cousins. In the bargain several new apartments and outhouses cropped up in the garden of Ranjit Singh, but the outer fortification wall and the lofty gateway is preserved to this day, though a substantial slice of the property has been sold off by one of the owners.

Ejazullah remembered that in his childhood he had seen most of the rooms resplendent with paintings. However, in the early 1970s, someone in the family, overcome with religious fervour, had the rooms whitewashed. All would have been lost had Ejazullah and a few others of his generation not stood up against this modern day iconoclasm. However, they were not able to save the paintings in any room other than the tower. For this act of prudence, one can never be sufficiently thankful to Ejazullah and his partners in resistance.

Through the 1990s I returned several times to Musamman Burj always to be warmly welcomed by Ejazullah. Several times I took friends as well. But time passes and families grow. Today the tower with its paintings is in the possession of a younger member of the family who keeps it locked while he himself resides in Lahore. I am told, however, that the paintings are still preserved. One can only hope that the good sense of keeping the two century-old frescos will persevere. It would be even better that the Raja family remain as open and welcoming as Ejazullah was in the 1990s and permit visitors to appreciate what they have.

∽

Sher Shah Suri may not have built the Grand Trunk Road, but he certainly was the one to order this post station. Standing across the road from Wazirabad railway station, it has long been neglected and was once used as billboard by local advertisers.

Wazirabad takes the name of Hakim Ilmuddin Ansari, titled Wazir Khan, one of the noblemen in the court of Shah Jahan. The man, a native of Chiniot town, for many years held one of the most important positions in the Mughal

Seven hundred and fifty metres, in a straight line, southeast of Sher Shah's
post station, outside village Bhattike, the Church of Scotland graveyard
once had beautiful tombstones. Today they have all been vandalised,
save those that are flush with the ground.

> A LIGHT FROM OUR HOUSEHOLD
> IS GONE,
> A VOICE WE LOV'D IS
> STILLED,
> A PLACE IS VACANT IN
> OUR HOME,
> WHICH NEVER CAN BE
> FILLED.

court, that is, Superintendent of the Imperial Kitchen. This entailed the emperor's fullest trust because in those dangerous times, regicide by poison was a favourite pastime of enemies and aspiring princes and since Akbar's reign, it was one of the highest positions a courtier could aspire for. Thereafter Wazir Khan served as the governor of Lahore. In June 1640, the last year of his life, he was ordered for a short while to the important fortress of Attock.

It is said Wazirabad owes itself to its supposed eponymous founder. However, the *Shah Jahan Nama* makes no such disclosure. It may be that shifting of the route from Sodhra to this side and the establishment of the way station by Sher Shah Suri may have caused the town to grow organically. It may have had another name at that time until Wazir Khan passing through on one of his journeys endowed it with his own name. But today the town looks well-ordered.

The cold-blooded Paolo di Avitabile, who we met in Peshawar gibbeting Pakhtuns suspected of wrong-doing, had earlier honed his hand at brutal governorship at Wazirabad. Having sized him up, the wily Ranjit Singh established him as the governor at the provincial little town of Wazirabad. Avitabile at once set to reordering his seat of governance. He tore down the old organic township and set out the new city in an oblong with two main streets cutting each other at right angles and a set of subsidiary alleyways all at right angles to each other.

Legend has it that when Ranjit Singh sent a set of prisoners with the instruction that they were to be kept restrained, Avitabile acted in his very own manner. He immediately ordered them to be strung up and left their corpses dangling from the gibbets. When the Maharaja asked why he had executed them, Avitabile is said to have replied that that was the only way he could keep them from escaping.

Long before it became a town called Wazirabad, this village, whose name is now lost in the mist of time, had a number of families working in steel and iron for we hear of much-admired 'many-bladed knives, paper cutters etc.'. From early British reports we hear that the nearby town of Nizamabad (now within the municipal limits of Wazirabad) was noted for 'the excellence and finish of its firearms and other warlike implements'.

Local manufacturers claim that they have been in the business of making the finest swords, armour and knives for a very long time. In Nizamabad, the family that leads the manufacture of the most bizarre-looking swords – and some truly exquisite ones with Damascene blades – that form the staple of Hollywood fantasy films, are Chadda Rajputs. Interestingly, their Bowie knives carry the mark of a famous German producer and are exported to that country to be re-exported elsewhere.

Many years ago, the Chadda patriarch told me that Alexander himself tarried a couple of weeks to have his armoury replenished by his ancestors. Somehow he was convinced that Greek histories note the iron working expertise of the Chaddas and no amount of argument could persuade him otherwise.

Even though he passed right by this place, Alexander's visit is fiction. What we do know from history is that King Louis Philippe I of France (reigned 1830–48) sent Maharaja Ranjit Singh a gift of a few sets of cuirasses. The Maharaja sent one set to Wazirabad for local steel workers to replicate. What came out, it is said, was rather to the liking of the Maharaja. Some would have us believe that the replica was celebrated for being finer than the original.

∽

Before finally setting off for 'Guseraoli' where Hari Singh Nalwa had a 'palace and garden', Carl von Hügel strolled through the Saman Burj grounds in one last ecstasy: 'I cannot express the delight I felt at seeing this Indian garden, with its regular little flower-beds and fountains. There is something very tranquilizing in these scenes, where the desire of embellishing life is displayed so tastefully.'

Other than telling us that the intervening country was 'poorly cultivated', von Hügel says no more of the nearly thirty-kilometre journey. He would have travelled past the little township of Nizamabad and by the side of the road would have seen the three-domed mosque on a high plinth. The lower portion forming two chambers might have been the resident priest's home, or it would simply have been a way of protecting the raised prayer chamber from the periodic flooding of the Palkhu stream.

Locals says it was built on the orders of Sher Shah Suri. And it might just as well have been for it clearly dates to that early period. Until two decades ago, it was impossible to miss as it sat just off the road to the right as one headed southward and was beautifully shaded by a clump of spreading *shisham* or Indian Rosewood (*Dalbergia sissoo*) trees. It was a lovely little edifice, the thick-walled and domed interior had an aura of serenity. The west facing mihrab was decorated with fading but delicate frescos. In 1991, an elderly couple lived in one of the ground floor rooms and stored chaff and hay in the other. The man said the muezzin's call had not sounded under those stout domes for as far back as he could remember.

South of Wazirabad, outside village Nizamabad, this early Mughal period mosque, once shaded by lovely trees, was visible from the road leading to Dhaunkal. It was disused and served as residence to an elderly couple. Today, the trees are cut but it is hidden behind housing and mostly remains locked. Local tradition attributes it to Sher Shah Suri.

The walls of the prayer chamber was covered with graffiti. Though it could not have been the work of a single person for the dates varied either by a few days or even by some years, yet it was all a fine, spidery hand in black

The Samadhi of Maha Singh, the father of Maharaja Ranjit Singh.

ink. Passage after passage in Persian prose, some one or two-liners, others longer. Some blocks of writing were clearly verse for they came in couplets. Totally illiterate in Persian, I could make out nothing save some dates of the Hijri calendar and a couple of names. The earliest I could decipher was from 1007 (1598-99) and the last 1104 (1692-93). Two discernible names were Mirza Sultan Mohammad Khan and Qadir Buksh Khan of whom nothing is known.

There were yet more, not in ink with the same beautiful hand, but scratched deep into the sixteenth century plaster. One dated to early June 1921 when it was Eid day and the other named Ghalib Shah who did his bit of vandalism sometime in 1940. The junior revenue clerk who had accompanied me said the man was a local landlord whom he personally knew and who had died in the 1980s. Finding the Persian writing was so like Raza Ali Abidi discovering history in the arch of Raja Man Singh's palace in Rohtas. But in my younger days when I thought things were immutable, I did not take pictures of the writing for decipherment.

Several years later, I returned again and thinking the mosque would still be visible by the roadside, managed to miss it. Again while working on this book, I returned to Nizamabad asking for the mosque of Sher Shah Suri. I drew blanks in the beginning, but eventually met a man who pointed me into a narrow alleyway. Wrong mosque, I said to him. The mosque stood in open fields just off the road from where it was visible.

'*Babeyo,* how many years ago was it that you saw it from

the road? This is 2019. Get with it!' Addressed as 'Old Man' was sobering enough to bring me quick into the present.

A short discussion ensued: three squat domes and a high plinth on which the edifice stood. The man nodded each time. Then I mentioned the little grove of *shisham* trees that covered its façade. The man said there were no trees and then went thoughtful. He said when he was a child he did see the trees. And that could not have been many years ago for he was in his early twenties. The man whose name I did not ask narrated a convoluted tale of two brothers or friends quarrelling over possession of the mosque which had led to it being permanently locked up. I could not make much sense of what the dispute was all about, but it seemed an attempt at land grab. He knew nothing of the elderly couple who once lived in the mosque.

I went into the alley, turned left as he had said and there, like a captive between ugly jailors, was the sixteenth century worship house caught between ungainly modern structures. Where open fields had stretched on all sides three decades ago, was now shoddy housing. Abutting on the left side of the mosque was one that smacked of the first attempt to take over a building that no one cared to own. The entrance under the portico and the two openings of the rooms that the elderly couple used three decades ago were now closed with steel doors, all padlocked. I could see that the three openings of the bays under the domes too were blocked by similar doors. The beautiful *shisham* trees were now stumps flush with the dry earth.

I knocked the door of abutting house and from behind the tattered sheets serving as screen from wandering eyes, a woman shooed me away saying there was no man at home to attend to me. I asked for the key to go into the mosque. That was a negative. I asked when I could return to go into the mosque and woman answered with her own question about the government department I belonged to. My young guide on the road had not been wrong about some vile activity underfoot.
'I am not from the government. I only want to photograph old buildings,' I replied.
'The government has never come here to see or repair the mosque, so what business do you have wanting to photograph it?' she said acidly.
'I want to photograph it so that when it eventually is no more, there should be some record of what once existed.'
'What good will that do? Here we have people dying like flies and no one cares and you worry for an old building!' The woman shut me up with an unassailable argument. I came away wondering if the graffiti were still there or not. More likely the latter case for it was certain the misplaced piety had caused the interior to be whitewashed.

A couple of kilometres southward was yet another signpost on the old Grand Trunk Road: a *baoli* with a fine little pavilion. The building which in my younger years I had mistakenly believed to be from the mid-sixteenth century is clearly later Mughal. Its base is eroding from the effects of water-logging and before long it will be a heap of old bricks. Three decades ago I was told that signs of an old caravanserai could once be seen here. But even then, and now evermore so, I believe that is fiction.

We know well enough that a caravanserai was no unguarded place but a fortified premises. What was described to me all those years ago seemed to be a largish house that just happened to be near the old well.

Carl von Hügel mentioned neither the old mosque where some Muslim in his retinue may have paused to put his forehead to the ground, nor the well where he surely would have halted if not for a drink himself then to water the horses of the carriage sent to convey him from Wazirabad to 'Guseraoli', that little fortified town that only eight decades earlier was just a collection of Gujar villages.

The year was 1739. Emboldened by the decay of the once powerful Mughal Empire, Nadir Shah the Afshar Turk who ruled Persia, led his first depredatory raid into India. It is said that in Delhi alone his soldiery ruthlessly murdered one hundred thousand humans regardless of age, gender or creed. From Mohammad Shah, the spineless Emperor of India, he stole the peacock throne and the Kohinoor diamond together with tens of thousands of captives to be sold into slavery. As his army made its way back across the riverine islands or doabs of Punjab, they were set upon by bands of hirsute horse-riders who plundered the baggage train of the departing looters, set many of their compatriots free and massacred any straggling foreigner they could lay their swords on. In Rachna Doab, the belt between the Ravi and the Chenab rivers, the man leading this merry band was Charrat Singh.

Followers of the Guru Nanak who had proclaimed a syncretic religion in 1499, the Sikhs were until then seen as deviants by Hindus and Muslims alike. Now they became fellow Punjabis for those who were liberated. In 1747, began the raids of Ahmed Shah Abdali, a Saddozai Pakhtun ruler of Afghanistan. In all of the nine raids by Abdali, his retreating army was harried by the Sikhs who did little damage other than relieving the outsiders of considerable plunder and freeing the captives being carried off to slavery. From freebooting desperados, the Sikhs began to be seen as Punjabi heroes. In the bargain, Sikh leaders like Charrat Singh enriched themselves. From this wealth, the man fortified a collection of Gujar villages.

It seems the original name Charrat Singh gave his fortress was Gujranwali, the diminutive or feminine form, the same as was used by von Hügel. This changed soon enough as the town grew in size. Originally from Sukerchak village not far from his fortified town, Charrat Singh became head of the Sukerchakia *misl* or confederacy. Each time Ahmed Shah Abdali led his forces down from the Suleman Mountains into the Punjabi plains, Charrat Singh's Sikhs spirited away into the forests. And when the Afghans departed, they set upon them looting their baggage and killing.

They say when you live by the sword, you die by the sword. Charrat Singh lived by it all right, but as much as any man in the Abdali army would have wanted, the Sikh did not die by their sword. He was killed when a faulty matchlock burst in his face. The irony of his death is that it did not occur in battle against his sworn enemies from across the Suleman Mountains, but fighting against his brother Sikhs of the Bhangi *misl*.

His son Maha Singh, just fourteen years old and armed with the daring and ambition of his father, took the chieftainship of the *misl*. Within the wide walls of his father's Gujranwali, he built a fortress calling it Garhi Maha Singh after himself. That was where Carl von Hügel was headed on that cold January day in 1836 for here Ranjit Singhs's favourite general Hari Singh Nalwa had a 'palace and garden'. Azeem, his assistant Ali and I followed up one hundred and eighty-three years and a few days behind him. If the Austrian suffered from the intense cold, we were bedevilled by rain.

The European visitor was completely taken by Hari Singh's mannerism and the splendid garden he maintained:

> The splendour of the rooms in the palace did not excite my admiration nearly so much as the garden, which was the most beautiful and best kept I had seen in India. The trees were loaded with oranges, of the same kind known in China as Mandarin oranges, but here much larger and finer, here called Santreh orange; Hari Singh has also transported the plane-tree from Kashmir, which seems to flourish exceedingly well in its new locality. An odour almost overwhelming ascended from the jonquils, which were in immense abundance, and of an incredibly large size. Nothing, in fact, could be more carefully adorned with flowers and plants of various kinds, than this garden, which evidently formed one of the chief delights, and sometimes the occupation of its owner.

Having earlier made inquiries about his intended host, von Hügel surprised the man by mentioning how the Sikh had earned the surname he carried: while still in his youthful years, the man had with a single blow of his sword split asunder the skull of a tiger (*nalwa*) that had him in its grip. That won the Austrian brownie points and the pampering of the guest began in earnest. Servants shuttled in 'twenty-five plates of sweetmeats, and a dozen baskets of fruit'. Hari Singh then showed his guest around the house where 'every room was hung and covered with the richest carpets of Kashmir and Kabul'. And when the traveller mentioned the cold he had braved over the past several days, portable braziers were ordered for the apartment where he was to sleep.

Von Hügel found Hari Singh a frank and affable person who was well conversant with the world:

> [The] conversation was very different from the majority of such interviews in India, and really consisted of a due exchange of ideas, and of references to events which had actually taken place: he is well informed on the statistics of many of the European States, and on the policy of the East India Company.

Hari Singh Nalwa, the man whose name rang in homes in Peshawar and Kohat to bring unruly children to heel a hundred and fifty years after he died, was not just a great general who fell in the fort of Jamrud valiantly fighting his Pakhtun foes; he possessed a green thumb, class and was a an intellectual to boot. With a degree of admiration von Hügel commented that the man could read and write Persian, a very rare thing among the Sikhs!

It was to this 'palace' I was headed in November 1991, my mind filled with great images of carpeted rooms and a garden. The streets were still uncrowded, and I had heard the old residence of the Nalwa was now called Anyaan di Maseet – Mosque of the Blind. In the place of Hari Singh Nalwa, the man presiding over more spiritual matters was the pleasant Maulvi Yasin. In the upheaval of 1947, the Sikhs left Gujranwala, and Muslims from East Punjab took over the properties they left. That was when Maulvi Yasin acquired the building and started his religious school. He called his son Mubashir to conduct me around the house. We ascended to the top floor from where, in my imagination, I would look down upon the garden Nalwa had once hoed and weeded. Instead a very warren of narrow streets bordered by blockhouses two or three storeys high stared up at us. Not a blade of grass or a flower was in sight. Downstairs Mubashir walked me from room to room where I imagined the Austrian's spirit would be seated sipping the brandy sent him by Ventura, the Maharaja's general in Lahore. But most of them stuffed with old and broken furniture. Just when I began to doubt if this really was Nalwa's house, we found in a room a marble plaque that read:

Residence of
Sardar Hari Singh Nalwa
A.D. 1791–1837

Below the English inscription was the same information in Urdu. This plaque was not the work of the local government or the deputy commissioner's office, it had been installed above the ground floor doorway during Raj times. It was removed when Maulvi Yasin did some repair work and placed in the room. On two later visits, the plaque was either missing or had miraculously reappeared until I requested Mubashir to please have it plastered into a wall before it was lost forever.

From the slim, shaven twentyish man I knew three decades ago, Mubashir is now a portly, full-bearded maulvi with a hefty paunch. Having proclaimed his late father a saint of sorts, he affects an air of spirituality, Thankfully, he still regards me a friend and remains always welcoming.

About twenty years ago, on another visit to Nalwa's home I had been caught in a traffic jam of humanity. So thick was the press of humans that it was impossible for several minutes for anyone to move. Now in January 2019, I had warned Azeem about it and we resolved to attack the place before the town woke. With rain pattering down at 6:30 in the morning we walked the deserted streets to the house and found Mubashir still groggy with sleep. But he was kind enough to entertain us and point out the marble plaque, now securely fixed in a wall.

The façade of the house, that could only be seen standing right below it because of the narrowness of the street, has completely changed. The mock pillars and arches are gone; the beautifully ornate timber bay window replaced by ugly steel fittings and the exterior plastered with modern cement, concealing the old brickwork. Happily the woodwork of the room where Maulvi Yasin held court, is still intact.

If this book aims to draw folks to our heritage, the Mosque of the Blind is the last place an ordinary tourist would muster the boldness to venture to through the workday press of humanity that leads to the old house. Only a direct descendent of the great general or a devout Sikh yearning for the lost glory of the time of Maharaja Ranjit Singh would enter those heaving rivers of humanity that those streets become during the day.

And then there was that yellow washed house in the vegetable market which had a plaque outside a first floor room proclaiming:

Maharaja Ranjit Singh
Born 2nd November 1780[1]

As on the slab in Nalwa's house, this one too had an Urdu translation. Again, this too was installed by some thoughtful Raj officer over a hundred years ago. With rain pattering down, Azeem, his assistant Ali and I squished through thick slush to the vegetable market. All was changed. The old house, once clearly visible, could not be seen. I asked one shopkeeper after another and all said there was nothing of the sort here. Not ever, one or two asserted.

I had photographed the house and the commemorative plaque in 1991. In 1996 or the year after, I heard land grabbers were hard at work to try and demolish the historical building and raise a monstrosity in its place. For a couple of years the struggle continued between those lusting for monetary gain and government officials trying weakly to resist the destruction. Then all went quiet. The foul deed was done, so I thought. And so short is human memory that within the space of a decade, what once was slipped from human minds. In fact, a portion of the building was damaged changing its outward look, the major part and the plaque inside remained intact and the district administration took custody of the building. At the time of this writing, it had been saved from further vandalism.

After the death of his father, Maha Singh, only fourteen years old, swiftly consolidated his power, increasing his armed followers to six thousand and acquiring additional territory around Gujranwala. Defeating the Kanhaya Sikhs and killing the chief's son, Maha Singh forced the old man to betroth his granddaughter Mehtab Kaur to his young son Budh Singh.

It was this Budh (Wise) Singh who was soon to be renamed Ranjit (Combat Victor) when his father returned from another victorious encounter against the Muslim Chatthas. In 1792, Maha Singh invested the nearby town of Sodhra, that old staging post on the Grand Trunk Road before Sher Shah realigned the thoroughfare to pass through where Wazirabad was later established. The Bhangi Sikhs holding the walled town resisted and the

---

1) The date is moot. Quoting earlier historians, Khushwant Singh tells us that it was more likely 13 November of the same year. It is also postulated that Ranjit Singh was not born in Gujranwala, but in the fortified village of Budrukhan in Jind for his mother, Raj Kaur, was the daughter of Raja Gajpat Singh of Jind and may have been in her parents' home for her first child.

siege dragged on for months. Maha Singh came down with a serious bout of dysentery and perhaps sensing that his end was near, proclaimed his twelve year old son Ranjit the chief of the Sukerchakia *misl*.

The siege was lifted and the ailing Maha and his young chieftain son returned to Gujranwala. Meanwhile, hearing of the illness of Maha Singh and that the *misl* was now led by a twelve year-old stripling, the Bhangi leaders of Lahore hastened to the aid of Sodhra. They had underestimated the mettle of young Ranjit. Ambushing them in the vicinity of Gujranwala, he routed the Bhangis. The last word the ailing and dehydrated Maha Singh heard before giving up his ghost was that his boy truly was the Victor of Battles.

Here was a mere lad, his face pitted by a childhood attack of smallpox that had left him blind in the left eye; if anything he was hardly impressive. The fatherless boy took no interest in the estate left behind by his father; instead he spent his time hunting in the riverine forests. On one such hunting expedition all by himself, he was attacked by a man who had suffered much at the hands of Maha Singh. The boy, then just thirteen, cut off the head of his adversary and carried it back to his camp impaled on his spear.

It seemed Ranjit Singh was on the way to making a small time gangster, at best a freebooter confined to Gujranwala, his immense genius and physical courage going waste. Without a mentor, he could well have been swept away by men more powerful than himself. Perhaps to give his life some direction, his widowed mother pressed him into marriage with his fiancée Mehtab Kaur when he was just fifteen. That done, he had the support of a dynamic and astute woman. If the young Ranjit Singh had directionless ambition, his mother-in-law Sada Kaur became his rudder to glory.

It was under her direction in 1799 that Ranjit Singh took Lahore in the debilitating summer heat of July. As he rode into the city from Lohari Gate in the south, Sada Kaur brought her troopers charging in from Delhi Gate. Lahore fell to the Sikh lad and with that fall there rose a Punjabi leader whose empire in thirty years would stretch from Multan to Kashmir and from Amritsar to the Khyber Pass.

A year later, having made peace with his erstwhile foe Shah Zaman of Afghanistan, Ranjit was caught in a web of intrigue: wary of his rising power and wishing to replace him as Punjabi leader, the other Sikh Sardars were intriguing to side with the Afghan should he venture another attack. Meanwhile, British agents were trying to keep Ranjit away from the Afghans. In October 1800, a meeting was held in Lahore to unravel the intrigue. Besides Ranjit Singh, his two close aides and the British agent, the only other person present was Sada Kaur.

History is silent on what part the astute and skilful widow played or how she prevailed upon the course of the decision made that day, but she would surely have been of great consequence. Ranjit Singh resolved that day to distance himself from the Afghans.

But things change and Sada Kaur who clearly propelled a young chief to become Maharaja of Punjab was soon estranged from her son-in-law. It was because while her own daughter Mehtab Kaur had failed to produce an heir, Ranjit's second wife Raj Kaur whom he married in 1798, had presented the Punjabi kingdom with prince Kharrak Singh in 1802. If hell hath no fury like a woman scorned, by 1808 there was no love lost between Sada Kaur and her son-in-law. The crafty woman conveyed to the British that should they attack Punjab, they would find her on their side. But it was too late. Maharaja Ranjit Singh was here to stay until death would tear him away in June 1839.

The house in Gujranwala where he was purportedly born, was saved from destruction by a hair's breadth. But the *baradari* with its rich frescos that Ranjit had ordered in his Sheranwala Bagh – Lion Garden – so named because, it is related, there he kept a pair of lions in a cage met with doom earlier in December 1992.

The building on a square plan with three doorways on each side had a smaller pavilion on the first floor above which stood yet another single room. The ground floor had a busy, ornate interior with few plain spaces. The frescos of platters of fruit with bulbuls and parakeets pecking at them amid irises, roses and intertwining vines were a lovely riot of colour. The building was entirely secular without a trace of Sikh or any other religious symbolism. Whenever I went there, I found students lounging in the cool shade cramming their lessons or men just loafing around. A junkie or two would complete the scene.

Early in December 1992, zealots in India tore down the early sixteenth century Babri Mosque for they believed it had been erected after razing an ancient temple of Lord Rama. The dust of the fallen mosque had barely settled when crazed mobs went for every Hindu, Jain or Sikh building regardless of the use it had been in. Among the hundreds of buildings destroyed in Pakistan, the beautiful baradari of Ranjit Singh too became a heap of masonry. It remained that way for a very long time.

But when Azeem, Ali and I went there in January 2019, a brand new baradari stood on the plinth where for two decades only a heap of masonry had been. Inside, an attempt to recreate the old frescoes has been made. The result is gaudy compared to the original, but I have no way of comparing what once was and what we have now. As we stood there, I lamented that all the transparencies from my 1991 work in Gujranwala were destroyed by fungus in the humid summers of Lahore.

I returned to Sheranwala Bagh a couple of years after the mindless destruction of its *baradari*. It was winter and a few middle-aged men were sunning themselves on the edge of the rubble heap that was once the baradari. After our preliminary pleasantries I asked if anyone of them had taken part in the demolition of the building.
'We, the four of us, grew up in Gujranwala. As children we played in these grounds and when we were tired, we rested in the cool shade of the building. It was always cool inside, even when it was hot out,' said one.

Then they all broke out speaking at once: it was madness to tear down the building. It was just like 1947 when lunatics ran wild across the country looting, burning and destroying whatever belonged to the other side. The destruction of this beautiful *baradari* was madness, they raved all together.

'Did anyone of you try to stop the hooligans?' I asked.

'Not just us. Many other older men joined us. We screamed ourselves hoarse to stop the madness but the mullahs leading the maddened mob screamed louder and rabidly. There were so many mullahs leading the attack, we did not stand a chance,' said the one who had spoken first.

They said the word was that a treasure was possibly concealed within the building. But the demolition was without any order and when the foundation was undermined, the whole came down rather swiftly. There were some vague tales of a move to turn the garden into a shopping mall but they could not say why that did not happen. They were just happy that they still had a tree-shaded open space to stretch their legs. As for the purported treasure, none was found when the rubble was removed to build the new structure.

Nearby, the lofty dome of Maha Singh's Samadhi sits above its tall octagonal drum. I was told that the mob did go for this building too, their goal was the two-tier metal finial above the dome. The word was that it was pure gold. Fortunately, however, by the time they were done with the *baradari*, a large police force had arrived to save the Samadhi.

There was another building that came under attack that December. The temple of Baddoke Gosaian, just off and to the west of the Grand Trunk Road near Gujranwala cantonment. We drove back in the direction of Wazirabad. Just short of Gakkhar Mandi, between the wall of the electricity grid station and the narrow distribution canal we took the road west to village Baddoke Gosaian.

In 1991, it was a lovely little religious monument standing in the middle of a square pond filled with blue-green water teeming with fish. The temple's porched door faced east and a walkway bridged over eight lovely arches connected it to the edge of the pond. The arches were strengthened by buttresses topped with stylised domelets. Surrounded by green fields where lowing cattle and the call of the bulbuls and mynas was the only sound, this was a very idyll.

The building was surprisingly free of expressions of love between various letters of the alphabet. Though a country road passed right in front of it, the temple seemed to have been forgotten by vandals. The sleepy watchman said he was there to keep people from stealing the fish, protecting the monument was not part of his responsibility, however. For someone with little interest in the house of worship, he nonetheless knew its story.

Though the temple is of more recent provenance, it is connected with an early sixteenth century saint. The old watchman was the keeper of the tale of Rama Nand: as a seven year-old he took his father's cattle grazing and routinely let them browse in the cornfields. When his father came to check the fields on the complaints of the farmers, he found the crops untouched. Daily farmers saw the cattle feeding in their fields and when Rama Nand took them away, the fields miraculously reverted to their original form. It did not take long for people to mark the child as no ordinary human.

Soon it came time for the saintly young man to be wedded. He refused saying he wished to follow the way of the *brahmacharya*, eschewing all pleasure and spending his time in the worship of his Lord. But the family would have nothing of that and a day for his betrothal was fixed. Rama Nand went that day to the village pond to bathe, so the tale goes. There he stuck his walking stick in the wet mud and disappeared into the water. All attempts to recover his body failed.

Time passed and Rama Nand did not return. Except that the staff he had stuck in the mud turned into a full-blown zizyphus tree. In the shade of this miraculous tree, the saintly youngster's mother daily came to grieve. One day Rama Nand appeared to her and told her not to weep for he would meet her every day. The condition was that she would keep these meetings secret. After a few days, the mother could no longer contain herself and broke her pledge. That was the last time the saint was ever seen.

The pond became sacred and sometime about the later years of the seventeenth century, the temple was raised in its centre and in time it became the site of a major religious gathering in the middle of the Punjabi month of Bisakhi (end April). In the 1860s, the affluent Diwan families of Eminabad executed the project of brick lining the pond. They also constructed a water channel to keep the pond full.

Interestingly, there is a zizyphus tree standing on the southwest corner of the temple, just by the side of the pond. It is huge in size with a thick trunk and clearly of a great age. In 1991, the watchman told me this was the very tree that had sprouted from Rama Nand's desiccated walking stick. Under it sits another small temple of a very recent date.

The temple at Baddoke Gosaian dedicated to the saint Rama Nand. The pond into which he miraculously disappeared is now dry, its water supply having been cut off years ago. In the 1990s, the pond was stocked with fish which was auctioned annually.

Shortly after the destruction of the Sheranwala Bagh baradari, I had returned to check out the temple. The old watchman was at hand to tell me how single-handed and heroically he had prevented the maddened mob from destroying the building. They made a deal with him: the temple would be spared if he permitted them to remove the 'gold' finial on the top of the spire. And so one man climbed up the roof of the portico and with the help of a noose brought down the three-tiered ornament. It turned out to be copper and in a fit of frenzy the mob beat it completely out of shape with clubs and bricks. The man was happy that the trade-off was good or there would have been no temple left.

On site with Azeem and Ali in 2019, I noted that the spire is now much desecrated with names and expressions of love gouged into the plaster. One wonders what manner of love it is that leads people to such vandalism. The beautiful painting of Surya the sun god in his chariot adorning the niche of the west façade has been rubbed out and there is considerable damage to the plaster all around. The saddest part is that the pond that was filled by an irrigation channel and once had fish enough to be annually contracted out, is now dry. And there is no watchman to tell stories.

∾

We gave up the modern Grand Trunk Road that passes through Kamoke to Muridke and on to Lahore. This was laid out in the 1880s when British civil servants turned somnolent little Kamoke into a grain market complete with a railway station and road connection. We took the old road heading for Eminabad. Just short of what was once a town rich with fabulous mansions and walled gardens, rises a chunky red building amid the fields. This is imposing gateway of Gurdwara Rori Sahib.

Sikh lore has Guru Nanak Dev passing through here on one of his many journeys. Wearied by a long slog, he sat down by a heap of refuse (*rori* in Punjabi). For those who followed the great Guru's way, the spot became hallowed and they began congregating here periodically. Sometime late in the seventeenth century, a baoli was built here to facilitate pilgrims. In the early 1990s, its water was polluted and it had not been in use for many years but it still had a beautiful multi-cusped arch where the stairway entered the well shaft. Since we have scant regard for historical buildings, at some point it was filled in and covered over.

In those days, the temple was deserted. The Muslim keeper said few pilgrims visited. And fewer still came to appreciate the fantasy of architecture that Rori Sahib represents. Work on the building began in the first decade of the twentieth century when the Spanish architect Antoni Gaudi had gained fame in Europe for his creative use of plastic forms of ornamentation. Had Gaudi passed along the Grand Trunk Road, the magnificent gateway would have astounded him for its beauty and flowing lines that seem to have been created from clay. But the material is all cut or moulded brick, finely baked to redness.

We do not know who the architect was. If he was trained at the Mayo School of Arts (now National College of Arts), Lahore, he would surely have been inspired by Gaudi. It is, however, more likely than not that the man was a mason – the traditional *mistri* – who had learnt his craft in the tutelage of local masters. In which case, he possessed a remarkably inventive and original mind for he created a very wonderland of curvilinear forms and Gurmukhi writing. All this in baked brick.

In the early years of the twentieth century, there was a class of British architects who dismissed the local *mistri* for being useless in the British scheme of architecture. But there were others who believed much was to be learned from local traditionalists. The nameless creator of this great fantasy outside Eminabad would surely have pleased the latter proponents.

The noted architect and architectural historian Kamil Khan Mumtaz is all praise for the unknown *mistri* of Rori Sahib. He says there is an 'amazing dexterity with which brickwork has been used to produce a plastic and almost sensuous quality'. In his view, the bold forms created thus are based on traditional practice but take the use of baked brick beyond known limits. Indeed, the building is a sight to be beheld, not merely to be read about or seen as an image.

Behind the lofty gateway stands the little gurdwara where the copy of the holy Granth Sahib rests. This building dates to the early nineteenth century. Nearby is the sacred pond for ablution and around it the architectural fantasy continues with more domes and free standing arches.

After years of neglect, the gurdwara is again a centre of regular worship and part of the pilgrimage circuit for local and visiting Sikhs. Besides the Muslim minders, it has a complement of resident Sikh keepers together with a Granthi (priest). If many years ago I had just wandered in, there is now an iron fence girding the grounds and the Muslim minders permit non-Sikh visitors in only after a bit of grilling.

Guru Nanak Dev went on to Eminabad. And so did we.

Once without doubt the most beautifully ornate *haveli* of Eminabad, this early nineteenth century building was home to the rich diwans who served the Dogra raja of Kashmir. With the family having left Eminabad in 1947, the building fell into the hands of refugees who cared little for it letting it crumble to pieces.

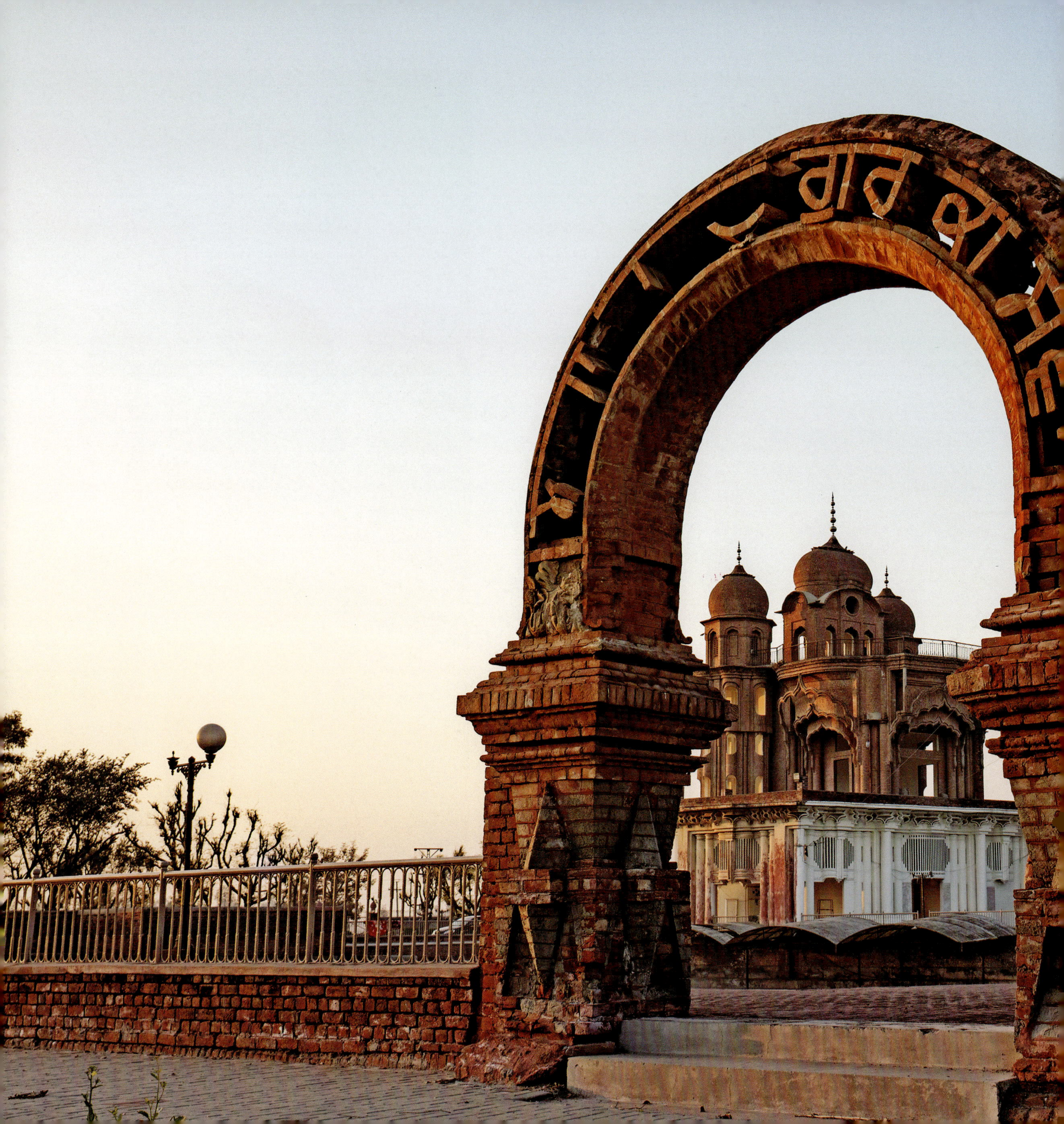

from Landi Kotal to Wagah | **187** | Maharaja Ranjit Singh Ruled Here

Gurdwara Rori Sahib, Eminabad in Gujranwala district is remarkable for its plastic forms created by cut and moulded bricks.

The last of the four corner turrets on the boundary wall of Begum da Maqbara (Tomb of the Begum).

The late Mughal period Begum da Maqbara - Tomb of the Begum - with the Lodhi mosque seen in the background.

But unlike the Guru we did not pause in town but drove straight around on to the old Grand Trunk Road leading to Wahndo and ever onward to the east. A few kilometres outside town stood the large tank fed by a natural waterway, its brick-lined sides and the stairs leading down to the water gradually crumbling. We were still a couple of hundred metres away when the squat dome of the mosque became visible.

'Pre-Mughal!' Azeem declared excitedly.

That meant the mosque was fifteenth century.

Tamerlane died in 1405. In the ensuing peace with no outside intervention, a family claiming to be Syeds (descendants of the fourth caliph) rose to power. Their weakness and ineptitude was soon noticed and taken full advantage of by the turbulent Khokhars of Punjab and for fully three decades the country lay in a state of turmoil. There now rose to prominence a man called Bahlol Lodhi, adept in the art of war and sufficiently canny to outwit and oust the Syeds and mount the throne of Delhi. He ruled from 1450, bringing peace to a country long brutalised by mindless bloodshed and established a dynasty to last six decades. Tamerlane had been dead a long time, Babur was still waiting to be born. In that period of peace the Grand Trunk Road going through Eminabad was a busy thoroughfare and the city earned a good deal of cess on passing trade. This made for affluence in the eighteenth century when several prosperous Hindu families of Eminabad served the Dogra rulers of Kashmir as ministers and advisors.

After Bahlol died in 1489, it took only a few more years for Babur to start breathing down the Indian neck. Therefore, if any major construction work was carried out, it was in this period of peace in Bahlol's time. In the collective memory of the people of Eminabad, this mosque casting a narcissistic reflection in the placid waters of the pond is 'Lodhi Mosque'. Azeem could not have agreed more with the Eminabadis.

Five and a half centuries on from the time the muezzin first called the faithful to prayer under its dome, the brickwork is still sturdy. When it was first built, the mosque had a pillared veranda in front for one can still see the remains of the arch where the cantilever of the portico sprang outward from the main building. The plaster is all gone except where it was protected by the overhang of the veranda. This is decorated with a repetitive leaf motif all around the building.

In 1991, the dome of the mosque had a wide cleft and I had gone away with fear that the building would not last many more monsoon rains. This time round we found the dome repaired. Though the work did not entirely meet Azeem's approval because of the use of modern cement, we were nonetheless happy that at least further damage from rainwater seepage had been prevented.

Facing the mosque is a ruined walled compound measuring some twenty metres square, its interior completely overgrown and its brickwork lying in heaps all around. When it was complete, the four corners of the compound were crowned by pillared chambers open on all sides and topped with domes. Of these only one remains now. In 1991, I had seen a simple grave in the centre of the compound. The elderly man living in the nearby house told me they called it Begum da Maqbara – Tomb of the Begum. Who the begum was drew a blank. Now the grave is no longer there.

The Lodhi mosque once had a large overhang on the façade which may have extended to form a pillared veranda. Now only a trace of the overhang remains and if there were pillars their foundations have been removed for cultivation.

Archaeologist friends in Lahore told me a certain Mir Ahmed Khan, a courtier in the latter years of Mughal rule, buried his wife here when she died on a journey between Lahore and Kashmir. The architecture is clearly late Mughal and the building seems to have not been of a high standard to have decayed so completely. Perhaps Ahmed Khan was not a man of means or of much significance.

∞

Rain cut short our fieldwork yet again and I returned to Eminabad a few weeks later, this time with Emily Macinnes from Scotland. She had come out to make a short film on the monuments of the Grand Trunk Road in Pakistan. We went through the Eminabad bazaar to the east end of town with its last remaining haveli from the early years of the nineteenth century. Local tradition attributes this beautifully painted, but dilapidated, building to the Diwans who served the Kashmir Dogras. Thirty years ago there were a generation who recalled those families and their departure in 1947.

Today Eminabad seems to be losing sight of its rich cultural and built heritage with most of its old houses demolished. But on this outing with Emily I had a pleasant experience. With her camera on the tripod, Emily was filming the painted façade of the ramshackle four storey house when a woman called out to me from a newish house on my left.
'You have to come see our house. It's very old and we have a cellar with a raised podium and a lovely arch.'

Telling Emily to carry on, I ducked into the house and Romila led me down a darkened flight of stairs composed of the old Nanak Shahi bricks. The cellar was square in plan and littered with old items of household use. In the dim light of my torch I could see the raised platform with two arches. The main arch was crudely repaired at some point while the smaller one to its right was in its original form. The platform, accessible from a doorway in the back which was blocked, was more like a small gallery to look down to where we stood. The walls all around had niches for lamps. Pointing to an opening on one side, Romila said that led to a well which too was sealed years ago.

When they had in-house wells, the cellar, with its temperature modulated by its nearness to water, was called a *sard khana* – cold room. The raised platform with access from the back would once have been suitably furnished for relaxation on hot summer afternoons. Servants coming down to fetch water would not have disturbed the repose of the master and his family for they would have used the same stairs as us. Above us, the ceiling had squinches on the four corners indicating where the dome sprang. But now there was none, only an iron grate cemented on to the opening left by the collapsed dome.

Romila is a most remarkable woman. Living in provincial little Eminabad she had somehow developed interest in history. 'I read, but I cannot commit to memory,' she complained. When she wedded her husband Naqib Khan in 2002 and came to this house, there were still multi-storey houses in this neighbourhood. Why, her own sister-in-law who lived across the lane had a five-storey house which she tore down. The timber alone, teak and pine, was sold for three million rupees, said Romila. This was perhaps the first time someone had come to talk to her for she was in a hurry to tell all.
'There is just no awareness, no sense of history or the value of what they have. And why would they? Those who were but servants and sharecroppers until August 1947 overnight became owners of great wealth they did not have to work for. They do not care for what they have. Anyone still living in an old house is waiting for money to tear it down and build anew in its place.' Romila was breathless with lamentation.

Naqib mentioned the discovery of some old coins when they tore down a wall. Excitedly I asked if I could see them. But he had given them to his sister, the one who had demolished her own house and moved away, and the coins were no longer traceable.

Curious about Emily's film making Romila asked what we were doing and I told the couple about the book on the Grand Trunk Road.

'Oh, the King's Highway,' said Naqib. I was rather surprised by his use of the English title for the road and asked him where he had heard it. He smiled and said nothing. Romila's enthusiasm for history seemed to have rubbed off.

The couple recalled the time in the early years of the century when art and architecture students from Lahore's various colleges routinely visited Eminabad. The students were very interested in the old architecture. By Naqib's account they ran amok across town making sketches, measuring and taking notes.

'They raced down the stairs into our basement. And they went to every old *haveli*,' added Romila. 'Alas, nothing is now left. And we haven't seen students for years.'

∽

The road east from Eminabad leads to Wahndo. Ask anyone for Kotli Maqbara and directions will be forthcoming. But ask for Deo Minara (Minaret of the Giant or Djinn) and you draw blanks. Thirty years ago, the story was that djinns were assigned to build a mausoleum. Being djinns, they worked secretly during the night and went into hiding before daybreak. Their alarm clock being the noises of people waking to begin their daily routine. One morning, well before sunrise, a woman who kept a herd of camels roused from sleep early and thinking it was time, set to work her milk churn.

Panicked that they were caught working late, the djinns fled. But they soon realised their error and cursed the woman, 'May your milk never yield butter.' The story went that it was since that day camel's milk has ceased yielding butter. This is not an original Gujranwala tale, however. It is a recurrent theme across several areas of Punjab and Sindh. Nevertheless, Deo Minara, clearly a late Mughal period monument, retains its aura of mystery.

Well off the main axis of the modern Grand Trunk Road, the tomb sits on the direct line between Eminabad and Amritsar and thence on to Delhi. It would be folly to say that such an alignment did not exist for we know that the Rajapatha even in ancient times followed at least three parallel lines in Khyber Pakhtunkhwa and Punjab. As well as that, there were a number of subsidiary byways.

In 1991, when my wanderings first betook me to Deo Minara, all my queries about the three burials in the subterranean vault turned up blanks. 'This building has stood here since the time of our grandfathers and no one knows whose remains it contains,' was the refrain of anyone I asked. To invoke the grandfathers was to indicate an age of 'thousands of years'.

Then one man told me of the woman who came dancing one day. She unshod herself a hundred metres from the tomb and with a great show of reverence came up to put her forehead on the entrance to the underground burial chamber. Curious locals were told that it had been revealed to her in a dream that three holy personages reposed under the imposing dome and she had been ordered to be the keeper of the shrine.

Thereafter she returned every Thursday in a van with a cauldron of food to distribute to the locals. Amused by my narration, friends in the district administration and police, Kamran Rasool, the commissioner and Iqbal Malik, the senior superintendent of police, set the state machinery working to unravel the secret of the dancing woman: she turned out to be a courtesan from Chhicherwali, a village just outside Gujranwala.

Having reached her fifties, an age where such persons retire, she had claimed the tomb as her source of perpetual income. With no other 'descendants' since the 'time of the grandfathers' to dispute her stake, it worked. In a society as superstitious and quasi-religious as ours, nothing could have been easier. The weekly investment in food for locals paid off and when I returned exactly a year after my first visit, I was told that the village was blessed by the presence of three holy burials. But only last year they were unidentified, I protested.
'What are you talking about? These holy men have been worshipped since the time of our grandfathers!' came the rebuke.

People now took off their shoes below the plinth and the boys who once played cricket in the open ground floor space under the dome were no longer permitted to desecrate the newly hallowed ground. There were no names for the three holy persons, however. I returned again after a gap of nine years. The new century had dawned and on the entrance to the subterranean chamber stood a sign in Urdu: Hazrat Pir Makki Shah and Hazrat Pir Atray Shah. It was only logical for a holy person to be Makki – from Mecca, but Atray was inexplicable. The woman who visited weekly was still around and she had planted the sign some years previously. For some curious reason she had failed to conjure up a name for the third grave. All three graves were covered with cheap shiny satin with Quranic verses and images of the Ka'ba. The apotheosis of three very worldly men was complete.

I returned to Kotli Maqbara in March 2019 and parked the car near two men about my age. Atray Shah? Makki Shah? They looked at me as if I were stupid.
'This is just a Mughal tomb,' said one. 'A man once came here many years ago telling us the name. But we forget now. It doesn't matter as long as we know it's Mughal.'

For Mughal, he used the word Chagatta with the accent hard on the final syllable. This term used for Mughals derives from Chagata Khan, the second son of Chengez Khan.[2] I have always felt Chagatta has a derogatory undertone and goes back to the time when the Punjabi peasantry chaffed under the strict Mughal taxation system.

I insisted it was a holy burial and the grey-bearded one smiled wryly, clearly not believing me. Surprisingly, nei-

---

2) Chengez being closest to the actual pronunciation of the Mongolian name, I prefer it over the accepted Ghengiz Khan.

ther man recalled the dancing woman or the van with the cauldron of rice and chicken she brought on Thursdays. Both men insisted the building had always been secular and that boys played cricket under its dome. Indeed, even as I went in and out without taking off my shoes no one objected.

It is surprising how short-lived human memories are. I imagine the dancing woman died sometime after my visit in 2001. The weekly parties ceased, over time the sign with the names rotted and the tomb went back to being what it had always been. Within years everything was forgotten.

In 1991, having never read of this building or seen its images, I ran off with the notion that I had discovered a hitherto unknown monument. Gloating, I went with images to my mentor Dr Saifur Rahman Dar. Just a short phrase from him killed my euphoria, 'Well,' he said, 'it so happens that the building has been discovered by others before you.'

Diwan Abdul Nabi Khan, who served Shah Jahan and his son Aurangzeb in ministerial positions died on his passage through the area. According to Dr Dar, it is not known if he was travelling through or hunting in this area. But we do know that before the canals transformed primal forest into farmland in the closing years of the nineteenth century, this country was rich with forest and wild animals, especially ungulates the favourite prey of Mughal hunters. In fact, hog deer and blue bull were quite common until fifty years ago. My mentor believed there was every chance that Abdul Nabi was hunting here. But it is not known who the other two lie with him.

∞

Southeast of Eminabad, seventeen kilometres by Google Earth, but a little more through Sadhoke and Gunahor, the old Rajapatha crosses the Degh, properly Devka, rivulet. Washing the foothills of Jammu, the Degh had long been infamous for its monsoon floods that still flow the colour of the milk tea so popular in Pakistan. Then it is known to claim lives. When not in spate, it is languid with blue water, fish, turtles and boys splashing around in it. Nearer the modern Grand Trunk Road, it turns into poison from the several factories that dump their untreated waste into it.

In Gunahor people have a vague inkling of the old road passing by and crossing the Degh by what they call the Shah Daula Bridge. They attribute it to the generosity of the saint of that name buried in Gujrat. From the *Tuzk e Jahangiri* and the *Shah Jahan Nama* we know that both father and son, on their respective journeys, suffered from Degh floods. In October 1620, Jahangir was greatly vexed on his journey from Sheikhupura to Lahore when the downpour would not cease and the intervening Degh would not permit crossing. Not even on elephant back. For four days the king, his wives and the court hunkered in sodden tents until the stream abated. That year Jahangir ordered the construction of the bridge outside the village of Kot Pindi Das, many meandering kilometres downstream of this point.

Of the Shah Daula Bridge we have no definitive date, but

Tomb of Diwan Abdul Nabi Khan who served Shah Jahan and his son Aurangzeb. An attempt begun in the early 1990s to deify the tomb continued for a couple of years into the present century but failed to make the desired impact and was abandoned. Now everyone regards it as a Mughal tomb.

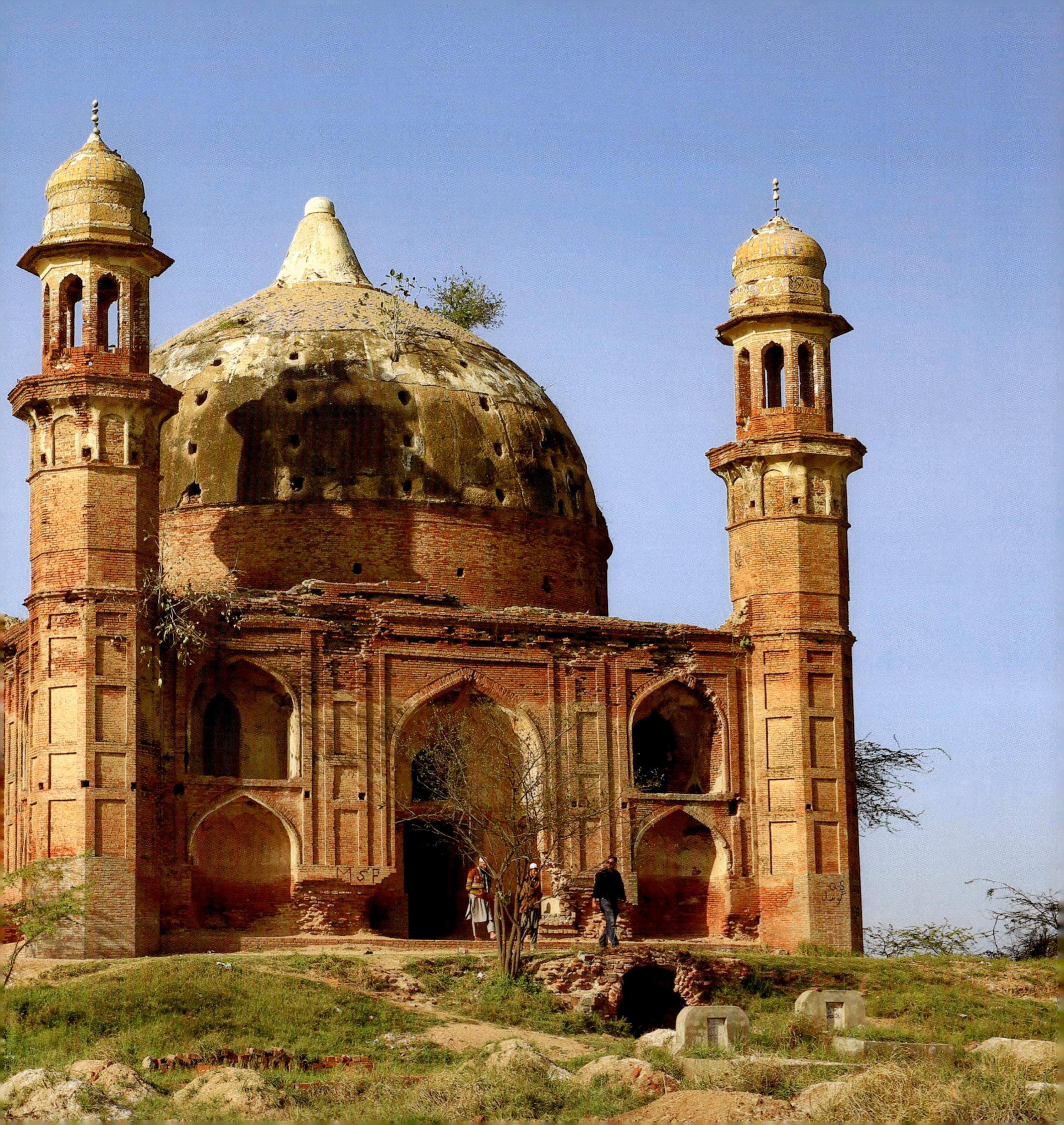
MSP

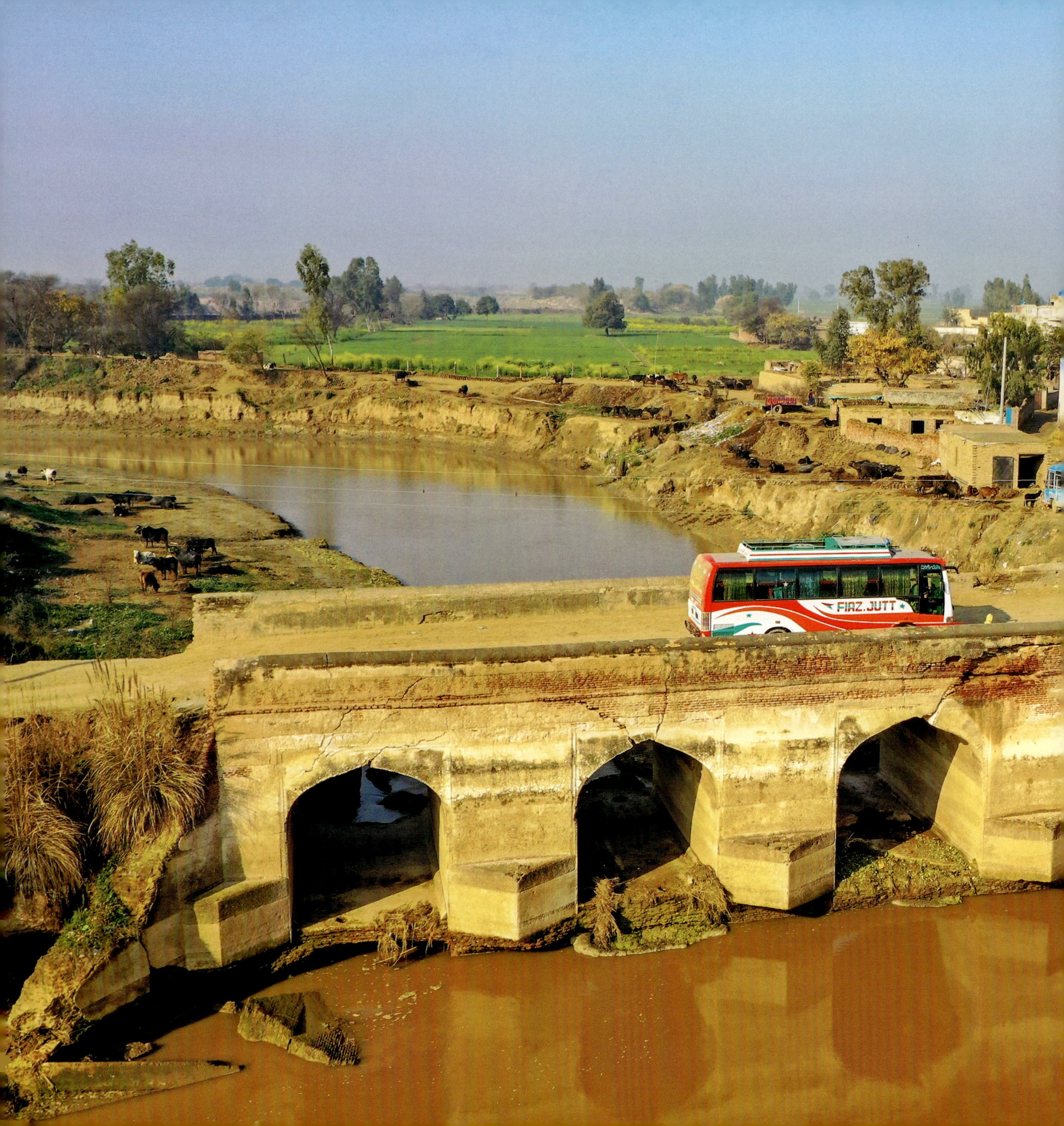
FIAZ JUTT

from Landi Kotal *to* Wagah

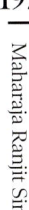

Maharaja Ranjit Singh Ruled Here

Four hundred years on and Shah Daula bridge spanning the Degh River shows no signs of sagging. Not even under the weight of heavily laden lorries or a bus as seen here.

going by its architecture, one can say it is of the same age as the other one. Here, just downstream of the bridge, there lies in the stream-bed the debris of an earlier structure whose story I heard from a young man more than a

The parapet of the Shah Daula bridge was once adorned with four mock turrets. Of them, this is the only one remaining.

decade ago. He said his grandfather who died at age one hundred and thirty (in Pakistan many seventy year-old persons claim that longevity), told him the story of the old bridge as he had heard it from his elders. The spans, said the youngster, were closed by gates carved out of solid blocks of rock. Their small openings let only a limited quantity of water through.

One summer a great flood bore down the river and there was every danger of the village being washed away. Yet with the water building up upstream no man dared enter the river and undo the sluices. When it seemed something drastic was just about to occur, one elderly man went in and no sooner had he undone the gates that the surge of water swept away the entire structure. In that outpouring the brave old man was also lost. The teller of my tale said his grandfather claimed that even his grandfather who, I presume, was also a few hundred years old, had not seen the original bridge.

My archaeologist friend, the soft-spoken late Tariq Masood was the keeper of the true story of Shah Daula Bridge. Quoting from a legend as recorded by A. C. Elliot and published in *Indian Antiquity* (February 1909) Masood tells how, Shah Jahan, as he journeyed to Kashmir, once lost several laden pack animals to a flood in the Degh. The administrator of the district, a certain Mirza Badi uz Zaman, was ordered to immediately build a bridge and have it ready before the emperor's return journey.

That very likely being monsoon season when kilns traditionally shut down in Punjab, the Mirza was hard put to procure fired bricks. All he could come by were mud bricks useless for bridge building. In a fit of rage he imprisoned all brick-makers and when the emperor returned was nowhere near beginning construction. Upon being rebuked, the Mirza is said to have told the emperor that it was only Shah Daula, the doer of public works, who could build the bridge. And so the saint was called for from Gujrat and the bridge constructed under his supervision.

The origin of this legend lies in the reputation of Shah Daula as a great patron of public works in Sialkot, where he first lived, and in Gujrat subsequently where he was buried. The chronology placing him contemporary with Shah Jahan is not incorrect: having been born in 1581 during the reign of Akbar, Shah Daula lived through the reigns of Jahangir, Shah Jahan and Aurangzeb until his death in 1676.

The king's summons for him to come build the bridge could just be legend that plays on a reputation for public service that Kabiruddin, a Lodhi Pakhtun, better known to us as Shah Daula, had made for himself even before Shah Jahan's time. He is reputed to have built scores of inns, bridges, roadways, mosques, water tanks and wells for public use, acts for which he was much admired. Surely this tireless public service earned him the status of a saint. History tells us of devotees bringing him valuable gifts all of which the selfless and generous Kabiruddin Lodhi a.k.a Shah Daula spent on public works. On the other hand, it could be that the king trusted the experienced man to be able to do his bidding and ordered him to it. However, going by the architecture, the king would have been Jahangir and not Shah Jahan.

The *Khulasa tut Twarikh* (Compendium of Histories) of Subhan Rai is one source that definitely assigns this bridge to Shah Daula. It mentions a bridge built by him at a distance of five kos (about sixteen kilometres) from Eminabad on the highroad to Lahore. However, we get no date from this work.

It is said, Masood told had me, that the original name of the bridge was Pull (Bridge) Saadullah or Saadullahpur after Shah Jahan's prime minister and trusted general. But history does not mention the undertaking of a bridge building project in this area by Saadullah under Shah Jahan's orders. I would say that the bridge, already in place for a couple of decades, was named after the prime minister for a short while. But Saadullah meant nothing to the peasantry who used the facility. To them it was Shah Daula first and last. Also, the names sounding alike, the new name would have only seemed a mispronunciation of the original.

The most interesting bit from my late friend Tariq Masood concerned the events of the spring of 1707. It was noised that the aged Aurangzeb had finally given up the ghost. In their unholy haste to have themselves crowned king, his sons tripped over themselves and over each other. While Azam Shah quickly donned the crown in Ahmadnagar in the Deccan and hastened for the capital, Shah Alam turned to Agra from his posting at Jamrud outside Peshawar. As he arrived at the staging post of Shah Daula Bridge, word arrived from the east that his brother had already been crowned.

In order that he may enter the city of Lahore as a crowned king, Shah Alam went through a coronation ceremony at the bridge. Since the bridge is at most two days' journey from Lahore, the coronation would have taken place on the last day of April for history tells us that Shah Alam entered Lahore as another king of the sagging Mughal empire on the third day of May 1707.

But that was the past. Nothing spectacular or earth

shaking happens at Shah Daula Bridge anymore, except that fully laden Bedford trucks with axle weight of over fifteen tons still routinely pass over the four hundred year old bridge. However, in 2015, something mindlessly drastic came within a hair's breadth of occurring. With a brand new concrete bridge completed a couple of hundred metres upstream, the Punjab Department of Irrigation was in the process of beginning demolition of the historic span. It was a fortunate fluke of chance that I went to the bridge to photograph it digitally and heard from local men of the folly about to occur.

In a fluster I went to see the secretary of the department to plead for the preservation of the bridge. I was stunned by the man's contention: 'The old bridge constricts the passage of floodwaters. Since the new one is now in place, it is only logical that we tear down the old one.'

For four hundred years, I appealed, the bridge has weathered as many monsoon floods and there has never been any threat to life or property because of it. Why, even today laden trucks pass over it as testimony to its robustness. It still has decades of useful life. And when that life comes to an end, we yet need to preserve it as a model of seventeenth century civil engineering for students to learn from. It has never worked in my life, but this time my frantic and passionate pleading did.

Credit goes to Saif Anjum for my raving to have affected him. He called for the file and added a note to it to let the bridge be. He has moved on to other assignments and happily the bridge is still there and locals still congregate on its brink to sun themselves in winters or take the air on summer evenings.

For me there is an element of tragic irony. The good Kabiruddin Lodhi is celebrated not for the public service he did in his long life (1581–1676), by some quirk of fate he is remembered as Shah Daula and his shrine in Gujrat is the centre for parents to abandon their microcephalic children. These unfortunate children, the result of generations of inbreeding, are known as the 'rats' of Shah Daula, believed to have been begotten by the blessing of the long dead man.

The irony is only offset by his lingering association with the bridge. Those who use it, or live nearby, invoke his name even today. Through them his spirit of public service lives on.

∞

The Rajapatha of the classical age and our Grand Trunk Road on the bridge of Shah Daula would have placed Shah Alam within twenty-seven kilometres of Lahore Fort. We too headed the same way, but ours was no unholy haste, nor did we lust for a crown. And so we paused at Shahdara – Royal Gateway – on the right bank of the Ravi. Shahdara is now identified by the spreading quadrangle where Akbar ordered a caravanserai and which later became famous as the last rest place of his son Jahangir.

The exquisitely beautiful single-storey edifice, with four towering corner minarets is resplendent with white marble pietra dura on red granite. The red and white is offset by the yellow, brown and white chevron patterns that march up the four minarets. It is clear that a great deal of thought lay behind the architectural scheme. And it came from none other than the remarkable Nur Jahan.

Born in Kandahar to Mirza Ghias Baig, a Persian nobleman, and Asmat Begum as the couple journeyed to India, she was named Mehrun Nisa – Sun among Women. When still in her teens, she was wedded to Sher Afgan who was later in the service of Jahangir. In 1607, Sher Afgan was killed while on a mission to Bengal on behalf of his king. Some say the king had much to do with the dubious manner of the man's death for he was already besotted with the round-faced, full-lipped, almond-eyed beauty Mehrun Nisa. Four years later, in 1611, Mehrun Nisa became the last, and favourite wife, among seventeen others, of the emperor. As the queen she was first called Nur Mahal – Light of the Palace – and elevated a few years later to Nur Jahan – Light of the World. Her father became a trusted courtier titled Itamadud Daula and her brother Asif Khan also got high office.

Jahangir's fondness for Nur Jahan is demonstrated by the authority vested in her to sign royal *firmans* (decrees) and the coins he minted in her name. Indeed, Nur Jahan was no ordinary woman. Extremely athletic, she was a fine rider and a good polo player; in matters of administration and dealing with the court and visitors she was admirably competent. Nur Jahan was a first-rate marksman as well. On a hunt with the king on elephant back, she killed a tiger with a single shot from her musket. This won her much admiration from her husband and the event passed into the *Tuzk*. Had it not been for Jahangir's granddaughter Jahan Ara, I would have no quarrel with Annemarie Schimmel who terms Nur Jahan 'undoubtedly the most dynamic woman in the history of the Mughals'.

Jahangir's tomb

When Schimmel writes, 'Ineffectual aesthetes were no match for this cunning and energetic woman, who exploited their weakness for drugs and alcohol', she refers to Jahangir's dependence on an overuse of opium and alcohol. While the king, who on his travels became a naturalist but in his capital remained doped, it was only normal for the talented and vigorous queen to come to the fore. In this she was ably assisted by her brother Asif Khan. She was a rare queen who besides actively engaged in running the empire, managed an orphanage for girls and also traded in indigo grown on her own farms near Agra. The export of this commodity was overseen by her brother.

A general view of the Jahangir quadrangle from above the imposing inner gateway. The tomb itself is in the background.

Top Left: Looking east through the gateway leading into the garden quadrangle of Jahangir's tomb. Nur Jahan's fine taste is evident in the pietra dura and the overall architectural detail of this building.

Bottom Left: Jahangir's mausoleum in the middle of the traditional garden of four quadrants.

Top Right: Detail of decoration in the passageway leading to the cenotaph. Though the actual burial is in the basement below, the chamber in the background contains the ornate sepulchre.

Bottom Right: The form and symmetrical grace of Jahangir's mausoleum marks the zenith of architectural development during the latter years of the Mughal era.

In 2019, the tomb of Nur Jahan was under restoration work. Years earlier it had been a rather sombre brick structure devoid of its original decoration.

Interior of the tomb of Nur Jahan.

As a connoisseur of the arts, Nur Jahan displayed educated interest in textiles, both native and British imports. Schimmel believes that her appreciation of British needlework introduced new designs to Indian carpet manufacture. Unsurprisingly, when her husband died in October 1627, the grand mausoleum sitting in the centre of a spacious walled garden on the banks of the Ravi just outside Lahore was raised under Nur Jahan's instructions.

She survived her husband by eighteen years and her brother by four. And when she died, Nur Jahan, the builder of the magnificent Nurafshan (Light Scatterer) Garden on the Yamuna River near Agra, was buried in a simple single storey tomb, a hundred metres west of her king's burial place. The brick edifice was faced with marble which was plundered during the reign of Maharaja Ranjit Singh. The stone has since adorned Harmandir Sahib at Amritsar.

Images of the queen's tomb from my childhood have a dismal and lonely brick building exuding sadness. In life Queen Nur Jahan towered above Jahangir, who was scarcely worthy of her, in death she reposes almost under the shadow of the lofty minarets of the emperor's mausoleum. As if to accentuate the intellectual difference between the woman and her man – which was immense – the British separated the two by a railway line they put through what was once a magnificent Mughal garden.

Nowadays the garden around Jahangir's tomb is a picnic place. Every morning and evening men and young women walkers do their frantic circuits on the paved walkway

Tomb of Asif Khan. Originally heavily ornamented with marble and coloured stone, it was vandalised heavily during the reign of Maharaja Ranjit Singh.

around the tomb. For some reason, the younger lot and most men prefer circumabulating Jahangir's tomb while waddling matrons like going up and down the path leading to Asif Khan's separated from Jahangir's by the wide quadrangle of Akbar's caravanserai. A person with a camera on a tripod becomes a foreigner and a centre of curiosity for the bored 'aunties'.

Since a foreigner illiterate in the local language is understood to comprehend only if shouted to, the fat old women throw their first volley, in Punjabi, at the top of their voices. Addressing me with the traditional Punjabi *'Vay'*, one of them said 'No movie, no movie!' A response in Punjabi that I was not filming drew loud guffaws and jabs at each other with a surprised *'Nee*, he's a Punjabi!' The questions were mostly what and wherefore and ended with the emoluments to be gleaned for 'this work'.

I asked if they knew whose tomb they had at their back. 'Must be some Mughal prince. They say he was called Asif Khan,' said the eldest among the four. Her attitude was clearly don't-give-a-damn-if-he-was-someone-else.
'He wasn't a Mughal, but he was related to Jahangir's wife Nur Jahan,' I hinted.
'Must have been her boyfriend!' chirped the youngest of the lot, herself in her fifties. The dames exploded with laughter, their midriffs jiggling, even as they mock admonished the younger one.

Oh, the freedoms an eastern woman enjoys once past child-bearing age!

Younger girls, some in their teens, also came up to chat. They wanted to know which media house I represented. A writer was a bit of a disappointment, though. They asked if I was writing a television play, apparently the only redemption for me. I must have broken their young hearts with a negative.
'What *do* you write?' asked one.
'I write about history. And culture.' I never use the Urdu word for travel writer because that leads folks to equate me with one I label a scam for his misleading and totally faux work. The girls gave up on me and with polite good-byes walked away.

In sharp contrast to the liveliness of Jahangir's side, across the railway line Nur Jahan's tomb remains forlorn. Strangely so when it has recently been redone with red granite and white marble inlay and even a surrounding well-tended garden. It may be that the queen foresaw the abandonment that was to be her lot in death: for her tombstone she composed a verse dripping with melancholy. Annemarie Schimmel translates it:

On mine, the outsider's grave,
No candle and no light,
No burnt moth wings,
Nor nightingale song .....

The sun was setting when we left this sad premises. Azeem was in full flow with his tale of the outwitting of Shah Shuja by Maharaja Ranjit Singh. But that happened on the far side of the Ravi. That happened in the city that Raja Loh is supposed to have built.

A drone's eye view of the eastern part of Lahore walled city. Taken from just inside Delhi Darwaza, the view looks westward with Wazir Khan's mosque dominating the view. Though some few remain, most of the older architecture of the narrow alleys in the background has been replaced with modern structures, taking away much from the city.

The City that Loh Built

The monk Xuanzang whose innocent piety never fails to move me, set out of the monastery of Chang'an (modern Xian) in early 630 CE. He braved a hazardous journey across deserts, river valleys and high mountains, his heart set on India, the home of his Lord and Master the great Buddha. As a teacher and Master of the Law, Xuanzang was painfully aware of the deficiencies in the copies of scripture his school used. His quest was for the true word of Buddha. And so, for sixteen years the pious monk travelled around India collecting books, flower seeds and other relics connected with his Lord.

Back in Chang'an, Xuanzang wrote up a detailed account of his journey that we today know as *Buddhist Records of the Western World*. Since he would also narrate travel stories to his acolytes, one devoted student, the shaman Hwui Li, took careful note of every word the master uttered. After the master passed away, this man produced a book that comes to us as *The Life of Xuanzang*. Both works were translated from the original Chinese by the Orientalist Samuel Beal in the nineteenth century and reading them in conjunction, one learns a fascinating lot about life in our part of the world a century after the savagery unleashed by the Huns.

Hwui Li tells a very interesting story of his master's journey from Sialkot to a nameless city en route to Jalandhar. A day's journey short of this nameless city, as the pilgrim's caravan was passing through a dense forest, it was beset by robbers who took everything, including the clothes of the travellers. The day after the robbery, the caravan reached a 'great city' with 'several thousand dwellings'. The people of this nameless place, mostly Buddhist with some 'heretics' (Hindus or Jains) were a remarkably kind and hospitable lot. Upon hearing of the travellers' plight, a public request was made by the chief to recompense them. 'All hostile religious feeling was laid aside' and three hundred 'people of distinction' came forward with liberal donations of bolts of cotton, food and drink.[1]

Unsurprisingly, the master remained in this city a whole month, spending his time in religious study. From here he made his way to Che-lan-t'o-lo as the Chinese rendered Jalandhar in their phonetics. Beal believes the city of hospitable people was Lahore.

Born in 100 CE, Ptolemy, the Greek geographer and mathematician, wrote his *Geographia* about the middle of the following century. In it he mentioned Labaka, a city that some scholars believe would be Lohkot or Lavakota – the Fort of Loh or Lava. Now, Loh was the son of Lord Rama who is credited with founding Lahore that still carries his name. That alone does not indicate the city's great age, for any king or chieftain establishing their seat could name it after any religious figure regardless of how much they were separated by time. The question then is: how ancient is the city of Lahore?

---

1) The existence of 'hostile religious feeling' in that far off time marks social decline since the time of Alexander's sojourn in Punjab a thousand years earlier. The Macedonian's historians tell us that three communities, namely, Buddhist, Hindu and Zoroastrian lived in complete amity in Taxila.

Hard core Lahoris love to proclaim their city as the only one in Pakistan in constant habitation for the last five thousand years. In 1989 or the year after, the government of Punjab planned to celebrate Lahore's five thousand-year festival. Accordingly, a prominent archaeologist-historian was asked to write up the history. Unaware of the desired view, the scholar wrote the truth: that Lahore was at most two thousand years old.

He was requested to re-write his history to 'set the record straight'. Another paper was produced declaring Lahore five thousand years old! It was only our great good fortune that the festival was never held.

That was the beginning of the myth of Lahore's longevity.

Standing outside the east wall of Lahore Fort, Azeem told me of the exploratory trench made in the fort back in the 1960s. The deepest cultural layer dated to the Indo-Greeks who had annexed this part of the subcontinent around 180 BCE. Megasthenes, playing ambassador from Seleucus Nikator to the court of Chandragupta Maurya, was in India BCE 300-285. In his tenure, he travelled extensively around the country. Though he made repeated reference to the Rajapatha and the cities it traversed, he made no mention of the name Ptolemy mentioned four hundred years later.

Also, Xuanzang despite having been done a good turn by the city and the fact that he tarried here a whole month did not even bother to name it. In fact, in his own work he omitted the whole episode of the robbery and had Hwui Li not been attentive to the master's stories, we might not have even heard of it. Xuanzang's omission seems to signify that a village, home to kind and helpful people, became a city of several thousand houses in the imagination of Hwui Li. And that only because of the kindness shown by its people to his revered master.

The insignificant Greek settlement of the second century BCE, that still slumbers under Lahore Fort may well have been named Lohkot or Lavakot or Labaka by local people, but the truth is that Lahore came of age in the Middle Ages. We first hear of its name from Abu Rehan Al Beruni who came across the Khyber Pass in 1017. Over the next several years, he travelled extensively across India and wrote a most informed masterpiece *Kitab al Hind* – Book of India – covering a truly amazing range of subjects. At a few points in the book, Lauhawur 'east of the Irawa[ti]' is mentioned, but always in passing. It seems to be a city that did not much impress our savant. It was clearly not a place of learning where this brilliant and ever inquisitive man would have wanted to tarry a while.

By the beginning of Ghaznavid control over Lahore in the early eleventh century, the Indo-Greek city on the left bank of the river they called Hydraotes would have long since decayed and reduced to a mound. This eminence right by the river that was once again known as Iravati on the very spot where a ferry had plied since times immemorial was the place to raise a citadel. The populace, wearied by two decades of periodic pillaging, seeing the walls going up would have been lulled into believing the city was coming in for better, more secure times.

Mahmud Ghaznavi's sons ruled over Lahore in comparative peace only because there was no other contender. His grandson Behram struck the first Ghaznavid coin in Lahore in 1123. It was stamped 'Dar us Saltanat e Lahore' – capital of the kingdom of Lahore – and things seemed on the right trajectory. However, some cautious believers would have found the inscription on the reverse to be flying in the face of God: 'A Proclamation issued from the Seven Heavens, that Behram Shah is King of the Universe'!

How could he, a mere mortal, arrogate for himself the claim of being King of the Universe? Why, that was for God alone. Surely tongues would have wagged and wise men would have met in the streets of Lahore to put their heads together and solemnly whisper that the time of the Ghaznavids was over. It did not take long for that to happen.

In 1181, Muizuddin Ghori appeared before the walls of Lahore at the head of a sizeable army. Our source, the *Tabakat-i-Nasiri*, is silent on his treatment of the city. We only know that the Ghaznavid ruler Khusrau Malik was treated shabbily and besides the tribute of an elephant, his son Behram Shah was taken to Ghazni as hostage. Ghori returned four years later. From the now tall ramparts of the fort of Lahore, Khusrau spotted the dust of the advancing horde and fled, abandoning the city. Lahore was pillaged and sacked. Ghori seems not to have seen any strategic use for Lahore which he disregarded. Instead the thousand year-old fortress of Sialkot, then crumbling, was restored that same year and a governor left there.

The next year, 1186, the Ghorids were again at the ferry of Lahore when Khusrau Malik sued for peace. Muizuddin summoned him to his presence on the pretext of negotiations and there, outside the walls of the fort of Lahore, Khusrau was treacherously seized and imprisoned. When the Ghorid leader returned to Ghazni, he took the hapless man back to the place where Khusrau's ancestor Mahmud had first got it into his head to possess India. Khusrau and his son Behram, already held there as hostage, were kept imprisoned and eventually cruelly executed.

Under the Ghorids, toward the end of the twelfth century, Lohawar became 'the place where the throne of Sultans had been established'. After the Khokars despatched Muizuddin at Dhamiak in March 1206, the late king's brother established the slave Kutbuddin Aibak as Sultan at the *kasr* – castle – of Lahore. The people of Lahore had known only seven decades of relative peace under the Ghaznavids before the turmoil began anew with the Ghorid influx. With Aibak on the throne, they would have imagined another peaceful interlude.

Taken from Turkestan as a child and brought up as a slave, Aibak rose through the ranks and as king is said to have been just and generous to a fault. But he did not get long to rule over northern India. Barely five years into his reign, while playing polo in Lahore his horse tripped and rolled over. Aibak was caught under his mount with the raised and hardened front part of the saddle crushing his sternum. He did not stand a chance.

Any child growing up in Lahore in the 1960s would have known the dilapidated brick structure near the north end of Anarkali bazaar as Aibak's tomb. Some might have wondered why a Sultan, supposedly great, had such shabby treatment in death. Somewhere this thought appears to have resounded: in the 1980s the drab brick veneer was made over with marble, stucco and sandstone to look its part as a bygone ruler's resting place.

Aibak was survived by three daughters and an adopted son, Aram Baksh, who rose to the throne as Aram Shah. And here began a long period of misfortune for the city of the divine Raja Loh, the son of Lord Rama. Aram Shah was inept and, contrary to the dreams of its people, Lahore became a ping pong ball in a bloody three-way tussle between Tajuddin Yalduz, the very man who had tearfully buried Muizuddin Ghori in Ghazni, Nasiruddin Kabacha ruling over Multan and Sindh, and Shamsuddin Iyaltimish who was Sultan at Delhi. Interestingly, the last two were both sons-in-law to the late Aibak. As each man took his turn wresting the city from the other, innocent blood spilled freely in the streets of Lahore.

That was not the end of it, however. Over the next three decades, even as the able Razia Sultana, daughter of Shamsuddin Iyaltimish, rose to her brief stint in power, peace did not return to Lahore. In 1240, she and her husband were killed in battle against her own brother Muizuddin Behram Shah and, the following year, the scourge of the Mongols that had waited on the western horizon, broke over Lahore three days before Christmas 1241. Lahore was unprepared. Its wall was in disrepair; Behram Shah's governor for the city, the Turk Ikhtiyaruddin Karakash, commanded an ill-equipped force and there were not enough provisions should a siege ensue. Kinsmen though they were, there was a simmering friction between descendants of the Ghaznavids and those of the Ghorids who still held positions of power and city administration.[2]

Minhajuddin Siraj, the writer of *Tabakat-i-Nasiri*, complains that the population was not of one mind and 'did not harmonise together'. Worst of all, they were opposed to their governor Karakash and were unwilling to stand with him. Influential persons, probably the very ones whose ancestors were among the three hundred who came forward with assistance for Xuanzang and his party just six hundred years before, all being merchants, were away travelling in Khorasan and further north. Ironically enough, the traders were under protection of the Mongols poised to sack their city.

The horde crossed the Ravi and the walled city was girded by Mongol trebuchets in 'a great number' as they began to pound the defences. In this crisis, there appears to have been a change of Lahori heart, because we now hear of a spirited resistance led by Karakash himself. Even as he guided operations from the battlements, the man knew the approaching end was going to be disastrous for he was aware that preserving the city was beyond his power and capacity.

---

2) Spelling of all personal names (Kutubuddin, Iyaltimish etc.) in this chapter follow Henry Raverty's translation of *Tabakat i Nasiri*.

The *Tabakat-i-Nasiri* tells us that Karakash came out 'under the pretext of a night attack', made a dash into the sleeping Mongol camp killing many and losing some of his own troopers as well as his harem before fleeing east to Delhi. Minhajuddin Siraj was a loyal servant of the Turks, as had been his father before him, and he habitually glossed over every action of his masters. Therefore it seems probable that Karakash made no attack but simply stole away in the dark of night. Lahoris woke the following morning to find their city bereft of its ragtag army. And so did the besiegers. As the Mongols poured into the city, something stirred in the collective Lahori heart and the streets 'in every quarter' rang with the din of hand to hand combat.

Siraj celebrates two groups of 'Musalmans' for having 'firmly grasped the sword' and gallantly fighting to the end. The leader of one of these groups was the heroic Ak Sankar – White Falcon – the Turkish seneschal of Lahore, equivalent to our deputy commissioner today. The other group was led by Dindar Mohammad and his sons. The man was no soldier, but a supplier of fodder for military animals. All these men died in the fighting.

Siraj says thirty or forty thousand Mongol cavalry men with twice as many horses 'went to hell'.[3] It is surprising that when it came to actual fighting, a population of disaffected Punjabi civilians and their Turkish overlords gave a heroic account of themselves for we are told that not a single Mongol trooper was without an arrow, sword or other wound. Ak Sankar matched lances with his Mongol counterpart, both mortally wounding the other, they died staring into each other's eyes. Since all the 'infidels were hell-bound', it was only natural that the Muslims went the other way: 'One company to heaven; one to the flaming fire', Siraj quotes from the Quran.

As for Karakash, he had fled only as far as the near shore of the Beas River when he received word of Mongol withdrawal. He hurried back. And he was in a right haste to retrace his steps for in their terrified flight, his wardrobe-keepers dumped a good deal of 'pure gold, and other valuables' just outside Lahore. They had fortuitously marked the spot for later recovery. In the melee with commoners fleeing for their lives, no one had noticed the fresh grave, incorrectly aligned, housing the treasure which was duly restored to Karakash.

The Mongols left Lahore a smouldering ruin. Siraj tells us that it was after their withdrawal that the Khokhars – many of whom still kept the old religion – and Gabrs (Fire-Worshippers) from outlying towns flocked into Lahore and set to plundering and destroying what little was left of the city. As always the good Karakash got back just in time and despatched the lot to hell. Then, perhaps fearing a Mongol reflux, he immediately fled back to Delhi.

Lahore may have suffered and remained in a ruinous state for nearly three decades after the Mongol strike, but Minhajuddin Siraj finds one silver lining in the sacking of Lahore. He records a 'tradition of the ancients' that when the 'narrow-eyed should seize upon the universe', their dominance will go on the decline after they reach Lahore.

---

3) We know that each Mongol cavalryman had a spare horse.

He claims that as a child of seven, he heard the imam of Bukhara under whose tutelage he sudied, pray that may God speedily send a Mongol army to Lahore.

It is not known if the imam had ever travelled to Lahore, but surely some Lahori trickster seems to have comprehensively duped him, perhaps even in his native Bukhara, for the man to hold such a cavil against Lahore.

Whatever the case, the fulfilment of the prophecy, according to Siraj, was that Chengez Khan's son Ogodai Bahadur died within days of the sacking of the city. Sadly for the imam, however, Lahore's misfortune did not bring Mongol power to an end.

Incidentally, Ogodai's death was ignominious. Given to drinking in gross excess, his brother Chaghata Khan appointed an intendant over him to see that alcohol stayed within a stipulated limit. But Chaghata was apparently not a great judge of men for the overseer was soon partying with the prince and may in fact have hastened royal demise.

Meanwhile, back in Lahore, those who had managed to flee the massacre began to trickle in to rebuild their shattered city and lives. This was without support for Sultan Abu'l Muzaffar Mahmud Shah, grandson of Iyaltimish, who now sat on the throne at Delhi, had temporarily shifted his focus to Rajasthan, Multan and Uch. For the next century and a half Lahore limped along in poverty and obscurity. Sitting on an important ford of the Ravi, the only royal favour Lahore received in this period of adversity was that its fort was rebuilt. This was in 1266, a quarter century after the Mongols had departed.

In 1296, yet another Mongol inroad occurred under Katlagh Khwaja. The *Tarikh-i-Firoz Shahi* tells us that Delhi being the objective of this campaign none of the territories bordering the line of march were attacked. Lahore certainly lay on the route and was spared because it had little to offer. The Khokhars continued to hold sway and from time to time rise up to vex imperial power then seated in distant Delhi. The talented but cruel Mohammad Tughlak was on the throne and about this time Alaul Mulk, his police superintendent, advised him to reduce contumacious provinces to 'such obedience that the name of rebels should never be heard'. Lahore was included in the list of other Rajput controlled areas to be severely chastised.

The great traveller Ibn Battuta was in our part of the world in the 1330s, and he missed Lahore. He seemed to care little or nothing for the city and expressed no desire to see it. His only mention of Lahore was in connection with a native of the city: Malik Qabula, the much-favoured Fly-Whisk Bearer to Sultan Mohammad Tughlak. In those decades, Multan, Depalpur, Uch and even the now provincial little town of Tulamba were more prosperous and, therefore, in the sights of Delhi monarchs and plunderers alike.

The Barlas Turk Tamerlane who boasted that he had two reasons for coming to India; one, to win merit in the afterlife for waging jihad against infidels and, secondly, to gain plunder which was 'as lawful as their mothers' milk to Musalmans who fight for their faith', missed Lahore.[4] And thankfully so for we know well the rape and massacre that Delhi suffered under his sword. However, in February 1400, while in Kashmir, Tamerlane sent an expedition to Lahore to arrest Malik Shaikha Khokhar. This man's brother Nusrat was governor of Lahore who had shortly before been defeated and killed in battle against Tamerlane's forces.

Shaikha was perhaps a tad more perspicacious than his brother for he immediately submitted to the Turk and waited upon him on his way to Delhi. But how long could a proud Rajput feign allegiance to an alien he considered an upstart savage. Soon wearying of the endless obeisance and salaams demanded by the Barlas, Khokhar asked for permission to return to Lahore.

The *Tuzk e Timuri* tells us that a party of Turks leaving Tamerlane's perambulatory court on their way back to Samarkand was shown 'no attention' when they passed through Lahore. 'The defection of Shaikha Khokhar had become clear', wrote the Barlas. For this breach of decorum by their governor, a sizeable ransom was levied on the struggling populace of Lahore. Shaikha was put in chains to be returned to the court and for sport to compensate for the time spent on the expedition, on their way back the raiders plundered the country around Lahore.

Not until the middle of the fifteenth century and the relative peace and better administration of Bahlol Lodhi did Lahore come into eminence again. But now Babur, ousted from the land of his forefathers in the Fergana Valley was partying in Kabul and Bamian even as he made exploratory forays into Peshawar. Then, as he set his eyes on Delhi, he famously uttered words that have entered the common lexicon of our part of the subcontinent in the original Persian: Delhi is yet distant.

Between Babur in Peshawar and Delhi in the east lay the doabs of the five rivers of Punjab. And snuggling in the Bari, the doab between the Beas and Ravi, sat Lahore, now fast becoming a jewel polished by six decades of peace under the Lodhis.

∞

Growing up in the city, I experienced a unique Lahori persona exemplified by lively humour and jocularity. A memory that refuses to leave me goes back to September 1968. A friend and I, teenagers still, stood in the veranda of Tollinton Market in downtown Lahore talking of the mellowing post-monsoon weather. I remarked how the strength of the heat was 'broken'. A man passing by overheard, stopped and turned to us.
'Yes. Broken it certainly is. It's in two halves.' He held up two fingers for emphasis, eyes wide with mock awe. 'It's lying there on the far bank of the Ravi. I was just there to see the broken bits!' Deadpan the man delivered his line,

---

4) It is another thing that infidel and Muslim were equal fodder for Tamerlane's war machine. His humiliating treatment of fellow Muslim, the Ottoman Sultan Beyazid I, who, after his defeat and capture, was borne around in a cage casts the perfect image of the brutal savage that Muslims now hail as a Champion of the Faith. Among other infringements, one can also not forgive the wanton massacre of twenty thousand Muslims in Tulamba near Multan.

turned on his heel and walked off leaving the two of us in stitches.

Even earlier, when I had first learned to cycle at age eight, I would pedal from our Durand Road home to the old city. The oldies sitting around chatting on the *tharas* – those cement concrete ledges extending outward from the buildings in the narrow streets – would spot me as an outsider. They asked where I was from and what business brought me to their part of town. Then, without fail, they ordered *lassi* – buttermilk which came in a tall bronze tumbler – and *kulchas* – the delectably fluffy and scrumptious round bread sprinkled with sesame seeds served on a piece of yesterday's newspaper – steaming hot from the clay oven. Their order to the *tandoorchi* was always to bake it red. Now, six decades later that is my instruction at the tandoor.

Nowadays the oldies still hang around street corners the same way and as I go past greeting them I half expect to be stopped and offered the same fare. But I suppose another man their age no longer interests them.

Then there was the Lahori empathy. Long before life became all speeded up, anyone anywhere in Lahore looking lost, confused or worried would be approached by a total stranger to be asked if everything was all right and if they could be helped. Within seconds there would be a dozen or more people crowding around. The person would be given a drink and helped in every possible way.

Several years ago, with a pair of shoes needing repair and with so few repairers left in this age of disposables, I was guided, after much asking around, to Chowk Old Anarkali. With the footwear hooked in my fingers I stood on the pavement looking around.

'*Bao ji!*' I heard someone call out. It was the man in the milk shop. 'You need to go there,' he said pointing across the busy street. There, in what was no bigger than a crack in the wall, sat a man surrounded by racks of old shoes.

For the first formative centuries of its life Lahore was repeatedly ravaged by outsiders. That should have left its people brutalised. That did not happen. The spirit of Lahore was extremely resilient. Lahore is accused by natives of other cities of always having succumbed without a fight. Though they did fight when the chips were down, their way of resistance was to keep the spirit alive. Surely, even during the shortest peaceful interlude, Lahoris would have reverted to their fun-loving ways. The humour, the compassion and the fellow-feeling never left the soul of Lahore and are still a tangible part of the Lahori character. This spirit has now been badly dented by the ingress of outsiders to whom the city is not the mother but a courtesan to be used for their own advancement. Rubes from outlying villages, lacking the sophistication to understand the city's ethos have taken over. In a word, Lahore has become ruralised.

∞

The foundation laid by Bahlol Lodhi had eroded by the time of his grandson Ibrahim. In 1520, the sultan's own governor of Lahore Daulat Khan Lodhi, a kinsmen to boot, treacherously invited Babur to take the city. Lahore fell again, but thankfully not as violently as three centuries earlier to the Mongols. It rose soon enough under a Mughal feudatory. In the decades of Lodhi reign, Lahore had become a rich mercantile city and in 1525, while Babur was still in Balkh, his administrator in Lahore sent him tribute in gold and silver coin equivalent to twenty thousand shahrukhis.[5]

Although historically dubious, a desire attributed to Sher Shah Suri was to depopulate Punjab between the Indus and Lahore and replace indigenous peoples with Pakhtuns who would stand against the exiled Humayun should he attempt a comeback. At the same time, Sher Shah is said to have considered razing Lahore because a city as large and prosperous sitting on a main artery into India would always be lure and help to invaders. Doubtful as this bit of history is, it must have been the gossip of Lahore in the mid-sixteenth century because when Humayun did return in February 1554, he was accorded a resounding welcome by the 'illustrious city of Lahore …. which is in fact a great city of India', so Akbar's chronicler Abu'l Fazal tells us.[6]

Humayun might have considered repaying Lahore, but he got no time for within the year he was dead. His son Akbar made the city a strong cantonment and a regular stopover for the journey from the Afghan highlands to Agra which he preferred as a capital. The huge caravanserai that is now part of Jahangir's Quadrangle in Shahdara on the far side of Ravi dates from his time. As too does the Divan e Aam in Lahore Fort. The red granite and the Vedic iconography on the balconies is noteworthy.

I had my camera bag when I went looking. Just past the ticket booth where the man wanted to charge me the higher foreigner's fee until I spoke in Punjabi, I was accosted by one of the several 'guides' hanging around. I took the man aside and asked him about the tunnels that connected this fort with the one in Sheikhupura and with Red Fort in Delhi.
'The tunnels are there all right, but they go only a short ways before being blocked,' he said, a picture of solemnity.

The tunnels are ubiquitous. They are under every fort in Pakistan and everyone knows of them. No matter how hard one tries to convince believers that the Mughals simply had not mastered the art of tunnel building, they continue to believe. Contemporary sources do not mention any tunnels. On the other hand, they do tell us of the troubles Mughal kings faced during journeys above ground in inclement weather. But this has zero effect on the so-called guides and for them the tunnels remain firmly hidden under the ramparts of our forts or any other historical building. Having said that, I had always wondered where the inane stories originated. The truth dawned in the course of research for the present work.

The well-known Urdu magazine *Naqoosh* published in

---

5) In Babur's time the shahrukhi, a silver coin, weighed 4.69 grams.
6) Clearly the fear of the city being razed was common in the Lahori mind for Abu'l Fazal tells us that the thought occurred not to Sher Shah but his son Salim when he was in power.

1962 a *Lahore Number*, a detailed compendium of the city containing articles by various writers on its history, monuments and persons connected with it. These articles had all been published earlier in other journals and reportedly edited by the learned historian S. M. Latif who died in 1902. In an article on Dara Shukoh we are told that after his defeat at Samugarh (near Agra) at the hands of his younger brother Aurangzeb, the beaten prince repaired to Lahore, his fief since long by a decree of Shah Jahan.

Here Dara Shukoh found refuge in Shalimar Gardens from where, the *Naqoosh* story informs us, he 'took the underground tunnel to Lahore Fort to recover his treasures' before fleeing to Sindh. There never was any subterranean passage. The writer merely used his licence to add drama to a story that needed no additional spice.

The trouble with these so-called guides is that they have no idea of history and they take no pains to learn, nor too are they regulated by any authority. With nothing else to do, unemployed men, their only facility being glibness, take on the role to fool unsuspecting tourists both local and foreign. Sadly, it is the local variety that falls for the stories they are fed and the myths magnify basements to become hundreds of kilometres long tunnels.

For Akbar Lahore was just a way station, but his son Jahangir made it his capital. While residing here Jahangir's mother Mariam Zamani (Mary of the Age) nee Manmati endowed to the city the most exquisitely decorated mosque of the time.[7] Sitting under the shadow of the east gate of Lahore Fort, it was constructed during 1611-14 and known as the Begum Shahi Mosque. Nowadays it is simply Mariam Zamani Masjid. For two decades after being built it was the most ornate Muslim prayer house in Lahore until it was outdone by the magnificent splendour of the mosque of Wazir Khan who served under her grandson Shah Jahan.

Situated in the west side of the old city facing the fort, the Mariam Zamani mosque vies with Wazir Khan's mosque on the other side for beauty of its frescoes.

In 1991, having read *Lahore* by S. M. Latif (published 1892), some friends and I went looking for Mariam Zamani's mosque. The mosque, fronted by an open piazza, was visible from the road passing under the east gate of the fort. In the open space, old men were sunning themselves while some youngsters played cricket. The exterior was

---

7) Manmati, Akbar's first wife (five more followed) who bore him Jahangir, was a daughter of Raja Bhagwandas of Amber in Rajasthan. Some sources refer to her as Jodh Bai. I follow Dr Annemarie Schimmel (*The Empire of the Great Mughals*) and prefer Manmati.

Detail of the vault and spandrel of the main entrance to the prayer chamber.

Main prayer chamber of Mariam Zamani mosque.

drab bricks, and the frescos inside were frayed and fading with very few bits left intact. The mosque seemed to be in disuse; the three bays of its prayer chamber littered with wind-blown debris and pigeon droppings. If memory serves, there was a plaque on one of the walls saying, in English, that the building had been used as an orphanage in the 1880s.

Fast forward to 2019 and the mosque is no longer visible from the road where they sell used tyres and rims in makeshift kiosks. The open square was now choc-a-bloc with cubicles selling cheap footwear, leaving a narrow lane to reach the mosque. One wonders where the old men now sun themselves. Inside, the mosque façade was scribbled with electric cables and metal fixtures hammered into the frescoed mortar as anchors for canvas *shamianas* to shelter worshippers from the sun. However, the frescos in the arch of the main entrance were clearly redone. A thoughtless scrawl of a couple of wires right across them marred their beauty.

The interior was a rhapsody of colour and form, resplendent and radiant, that defies description. Having seen dozens of attempts at 'restoration' that have only ruined what once was, I was in a state of ecstasy. For a moment I thought these were the original that had dimmed only in my three decade-old memory and that they had always been like this.

Azeem corrected me. The mosque had never been out of use. It was very likely undergoing restoration when my friends and I visited. It is remarkable that the team of restorers has done a job to be celebrated: they have recreated the entire original from only a few surviving scraps. Clearly, when there is the will, there are experts in the field who can bring back a building from near demise.

Manmati or Mariam Zamani who, according to Schimmel, was one of 'the most influential women', did not convert to Islam. That she ordered a mosque as beautiful as this shows that Akbar's attempt at religious integration was working to some extent. But that was the past and as they say the past is another country. As we were leaving I stopped at one of the shoe stores pretending to check out the wares. The salesman did not know what the mosque was called. I told him not only the name of the mosque but that the builder was a Hindu. That Akbar had married her when she was Manmati or, as some say, Jodh Bai, and titled her Mariam Zamani.
'How can that be?'
'That was. And that too was once this country,' I said and left hoping he would reflect.

On the far side of the old city, the gate facing east is Delhi Darwaza. Inside it is the jewel of Lahore that outshone Mariam Zamani's mosque. Shah Jahan's most reliable Hakim Ilmuddin became associated with him during his early youth when he was yet Prince Khurram. Quickly Ilmuddin rose in trust and rank to be titled Wazir Khan. As Shah Jahan's physician and governor of Lahore, he endowed the city with the mosque inside Delhi Gate that bears his name to this day.

A walk through narrow alleyways, once lined by houses

three hundred years old and ornate with carved bay windows and doors to die for, is now a good deal more modern – and uglier – with steel fixtures instead of the old timber. Façades with colourful bathroom tiles are frequently seen. Despite all the mindless vandalism, it is yet a delightful walk ending at Delhi Darwaza of the old ramparts. The attraction on the way is Lahori street food.

Here men with weak flesh but a bucking spirit can still buy 'snake oil' – actually oil extracted from the *sanda (Saara hardwickii)* or Hardwicke's spiny-tailed lizard, a native of the subcontinent's arid regions. To underline authenticity the so-called medicine man has a number of lizards on display, alive but cruelly immobilised with broken spines. There is also a choice of luridly coloured capsules whose efficacy the seller exhibits by lifting them with a magnet. 'Pure iron', he assures men of the weak flesh. And in these lanes traditional medicine men practice formulas 'perfected five hundred years ago by a grandsire who was a master hakim'. That medical science has moved ahead with new discoveries made in these intervening centuries makes no difference to the hakims or to their customers. Mostly sexagenarians, the users generally end up in urology wards, their kidneys demolished by mercury, arsenic and lead that constitute the base of these magic potions.

Somewhere in these lanes there was a medicine man that Shoaib Hashmi, teacher of economics, but an inveterate Lahori wit and story-teller, had discovered about three decades ago. The sign outside the establishment announced: Haemorrhoids and other Diseases of the Eye cured here! I failed to find him, however.

In my estimation Wazir Khan's mosque is matched in beauty by only one other mosque and that in distant Thatta. As Prince Khurram, Shah Jahan had revolted against his father Jahangir and found refuge for a short while in this Sindhi town where he was generously treated by the local ruler. The beholden emperor's offering to his erstwhile hosts is now one of the most magnificent monuments of Sindh.

Gateway leading into the courtyard of Wazir Khan's mosque

Built between 1634 and 1641, Wazir Khan's mosque, archetypal example of later Mughal architecture, sits above the fourteenth century burial of Mohammad Ishaq, popularly known as Miran Badshah. The subterranean burial accessible by a flight of stairs lies on the south side of the ablution tank. Three decades ago, a somewhat aggressive sort of attendant would exhort visitors to the mosque to first go into the burial chamber and do obeisance, calling down divine wrath on those who refused. Heaven help the person accompanied by white friends. The harangue was

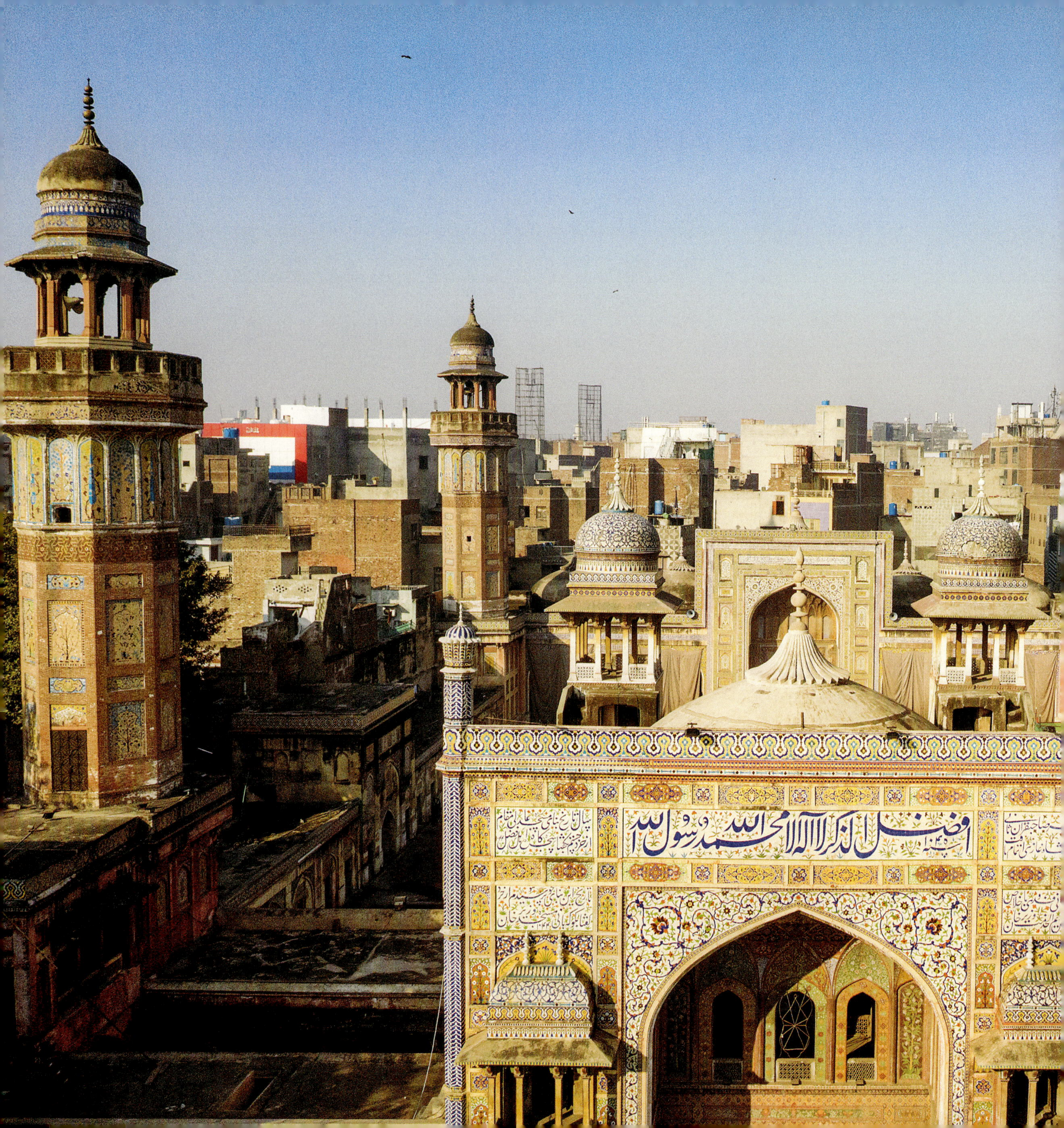

As governor of Lahore, Wazir Khan could scarcely have done better than gifting the city this exquisitely beautiful mosque.

then to convert them to the one and only true faith and win a place in paradise. Today the attendants are friendly.

Wazir Khan was a man who can only be termed decent; a meticulous man who would not leave anything to chance and possible wrangling after his death. The land for the mosque, its construction and exquisite adornment were all paid for by his 'best earned' wealth. His will explicitly laid down how the mosque and its officials, including the imam, two theological teachers and the muezzin, were to be maintained from the income of the shops lined along the outside wall. As one climbs up the stairs of the high plinth one sees small cubicles on either side in the veranda along the east wall. These, Wazir Khan's will records, were meant for book-binders and booksellers of religious works.

The fine Persian calligraphy bordering the main entrance reads, as translated by S. M. Latif:

> In the cornfield of this world, O well-conducted
> man, whatever is sown by man, is reaped by him
> in the world to come,
> In your dealings, then, have a good foundation in
> the world,
> For all have to pave their way to heaven through
> this gateway at last.

Like so many other monuments, this priceless building was falling into ruin. In the first decade of the current century, with funding from the Aga Khan Development Network, the mosque has been made over with such meticu-

Detail of frescoes and honeycomb in Wazir Khan's mosque.

lous care that the ghost of Wazir Khan would surely be pleased. Indeed, the entire area known as Chowk Wazir Khan has a new look. A nearby street once lined with tall, crumbling buildings is now a pleasant walkway.

In the late 1980s, architect and historian Kamil Khan Mumtaz wrote an erudite piece on interpreting the architecture and frescoes of Wazir Khan's mosque. The cube-shaped entrance chamber symbolises the temporal while the dome above represents the celestial. In the transition from the worldly to the everlasting, 'fruits of every kind on silver platters, the pitchers of wine and trees in pairs' are clear references to the Quranic paradise. Among other symbols, Mumtaz sees in the stately cypress the perfect man. Its top bent to one side as if in a breeze, we are told is sign of submission to God.

In March 1860, vicerene Charlotte Canning entered Lahore through Delhi Gate. She thought the streets 'so narrow that the elephants almost swept the sides full of people' was a sight 'really beautiful'. The houses were illuminated with oil lamps and every window faces 'all so merry & good humoured'. The vicerene conceded that she had 'never seen such a crowd in India or heard such a noise'.

Back at the west gate of the fort, Azeem spoke of Aurangzeb Alamgir's grandiose Badshahi Mosque fronting the gate and once the largest mosque in Pakistan. In 1986, the brand new Faisal Mosque of Islamabad stole this glory. In the grassy quadrangle between the mosque and the lofty gateway of the fort known as the Alamgiri Darwaza, sits the marble pavilion of Huzuri Bagh.

Before the pavilion was raised, this quadrangle housed a caravanserai which from available descriptions seems more of a military barracks than an inn for common travellers. Exiting from the Alamgiri Gateway of the fort, it was through this garden that Aurangzeb passed into his grand mosque at prayer times in right regal pomp. The hundreds of soldiers who lined the route seemed 'great and royal' to François Bernier, the French physician to Aurangzeb. The Frenchman does not comment on the incongruity of according such pageantry to worship – the supreme act of humble submission to the Maker.

The marble pavilion is now a single-storey building on a plinth with five doorways on each façade. Ornate and aesthetically pleasing it occupies the centre of a garden laid out on Aurangzeb's order. Photographs from the early part of the twentieth century show an equally lavish but smaller pavilion on the flat roof. The topping fell off in a severe storm in the summer of 1932; some say because of the force of the wind, others make it a victim of a lightning strike.

Azeem had a story to tell. It was here that Shah Shuja, the Saddozai prince of Afghanistan, then in exile in Lahore, was tricked by Ranjit Singh into giving over the Kohinoor diamond embezzled less than a century earlier from the moribund Moghuls by Nadir Shah, the ruler of Persia. Knowing that the Afghan kept the diamond concealed in his turban, the wily Sikh suggested the two exchange their headgear to cement their brotherly ties. Shuja demurred and Ranjit feigned offence. Why, Shuja enjoyed asylum in Lahore, and yet was showing lack of faith. Finding no way out, Shah Shuja made over his turban and the biggest diamond the world had ever seen to the Punjabi.

Historian and writer Khushwant Singh has a slightly different version in *Ranjit Singh: Maharaja of the Punjab*. Wafa Begum, Shah Shuja's senior wife, petitioned Ranjit Singh to secure her husband's release from Kashmir and subsequent safety from the inimical Barakzais. As recompense for this favour, she offered the famed diamond. The needful was done, Shuja was delivered to his wife in Lahore and the couple accorded housing in the lavish Mubarak Haveli. No sooner had that been done that Ranjit Singh's messenger demanded the diamond.

Wafa Begum denied the couple held the diamond saying it had earlier been pawned in Kandahar. Sensing subterfuge, Ranjit offered a token payment of three hundred thousand rupees together with an annual stipend of fifty thousand. When this did not work, the couple who had been royal guests until then were placed under house arrest. To further pressure the hapless Shuja, Ranjit ordered the family's daily ration supply to be cut drastically. Shuja eventually capitulated.

On the first day of June 1813, the Maharaja, followed by six hundred cavalrymen, rode out to Mubarak Haveli to receive the diamond. After the usual round of greeting and asking after each other's welfare, the diamond was brought out on Shah Shuja's order. Ranjit Singh undid the bundle of expensive cloth and took out the stone turning it around in front of his single eye. Then he gave it to a courtier of his who had seen the diamond earlier. Satisfied that it was the real thing, the Kohinoor was re-wrapped. The Maharaja got up 'and without a word of thanks or farewell, hurried out of the room', writes Khushwant Singh.

The marble pavilion of Huzuri Bagh was ordered by Ranjit Singh that same year as a triumphal symbol of regaining the jewel for India. It was completed in three years, the stone, it is said, appropriated from earlier Mughal buildings. If that actually is the case, Ranjit Singh's architects would have first checked out existing buildings, measured their worked stone slabs and then to that exact size, designed their own *baradari* of fifteen doorways. Unlikely that might be, but it would not have been a difficult job.

The lovely garden around Ranjit Singh's baradari was a place of great artistic and intellectual foment until 2003 or the year after. I first experienced the thrill of live Punjabi poetry recitals here in 1987 entirely by chance. One wintry Friday morning I went to the old city for a round of photography and at about nine ended up at Huzuri Bagh. It was crowded with people, mostly men, who sat in groups. Here was one group listening to a rendering of Waris Shah's epic love poem *Heer*, there another rapt in the words of *Mirza Saheban* and yet another swaying to the rhythm of the poetry of Shah Hussain of Lahore all performed.

Here, for the first time in my life, I also became acquainted with the nineteenth century *Jangnama* of Shah Mohammad. This epic ballad celebrates the cross-religious cohesion that once existed in Punjab and which was effectively dismantled by British rulers.

Huzuri Bagh was a place where Punjabi literature and culture were celebrated. The congregations, I later found out, were entirely spontaneous and that they had never been formally organised. In the beginning it was only a few men who came on the weekly holiday to recite and celebrate. Over time, the audiences began to grow until it became the very festival I saw in 1987.

I was not an avid or regular goer to this event, but was deeply saddened when in the early part of this century, the city administration banned the weekly (now on Sundays) gathering. The pretext was security. The only regular, and spontaneous, event in the entire province that introduced young and old alike to their language and literature was prohibited.

Maharaja Ranjit Singh was cremated in Lahore and his ashes went to the Ganges River, but the gleaming white and gold vault separated by the old Roshnai Darwaza from the Huzuri Bagh baradari celebrates him in death. In the cool and silent interior a Garanthi (Reciter of the Sikh holy book, Granth Sahib) fans the book. Second only to the holy buildings connected with Guru Nanak Dev, the Maharaja's Samadhi is the finest Sikh edifice in Pakistan. The foliated arches, the bay windows, the miniature replica of the fort's Naulakha Pavilion, and the parade of domelets along the parapet with the corner cupolas repeated on every façade create a delicate and pleasing effect. Between 1835 and his end four years later, the Maharaja suffered three strokes. The last in June 1838 rendered him incapable of speech. Only his trusted hakim, Fakir Syed Azizuddin could understand what the waning monarch said – and that with considerable difficulty. By June the following year, it was clear that the Lion of Punjab was on his way out. Meanwhile, the pundits continued to milk him by suggesting a 'continuance of liberal grants' for the best effect on the dying man's health.

Around the third week of June 1839, Maharaja Ranjit Singh complained of aching knees and pain behind his single eye. There was sudden onset of high fever together with violent epistaxis, typical signs of dengue fever. It was the man's iron will and constitution that kept him going until 26 June when he went into coma. The following day he had passed away into his long night. As with Alexander, so too with Maharaja Ranjit Singh, the empire died as his last rites were being performed.

∞

Ranjit Singh stands accused of having pilfered marble from earlier Mughal buildings to raise his pavilion in Huzuri Bagh and other buildings. In *Lahore*, S. M. Latif tells us the marble came from the tomb of Zebun Nisa, Aurangzeb Alamgir's eldest daughter who, by one source, was originally named Zebinda Begum. Born in 1639, she grew up into a very attractive tall and slim woman. Educated, very erudite and a gifted poet, she had delightful wit that shines through her verse even for one only marginally acquainted with the Persian she wrote in. There are examples, too, of her facility with the clever repartee – sometimes in verse.

From her half a million rupees annual stipend, she raised an elaborate garden with tanks, fountains and walkways which she gifted to her favourite attendant Mian Bai. The garden is today a warren of narrow streets discordant with the din of traffic and housing that is offensive because of its tastelessness. Only Chauburji, the imposing gateway leading into the lost garden, remains as a famous landmark of Lahore. This too now hidden from view because of the raised metro train track passing right in front of it.

South of this garden, Zebun Nisa ordered a chunky building tastefully decorated with worked white marble and precious stones. It was surrounded by a garden, fountains, water tanks and pavilions. This was to be her mausoleum and when she passed away in 1669, from a very young life (she was just thirty), she was interred under the ornate dome. Munshi Mohammadudin writing at about the same time as S. M. Latif, tells us that a certain Mohkamuddin Arain in the service of Sobha Singh of Lahore (and an associate of Ranjit Singh's) destroyed the waterworks around the tomb and removed the marble fittings to be sold. Since sources say it was the marble of this building used, in part, on the Huzuri Bagh pavilion, one wonders if the shrewd Mohkamuddin made some money from the pillage.

In the 1990s, Zebun Nisa was a forgotten princess. In life, her nom de plume was *Makhfi* – the Hidden or Unknowable. In death, she became just that: few locals knew who lay buried under the brick sarcophagus, even fewer visited the tomb close to the bus stop of Chhapar – stagnant pond. The building with its peeling plaster, broken stone grills and frescoes fading and marred by graffiti was a den for junkies.

The ruin was reclaimed by the Department of Archaeology in 2014. The marble could not be brought back from Huzuri Bagh but whatever else occurred came straight from some good heart. Red stone grills were crafted and affixed in the gaping openings. The few floor tiles that still remained in place were replicated and the floor rendered complete. Best of all was the restoration of the frescoes. The place has been cleaned out, the cenotaph now covered with the green velvet sheet reserved for the burial of Muslim saints.

Feigning ignorance and using masculine terminology, I asked whose burial it was.
'Princess Zebun Nisa, sir. She was a daughter of Aurangzeb Alamgir,' said Zahid, the young attendant from the Department of Archaeology.
'Have we turned her into a saint where people pray for sons and wealth?'
'Not yet. Some people do come to offer up prayers. I think they only do the Fateha,' he replied with a smile.[8]

Zahid had been with the department only two years and he simply shrugged when I commented on the encroaching housing. We were joined by a man in his sixties. Imtiaz Hussain Shirazi had been a teacher in Quetta where he was injured in a terrorist attack several years ago. He lifted his shirt and showed me the vertical scar on his abdomen. He lives in a recently built house that takes up a corner

---

8) Fateha – The Opening – is the first chapter of the Quran. It is recited at burials.

of what was once the garden of Zebun Nisa. I asked him about the sort of people who visited the tomb. 'Dervishes like you and I. No one else. Zebun Nisa is not known to many.' If he was aware that his house occupies a part of the princess's garden, he feigned complete ignorance.

∞

I had digressed in geographical terms. Back in Chowk Wazir Khan, Azeem and I set off east along the Grand Trunk Road. We rolled past the majestic crenelated and fortified railway station, less that more of a well-defended castle. When Raj engineers designed this building the thought foremost in their minds was to overawe natives with the power of the Crown. Surely, in the first few years it must have served the purpose rather well and one wonders if in the early years of the railway ordinary Punjabis would even have ventured anywhere near the station, much less on to its platforms.

Just before the University of Engineering and Technology, left of the road, stands the domed building that until the early 1990s was in the middle of large unkempt grounds. Now it had a steel gate guarded by a man from the Department of Archaeology. A narrow paved lane leads to the old mausoleum of Dai Anga set in the back. Here too the protected status came a tad too late: housing has encroached upon the surrounding garden (government land) and all but swamped a heritage site.

The civil engineer Kanhaya Lal, who wrote his *Tarikh e Lahore* (History of Lahore) in the 1870s and who was also tasked with restoring several crumbling heritage buildings, tells us of Mohalla (precinct) Dai Anga where Mughal nobility lived in the seventeenth century. As Mughal power waned, the area was walled and gated to keep marauders at bay. But precious little that did; the onslaught continued and over time residents moved away. In the early nineteenth century, European travellers passing en route to Shalimar Gardens noted the desolation of this area, then a suburb of the city, and wrote that Lahore was clearly a rich and splendid metropolis in the not so distant past.

About two decades before it came to be known as Mohalla Dai Anga, the area was famous for Gulabi Bagh – Rose Garden. Laid out by Mirza Sultan Baig, a Persian nobleman of the ruling Safvi family, who immigrated to India on the invitation of his cousin Ghiyasud Din holding office in the court of Shah Jahan. More importantly, Ghiyasud Din was also married to the king's daughter Sultan Begum. The

A decorative panel from the entrance of Dai Anga's tomb.

Tomb of Dai Anga.

Detail of frescos on the façade of the gateway.

garden was no longer extant in the late nineteenth century when Kanhaya Lal and Latif wrote; all that remained was its ornate gateway which exists to this day. In Latif's words:

> This picturesque gateway is remarkable for the profusion and excellence of its coloured pottery and enamelled frescoes, which are as vivid, and the decorations as perfect, as when they were made.

The description rings true to this day. The vertical and horizontal brick margins that separate the mosaic panels are the only element in the façade of the gateway that has been restored. Inside, the frescos of the domed ceiling have been faithfully redone. All else on the exterior, the flowing calligraphy, the sensuous curvi-linear forms and the blossoming plants, whether potted in fancy urns or sprouting from the earth, are as when the artist, having laid the last brush stroke, stood back to regard his masterpiece three and a half centuries ago.

Latif adds that the name Gulabi Bagh was also the chronogram for the laying out of the garden which gives us the Hijri year 1066 or 1655 of the Common Era. The writer appends an interesting little episode to his description of Gulabi Bagh gateway. Ghiyasud Din prevailed upon the king for the appointment of Sultan Baig as Admiral of the Fleet. Now, the admiral was an avid hunter to whom the emperor presented an English rifle. Eager to test it out, Sultan Baig betook himself and the firearm to the hunting ground of Hiran Minar outside Sheikhupura. It is not known what fortunate animal he had in his gunsight when the rifle burst killing the hunter on the spot. The poor man got to enjoy his Gulabi Bagh for just two years for he died his horrible death in 1657.

Dai Anga's real name was Zeb un Nisa and she was the daughter of a Mughal official in the court of Jahangir who earned the *dai* (midwife or nurse) prefix for being the wet nurse of the infant prince Khurram (later Shah Jahan). As she aged, Dai Anga became a woman of substantial wealth who gained considerable clout with the king. On her request, Shah Jahan arranged for her to travel to Arabia for the Haj.

Set a little way behind the Gulabi Bagh gateway sits the domed tomb of Dai Anga where she shares her last repose with her foster daughter Sultan Begum. If there were ever sarcophagi to mark the subterranean burials, they have long since been lost and replaced by rectangular markers of modern tiles. Interestingly, the tomb is referred to as Dai Anga's and not as that of princess Sultan Begum's.

Raised in 1671, the domed building is still an eye-catching sight. The dome ripples with blue chevron patterns representing flowing water, a much favoured adornment in the later Mughal period. On the corners of the rectangular building stand miniature domed and pillared pavilions whose once bright frescoes have faded almost to oblivion. Much of the decoration of the dome is gone, but around the parapet, especially on the eastern façade, there runs a lovely frieze of orange and white merlons stylised into floral shape. The orange being right side up, the white the other way.

As Azeem and I admired the excellent restoration work in the interior of Gulabi Bagh gateway, we lamented the extent of surrounding encroachment. Since 1990, housing around the heritage site has mushroomed so greatly that the dome of Dai Anga's tomb is no longer visible as one approaches it along the Grand Trunk Road. All that remains of the once grand garden laid out by Sultan Baig is something over an acre of a manicured lawn.

Common folks' cue to occupy heritage sites very likely came from what Raj officers themselves did. Fly six hundred metres due south of Dai Anga's tomb and you find the imprisoned tomb of Ali Mardan Khan who we first met in Peshawar for the lovely villa he built there. I say 'imprisoned' because the tomb is now surrounded by the high walls topped with barbed wire protecting the country's most elaborate railway workshop at Mughalpura. The only access to the heritage building is by a long and narrow alleyway walled in from both sides and roofed with iron bars to prevent ingress to the workshops. The alley can be entered from a barely noticeable door on the nameless road leaving the Grand Trunk Road opposite Singhpura bus stop to head south for Mughalpura.

Kanhaya Lal says this was the tallest mausoleum in the city of Lahore and that he had the responsibility of restoring it structurally. He laments the rape of this once beautiful monument by Sikh soldiery who 'heartlessly' removed the coloured sandstone facing of the octagonal façade. He does not tell us where the stone was used subsequently and looking at the scarred and pitted face of the building it seems to have been a case of wanton vandalism.

Gulab Singh Bhawandia, Maharaja Ranjit Singh's artillery commander, used the main building as arsenal. The still beautifully ornate entrance, now barred and looking into the railway workshop, served as residence for a colonel of the Sikh army. The glazed tilework here is comparable to that on the Gulabi Bagh gateway and despite centuries of neglect, the blues, greens, oranges and reds are still brilliant.

S. M. Latif waxes all praise for Ali Mardan Khan: '... the great Canal Engineer, who constructed the canal whereby the waters of the Ravi were conducted to Lahore..'. He also refers to him as 'the designer of the Versailles of the Panjab, as the Shalimar gardens are called'. Latif had a serious lapse of learning in the case of Ali Mardan Khan. For starters, he had nothing to do with the designing of the Shalimar, as anyone reading the sign outside the garden will know it.

As for Ali Mardan being Latif's 'great Canal Engineer', a critical reading of the *Shah Jahan Nama* clearly shows that the man was every bit a trickster. Since Babur's establishment of the Mughal dynasty in India, Kandahar had been in Mughal hands. In 1609, when Jahangir was on the throne, after a short spell of disturbance and subterfuge, Shah Abbas, the Safavi monarch of Persia, annexed the southern part of what is now called Afghanistan. This rankled greatly with Jahangir and after him his son Shah Jahan who considered ownership of Kandahar as a

The forgotten tomb of the princess who called herself Makhfi – the Hidden. Aurangzeb's daughter Zeb un Nisa was a cultivated poet given to the Sufi way.

Tomb of Malik Hussain titled Khan e Jahan Bahadar Zafar Jang and popularly known as Bahadar Khan was once faithful to Shah Jahan. He switched sides when Aurangzeb's star rose and became the man to arrest Dara Shukoh from far away Dhadar in Balochistan. Upon Bahadar Khan's death, Aurangzeb ordered this grand mausoleum for his loyal courtier. But the emperor passed away before its completion and the tomb remains as it was in 1707.

familial right. But neither was able to recover the distant Afghan town. In 1629, the aged Shah Abbas Safavi died after a rule of forty-two years, a crazed man who in his last days had blinded and murdered his own sons out of sheer envy. On his deathbed, he bequeathed his kingdom to his grandson Safi Mirza who took the throne as Shah Safi. He turned out to be no less paranoid than the late king and embarked upon a murderous spree that lasted the thirteen years of his reign during which he killed his siblings and cousins, both male and female, by the dozen. An equal number of his late grandfather's ministers and generals too tasted the executioner's blade on Safi's orders.

At this time, Ali Mardan Khan, a man of Turkish descent from the tribe Zik, had been governor at Kandahar for a number of years. Done with the nearer ones who he perceived as threat to his crown, Safi sent summons for Ali Mardan to present himself at Isfahan to kiss the royal threshold. This only meant that his blood too would colour the execution block. The wily man knew well enough how Shah Jahan coveted Kandahar and quickly shot off a letter to Saeed Khan, the governor of Peshawar that, in the words of the *Shah Jahan Nama* 'expressed his devoted loyalty to the crown and his anxious desire to surrender the fortress of Qandahar (sic) to His Majesty's servants'.

Before we go on, a word on the chronicle and its writer would be in order. Inayat Khan was Shah Jahan's chief librarian whose father Zafar Khan, a general in the Mughal army, served as governor of Kashmir and Thatta. Inayat Khan abridged the original three-volume *Padshahnama* of Abdul Hamid Lahori retaining the florid style then so much in vogue. As the original was in the process of being written by Lahori, it was read out to the emperor by the trusted prime minister Saadullah Khan. We are told that from time to time, the emperor ordered alterations. The book thus had royal approval and can safely be relied upon.

The chronicle tells us that Ali Mardan 'became apprehensive on his own account, and perceived that his only safety lay in allying himself to His Majesty's threshold'. To cut a long story short, even before Shah Safi could mobilise forces, armies from Multan, Bhakkar and Sibi under the command of able and trusted Mughal generals were hastened to the imperilled city's relief. The Persians capitulated and so, in early 1638, after a hiatus of twenty-nine years Kandahar and all of eastern and southern Afghanistan once again became a Mughal holding. The winner of this triumph was Saeed Khan whose gumption and diplomatic acumen took full advantage of Ali Mardan's insecurities.

In November 1638, Ali Mardan Khan arrived in Lahore for the 'honour of saluting the imperial threshold'. His offering to His Majesty was a thousand gold mohurs. In return a greatly beholden Shah Jahan lavishly presented him with a robe of honour, a gold-embroidered vest, a bejewelled turban ornament, similarly ornate sword and dagger, two horses with expensive jewelled saddles and four elephants. He also made over for Ali Mardan's residence the late prime minister Itimadud Daula's mansion. The man was given command of six thousand infantry and cavalry while his retainers received honours and gratuities commensurate with their status. Shah Jahan was falling over himself pampering the man whose loyalty, doubtful as the king perceived it, he was yet keen to purchase and retain.

There were clearly undercurrents that the writers of flattering hyperbole did not find fit to be aired for two weeks later Ali Mardan received more honours: ten bales of fine Bengal muslin and half a million rupees in cash. Again, a month later, Ali Mardan received a jewelled *pandan* (betel leaf box) and an enamelled salver with nine cups. Two weeks later, another gift of eighteen Arab horses, thirty Baloch camels, twenty piebald ponies of Bengal and an unspecified number of gold and jewelled articles filled Ali Mardan's already bursting coffers.

Having never been in Punjab before, Ali Mardan yet knew of the furnace summer heat of Lahore. In November 1638, as Shah Jahan was lavishing gifts on him, the man inveigled a posting as governor of Kashmir with permission to remain in Lahore until the end of the winter. Interestingly, the chronicler Inayat Khan's father Zafar was the governor at Srinagar at this time. In March 1639, Ali Mardan 'after being loaded with favours' was sent off to Kashmir while Zafar Khan was recalled to Lahore.

As the year drew to a close, Ali Mardan was summoned to the court at Lahore. Here he presented his usual one thousand gold mohurs, in return receiving several fold more in gifts. Also his rank was increased with the addition of another thousand foot and cavalry, making him a *haft-hazari* or seven-thousander. Inayat Khan does not tell us how it came to pass, but only that the crafty Ali Mardan was given the governorship of the Punjab even as he was persuaded to retain his Kashmir office. '[T]hus allowing him to pass both summer and winter in perfect ease and comfort by changing his residence from one province to another'.

The ornate gateway to Ali Mardan's tomb and the garden that once was. During Sikh rule, a military officer used this building as a residence. Now it stands between the tomb and Railway Workshop, Mughalpura.

I see just a hint of resentment in Inayat Khan's words when his own father was transferred to distant and rather insalubrious Thatta in the Indus Delta. But the grasping Ali Mardan was not satisfied with what he had. Inayat Khan writes:

> In these days [November 1639], Ali Mardan Khan represented to His Majesty that there was an engineer in his service who possesses eminent skill in the art of constructing canals, and that he had proposed to undertake the excavation of one that would supply water to the suburbs of the capital.

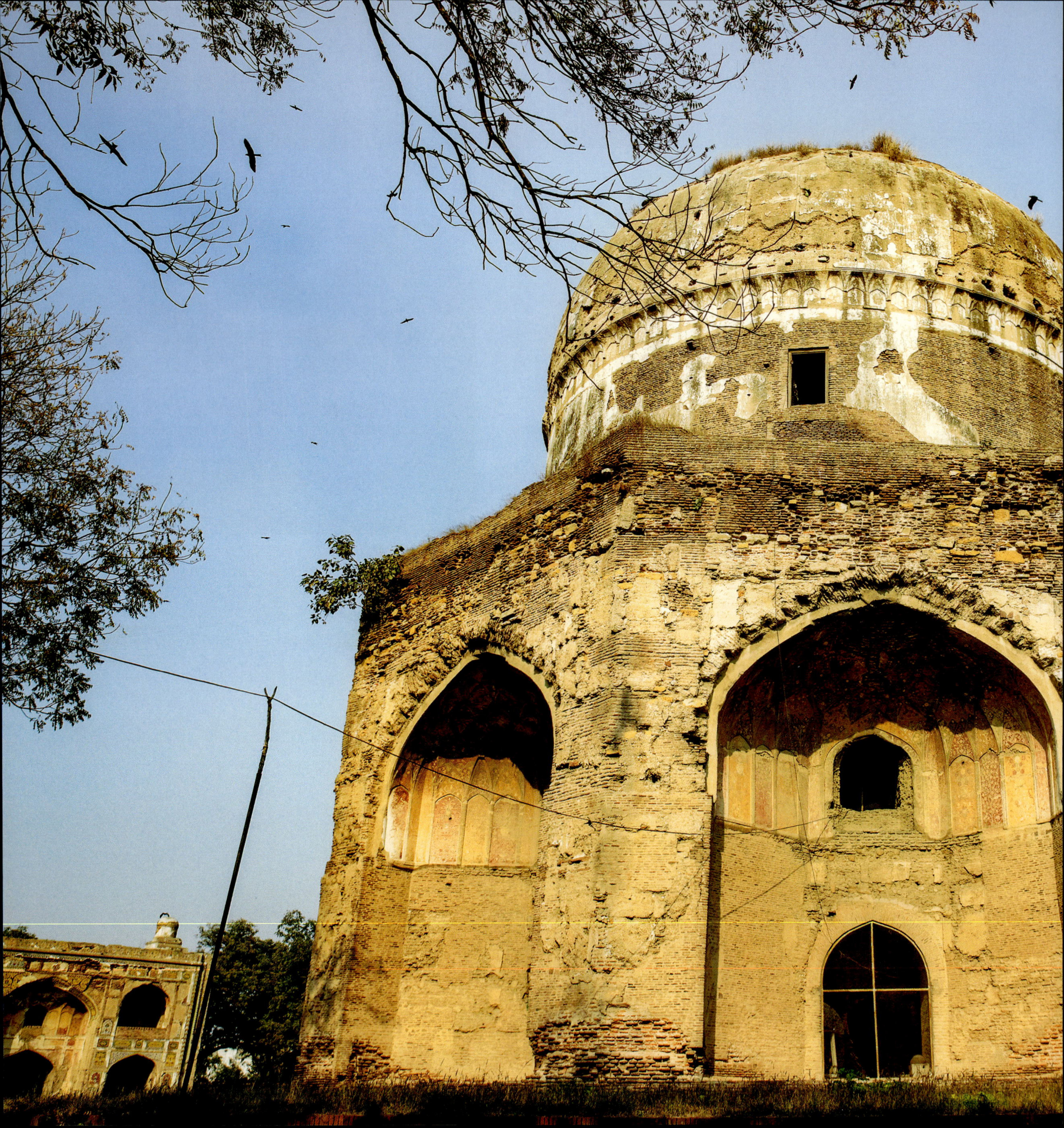

The brutally vandalised tomb of Ali Mardan Khan was once covered with marble and colourful frescoes. While the former was plundered by the Sikhs for use elsewhere, of the latter only remaining bits can be seen in the vaults above the entrances. The subterranean burial is visited by folks in the belief that Ali Mardan was a saint. The gateway to the tomb garden is seen in the left background.

Accordingly, one lakh of rupees, which was the sum estimated for the project, was delivered over to the said Khan; whereupon the engineer commenced excavations for the canal at a point where the river flowing to Lahore breaks through the hills into the level country, and which is about 50 imperial *kos* distant from the city.[9]

With the hundred thousand rupees in his pocket, Ali Mardan, master of the artifice, managed to get himself posted to Kabul. It goes without saying that he was seen off from royal presence loaded down with more precious gifts.

Meanwhile, in June 1641 Inayat Khan relays to us that the canal that Ali Mardan's servant had been digging was nearing Lahore. In his almost childish excitement, Shah Jahan ordered, just outside Lahore, the laying out of a lavish garden that the canal would water. Royal architects and engineers were directed to choose the site not far from the fort and on the banks of the canal that was promising to bring water to Lahore. The site having been selected, work began 'in a lucky moment' on the twelfth day of June 1641.

One wonders where our historian of Lahore, S. M. Latif got news of Ali Mardan being the 'designer' of the Lahore Versailles for at this time, even as his proposed canal threatened to reach Lahore, the man was miles away lording it over Kabul in summer and Peshawar in winter.

On the last day of October 1642, Shalimar Gardens with all its different levels, tanks and fountains was complete. Shah Jahan visited and was delighted to see the work. But, writes Inayat Khan:

> As a sufficient stream of water did not flow from the canal which had been completed under the direction of Ali Mardan Khan's servants at a cost of one lakh of rupees, another lakh of rupees was made over at different times to the engineers, in order that the water might be made to flow with the required volume. It chanced that through bad judgement, the engineers wasted fifty thousand rupees of this sum to no purpose in trying to improve the old canal. Ultimately, at the suggestion of several learned specialists who possessed great engineering skill, use was made of only five *kos* of the canal line laid out by Ali Mardan Khan's men; and a new channel of 32 *kos* long was excavated, by which a plentiful supply of water reached the garden without any impediment.

Apparently an old disused canal bed existed which Ali Mardan's so-called engineers wanted to utilise to save money. That did not work, however, and when skilled engineers came into play only five *kos* of the original excavation was useful and *a whole new dig of about one hundred and twenty kilometres had to be made*. Ali Mardan's men had not a clue about canal digging; they were clearly only fooling around.

---

9) The given distance would equal about 200 kilometres.

As Ali Mardan was now alternating between Kabul and Peshawar and rendering useful service against insurgents and trouble-makers in the Afghan highlands, Shah Jahan pampered him some more: he asked no questions about misappropriation of canal funds, but apprehensive of losing his doubtful loyalty, titled the grasping trickster *Amir ul Umara* – Lord of Lords.

Late in 1649, Ali Mardan was back in Lahore where Shah Jahan made him the feofee of Kashmir. The following spring, the man was weighed down with more gifts and packed off to his fief. Thereafter, Ali Mardan alternated between Srinagar and Lahore and was always at hand to help in quelling trouble in Kabul.

Early in April 1657, while on his way from Lahore to Kashmir, Amir ul Umara Ali Mardan Khan passed away from this life. His corpse was brought back to Lahore and buried under the dome where some years earlier he had interred his own mother. Shah Jahan, we are told, was 'much grieved' to hear of this transition.

Now, in those days, any dying nobleman's property automatically reverted to the crown. In the case of Ali Mardan it amounted to 'one crore' or ten million rupees. That was right royal affluence. In his benevolence, Shah Jahan gave half of it back to the man's son Ibrahim Khan.

Mountstuart Elphinstone mentions Ali Mardan's 'skill and judgement' in public works and tells us there is in Delhi canal named after Ali Mardan. I have serious reservations on that but it is difficult for me to explain how a canal got to be named after a man who comes across clearly as a fraudster. Other than a voracious appetite for lucre, a goodly store of guile and notable martial skills, Ali Mardan Khan has nothing to show for himself as a civil engineer. He found a king gullible and keen to retain his loyalty and Ali Mardan milked the opportunity to the end. Still it hurts to behold the pocked façade of his mausoleum from where the coloured sandstone was so brutally wrenched away two hundred years ago.

∾

Surely the most tragic episode of Mughal history is the end of the Sufi prince Dara Shukoh and his wife Nadira Bano Begum. In 1657, the aged and ailing Shah Jahan having ruled for thirty-one years was faced with the open rebellion of his sons led by the grasping and cruel Aurangzeb. The king preferred his crown to pass on to Dara Shukoh, the eldest. A bibliophile, artist and a devotee of the Sufi saint Mian Mir, Dara Shukoh, titled Shah Buland Iqbal (Lord of Exalted Fortune) by his father, was a liberal heterodox of kindly disposition. Like his ancestor Akbar, he together with his wife Nadira Bano and sister, the admirable Jahan Ara Begum, believed in religious syncretism rather than division. As the three stood beside the ailing king, Aurangzeb, whose religious views conflicted with those of his elder siblings, made ready to do battle.

The eighth day of June 1658, the seventh of the month of the fast, was a sad day on the field outside Samugarh. The imperial army led by Dara Shukoh faced off against the combined armies of the renegade princes Aurangzeb and

Murad Buksh. The intellectual prince was no match for the battle-hardened orthodox adversary and the defeat was nothing less than disaster. With Dara Shukoh in flight, hotly pursued by Aurangzeb's forces, the victor drove his father Shah Jahan to abdicate. Not two weeks had passed since his victory at Samugarh when Aurangzeb had himself crowned with festivities continuing for another fortnight.

Abandoned by his father's allies, Dara Shukoh fled south to Gujarat and then through Sindh towards the Bolan Pass in order to make Persia for refuge. His wife Nadira Begum had begun to show signs of exhaustion even as they traversed the unforgiving salt flats of the Great Rann of Kutch. At Dhadar, just short of the lower (south-eastern) mouth of the Bolan, the fugitive prince sought shelter in the house of the local chief Jeevan Khan. The prince thought he would be safe in this house because years earlier the man having been sentenced to death by Shah Jahan had found reprieve on Dara Shukoh's intervention. Here, Nadira Begum, her body consumed by dysentery and the fatigue of the harrowing journey, gave up her ghost.

Having performed her last rites, the heart-broken Dara Shukoh prepared his wife's body to be despatched to Lahore to be buried near the tomb of his religious mentor, the celebrated Sufi Mian Mir.[10] The funeral cortege was to be accompanied by the bulk of his remaining soldiery. No sooner was the prince's party stripped of its military strength that Jeevan Khan placed the royals under arrest and sent messages to their pursuers to come get them.

Bahadar Khan and Raja Jai Singh, both one-time Shah Jahan loyalists, hurried from the island fortress of Bhakkar between Sukkur and Rohri and on the second day of September 1659, took Dara, his son Sipihr Shukoh and the rest into custody. Six weeks later, Dara having reached the capital of Shahjahanabad, the spiteful Aurangzeb ordered public humiliation of his elder brother and nephew by being paraded in the city on elephant back dressed in mean and filthy garments, their feet bound, but their hands free. As Dara Shukoh passed through the bazaar stoically sitting in the open howdah with bowed head, a public outcry of sympathy stung Aurangzeb deeply.

That same evening, Aurangzeb sentenced Dara Shukoh to death for apostasy. He was beheaded and his headless and bloodied torso once again paraded through the streets. His blood lust not sated, Aurangzeb soon had his nephews too executed. He did not even spare the life of his confederate younger brother Murad Buksh.

Dara Shukoh was unceremoniously interred in a vault in the tomb of his forebear Humayun in Delhi. His beloved Nadira Begum lies close to the green-domed mausoleum of Mian Mir in Lahore. Her two-storeyed tomb, simple and without any ornamentations save some curvilinear forms in the dome most of which are lost to decay, exudes a sadness to reflect the tragedy of her life. Niccolao Manucci, the Venetian who had taken up service with Dara Shukoh

---

10) Breaking Mughal tradition where princes and kings had multiple wives, Dara Shukoh never married another woman. Throughout life, he and Nadira Bano Begum remained unstintingly devoted to each other.

and stayed loyal to the prince until his bloody end, has a differing report on the death of Nadira Begum. According to him, having made Dhadar, the princess was completely broken in body and soul. Despairing of the horrible end she knew was approaching her beloved husband and sons she took poison to end her life.

In the grounds surrounding Nadira Begum's tomb youngsters play cricket; the dried water channels serve as cemented pitches for them to practice bowling. Inside, the floor has recently been tiled with marble and the single sarcophagus made over and adorned with a marble plaque bearing the princess's name. With this makeover, the junkies who once used Nadira Begum's last resting place as their den have been ousted. The hour or so I spent sitting on the threshold of this forlorn house, no visitors came to raise up their hands in orison and send a blessing on the long departed princess. Only the sadness remains. And that is accentuated by the cooing of blue pigeons.

Shedding the gloom of Princess Nadira Begum's wretched end, we were making for Wagah. Driving east along the canal, on our left stood the lofty dome of an octagonal brick structure that I had seen all my life and never asked who gave it a name. We drove off to the left behind the railway officers' residences. I thought of the various Bahadur Khans in the service of earlier Mughal kings but as we neared the monument, Azeem indicated I consider the features on the building.
'Mature Mughal?' I asked still a little doubtful. Azeem nodded.

The sign said 'Tomb of Khan e Jahan Bahadar Zafar Jang Kokaltash'. He was reportedly a nobleman in Aurangzeb's court who died in 1697, ten years before his master. In

Nadira Begum who could have been empress of India, died a broken woman in faraway Dhadar in Balochistan. Her tomb is only a short way from that of the Sufi Mian Mir to whom she was much devoted.

Aurangzeb's estimation, this man, who started life as Malik Hussain, deserved a grand burial and the title Bahadur

Khan Zafar Jang. At the battle of Samugarh, he was one of the two generals leading Aurangzeb's forces to rout Dara Shukoh's army. He was the man who then relentlessly pursued the ill-starred prince across the country to Gujarat. As the prince and his retinue braved the burning salt flats of the Great Rann of Cutch, Bahadur Khan bided his time in the island fortress of Bhakkar in Sindh.

It was here he received the message from the treacherous Jeevan Khan to reach Dhadar and take the prince.[11] Bahadur Khan placed Dara Shukoh under arrest and escorted him back to the capital of Shahjahanabad where he led the humiliating parade of the defeated prince. And when Aurangzeb sought council regarding the fate of his elder brother, Bahadur Khan and five others loudly argued for his execution.

Upon Bahadur Khan's death in 1697, Aurangzeb ordered a majestic tomb for his mortal remains. But before the lofty domed edifice could be completed, the king himself passed away from this life. His sons, consumed by mutual rivalry and each ridden by the desire to be king, had little time for Bahadur Khan's mausoleum. The building, pocked with holes that held the scaffolding, shows that it was never completed.

∾

Upstream along the Lahore canal, we went to the very end where it takes off from the Bambanwala-Ravi-Bediañ Link Canal, commonly called the BRB. Azeem told the driver to stop and ordered all of us out of the car. There, about seven hundred metres to our east, standing tall above the trees, were two flagpoles, their banners swaying in the cold north wind. In the thick mist of late afternoon it was difficult to make out which was Pakistani and which Indian. But we knew the nearer one was ours. There we turned right on the far bank of the BRB to drive through the bazaar of Nathoke. Beyond the straggle of houses, amid well-worked blocks of agriculture, we spotted what we sought.

Having travelled around India as the ambassador of Seleucus Nikator, one of the inheritors of Alexander's empire, Megasthenes was well-equipped to write about India after his fifteen-year (BCE 300-285) sojourn here. He told us of stone pillars erected at every 'ten stadia' as distance markers. What we saw on our right amid the fields was the second and last one of the two stone pillars or *kos minars* that remain in Pakistan.

The other one accessible either from Garhi Shahu in Lahore or from the railway workshop of Mughalpura was once visible as one drove through the Garhi Shahu bazaar. Now it is caught between mushrooming housing and had the government not walled it off and nailed a sign on the brick structure declaring it a protected monument, it would surely have been razed so that the five hundred square metres that it occupies could be gainfully employed for construction.

---

11) William Irvine, translator of *Storia do Mogor* (History of the Mughals) of Niccolao Manucci, my source for this episode, writes that the name would correctly be Jeehan with a palatal n ending. Nowadays this is still a popular male given name among the Baloch.

The stone pillar we now approached outside Nathoke is still free standing among amid open fields. But I fear not for very long as housing schemes eat up this prime agricultural land and engulf the four hundred year-old monument.

Leaving the car on the tarmac, we walked a few hundred metres to it. Its height of about seven metres seemed exactly the same as that of the other one which might have been a laid down standard. But these pillars and the one I have seen in India near my ancestral village Uggi in Jalandhar district, do not date back to Chandragupta Maurya's time. Basing on the earlier tradition, they were raised during Jahangir's period. This was the third restoration of the furniture along the Grand Trunk Road; the second being during the zenith of the Gupta Period sometime between CE 319 until its decline in 543.

The raising of such towers to mark distances was not a purely Indian tradition. From classical times we know of the existence of at least three cities called Tashkurghan. The one in northern Afghanistan, another just across the Khunjerab border with Xinjiang province of China and the third in Fergana valley. In Turkic languages *tash* is stone and *kurghan* pillar. All these settlements take after now forgotten stone pillars that once stood there as ancient milestones.

We were joined by a local man with a few sheep. Haji Sadiq said this pillar marked the place where they had a sort of bandstand which would play when word arrived that His Majesty had set out from Shalimar Gardens to pass this way to Delhi or Agra. Azeem asked him where he had heard this.

'Oh, everyone knows it. That is what the elders always told us,' he said.

It was my turn to tell Sadiq that the elders knew nothing. They just made up stories. I told him also that historical stories remained valid only until the mid-1960s. The advent of television in Pakistan killed the tradition of stories being passed down from generation to generation. Poorly researched television reports did considerable damage to the telling of history. Sadiq, who was in his early fifties, did not remember the time before television.

Azeem, himself on his way to the pilgrimage in a few months' time asked him when he had performed the ultimate Islamic rite. With just a shade of contrition, he said he had only done the lesser pilgrimage, the Umra. I said he did not have the right to call himself Haji. Umri, perhaps, I said jokingly. But certainly not Haji.

'Here in our villages it does not make any difference. When I came back from the Umra everyone in the village was calling me Haji sahib. I did not object,' said the man.

'And then you appended the title to your name yourself as well,' I teased him.

Haji Sadiq shrugged and took off with his sheep.

Back on the tarmac, we returned the way we had come and hit the six-lane highway that heads for the border crossing at Wagah. For two countries perpetually in a state of war, this first-class high-speed highway is puzzling.

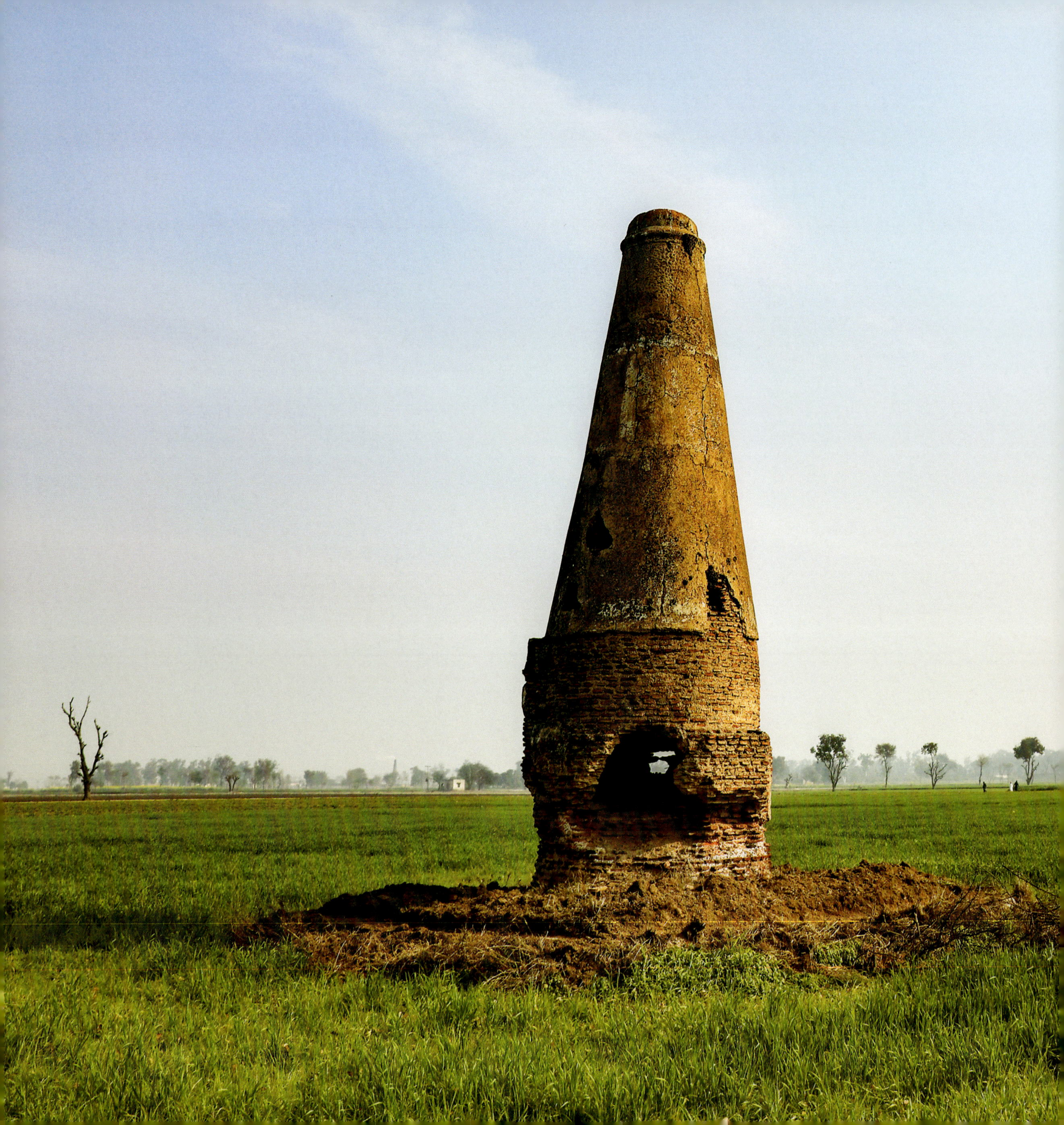

Strangely enough, across the border too the road heading for Amritsar is identical. It seems as if there was a fleeting moment in time when both countries almost came to peace. Then the usual occurred all over again.

We did not turn east. Our journey that had started at Landi Kotal in the purported jail house and gallows of Tamerlane had come to an end. But the Grand Trunk Road does not terminate at the post on the line drawn by Cyril Radcliffe in August 1947. It rolls on, across the great landmass of India all the way to the rain-drenched flatlands of Bengal. That is the Utra Rajapatha – Northen Royal Road – that Chandragupta's road building and maintenance department cared for. Across the gated and closely guarded border post lies the rest, more than two-thirds, of the grand old highway of history. And that is another story.

A few hundred metres short of the modern border post at Wagah, this Mughal kos minar stands amid cultivation. One wonder for how much longer for as the need for housing grows, it will be engulfed.

Photo Credits

All photographs in this book are © UNESCO/Asad Zaidi except for the photographs on the following pages which are © Salman Rashid.

Pages 56, 77, 104, 139, 142 (top right), 148, 159, 169, 189, 203 (bottom right), 204, 237 and 239

AFGHANISTAN

TORKHAM
LANDI KOTAL

Nawa Pass
BAJAUR

Ali Masjid

SWAT

MARDAN

Gurd Punja
Guide's Memoria

MICHNI
PESHAWAR
Bab-e-Khyber

NOWSHERA

KHAIRABAD

Attock Fort
ATTOCK   TAXILA

Mughal Bridge

Dharmarijika

PAKISTAN

Tilla Jogian

GRAND TRUNK ROAD

— GRAND TRUNK ROAD
~ RIVER

Badshahi Mo